D1416027

THE ARMY

OF

THE CUMBERLAND

THE ARMY

OF

THE CUMBERLAND

BY

HENRY M. CIST,

BREVET BRIGADIER-GENERAL U.S.V. ; A. A. G. ON THE STAFF OF MAJOR-GENERAL
ROSECRANS, AND THE STAFF OF MAJOR-GENERAL THOMAS ; SECRETARY
OF THE SOCIETY OF THE ARMY OF THE CUMBERLAND.

CASTLE BOOKS

CAMPAIGNS OF THE CIVIL WAR.—VII.
THE ARMY OF THE CUMBERLAND

This edition published in 2002 by Castle Books,
A division of Book Sales Inc.
114 Northfield Avenue, Edison, NJ 08837

First published in 1882.
Written by Henry M. Cist.

ISBN: 0-7858-1579-1

Printed in the United States of America.

PREFACE.

THE scope of this work precluded the entering into details as to the minor operations of the troops in the commands named. It has even been impossible to give the movements of troops on the battlefields in lesser organizations than brigades. The rosters of the several armies given in full in the appendices will enable those interested to trace the movements of the minor commands.

The subject is too great a one to be fully and justly treated within the limitations, both of time and space, which have necessarily been imposed here. Still, with the hope that the future student of history may glean something of value in this volume not found elsewhere, it is sent forth for the favorable consideration of its readers.

To the many friends who have kindly aided me in various ways, I return my sincere thanks. To Col. R. N. Scott, U.S.A., I am under special obligations for data furnished.

The maps for this volume were prepared by permission from those of Captain Ruger in Van Horne's "History of the Army of the Cumberland," published by Robert Clarke & Co., Cincinnati.

H. M. C.

CONTENTS.

CHAPTER VIII.

LIST OF MAPS.

General Map of the Campaign.

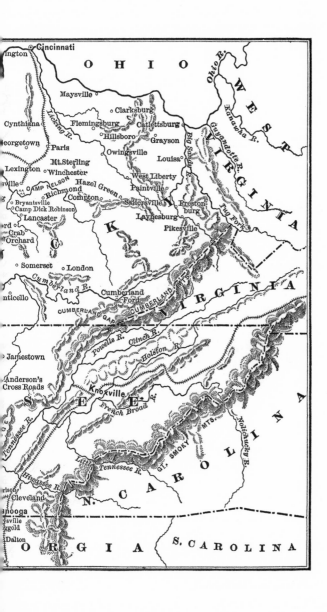

THE ARMY OF THE CUMBERLAND.

CHAPTER I.

EARLY MOVEMENTS.

IN Kentucky, during the spring of 1861, every shade of opinion prevailed, from the most pronounced Union sentiment to the most ultra secession sympathy.

The Government at Washington wished to enlist Kentucky heartily in support of the Union, while every effort was made by the rebel leaders to secure the secession of the State from the Union, and to have it join its fortunes to those of the South. These several efforts enlisted the active support of those in the State in sympathy with them, and Kentuckians became ultimately divided into two sharply defined parties. Under the peculiar doctrine of "armed neutrality" adopted by the local authorities, no serious infraction of the peace of the State was had until the fall. With the invitation given General Anderson to take command in Kentucky, by the State Legislature, the doctrine of "armed neutrality" came to an end. While it at times restrained prompt action on the part of the Union men of Kentucky during the first six months of the war, and hampered the Federal Government in the movement of troops in the State, still in the end it was of immense benefit to the cause of the Union, and

VII.—1

enabled those in support of it in Kentucky to unite and perfect their plans in comparative peace, unmolested by the rebels from Tennessee and their own State. Under cover of "armed neutrality" the Union men remained quiet until the time had arrived for prompt and decided action, with men, and arms for their support, in the measures they adopted to retain Kentucky in the Union.

In accordance with a general plan of operations adopted by General Albert Sidney Johnston, on September 18th, General Buckner broke camp with the rebel forces at Camp Boone, Tenn., near the Kentucky line, and marching north, occupied Bowling Green, throwing out his advance as far as Elizabethtown.

On receipt of reliable information as to Buckner's movements, General Anderson sent General W. T. Sherman, second in command, to Camp Joe Holt, with instructions to order Colonel Rousseau with his entire command to report at once in Louisville. The "Home Guards" were also ordered out, and they assembled promptly in large force, reporting at the Nashville depot, and by midnight they were started to the front by train. Rousseau's command followed at once, General Sherman being in command of the entire force, amounting to some three thousand men. The advance by train was stopped at the Rolling Fork of Salt River, about thirty-one miles south of Louisville, at which point the railroad bridge had been burned by the rebels. During the following day the troops under Rousseau forded the stream, and pressing forward occupied Muldraugh's Hills with its two trestles and a tunnel over fifteen hundred feet long. The Home Guards were left in camp at Lebanon Junction, some two or three miles in the rear, where Lieutenant-Colonel R. W. Johnson of the Third Kentucky Cavalry reported later in the day with some additional companies of

Home Guards, and, by order of General Anderson, assumed command of this camp.

This disposition of the troops caused Buckner to retire with his entire command to Bowling Green, where he strongly fortified his position.

The Kentucky State troops were under orders for ten days' service only, and their place was then filled by several regiments from the States immediately north of Kentucky. These troops were placed in camp, and there received instruction in drill, discipline, and camp regulations, waiting orders for the advance.

General Johnston, under his general plan of creating a defensive line from Columbus on the west, running through Bowling Green east to some point to be determined on, early in September sent General Zollicoffer with a force numbering several thousand men to make an advance into Eastern Kentucky by way of Knoxville, East Tennessee, through Cumberland Gap to Cumberland Ford, threatening Camp Dick Robinson. On the 19th of that month the advance of Zollicoffer's command had a spirited skirmish with the "Home Guards" at Barboursville Bridge. These troops were compelled to retire, which they did, to Rock Castle Hills, where they were reinforced by two Kentucky regiments under Colonel T. T. Garrard, of the Seventh Kentucky Infantry, who had received instructions from General Thomas to obstruct the roads and to hold the rebels in check. Garrard established his force at Camp Wildcat, behind temporary breastworks, where, on October 21st, he was attacked by Zollicoffer with 7,000 troops. Shortly after the attack General Schoepff, with five regiments of infantry, one of cavalry, and a battery of artillery, reinforced Garrard, and after a severe fight the enemy was repulsed.

After Buckner's retreat to Bowling Green, Zollicoffer

fell back to Mill Springs, on the southern bank of the Cumberland River, and soon afterward crossed the river to the opposite bank at Beech Grove, fortifying this encampment with extensive earthworks.

During the month of September, General George H. Thomas, who with General Wm. T. Sherman had been ordered to report to General Anderson for duty in Kentucky—at General Anderson's personal request of the President—was placed in command of Camp Dick Robinson, relieving General Nelson. The latter then established Camp Kenton in Mason County, three miles from Maysville, near the spot where Simon Kenton's station was erected in 1785.

On the 7th of October General Anderson, on account of ill-health, relinquished the command of the department, and General W. T. Sherman on the following day succeeded him. At the same time General A. McD. McCook was placed in command of the force that been ordered to the front under Sherman.

During the month of October the rebel Colonel J. S. Williams was organizing a force of some two thousand troops at Prestonburg, on the Big Sandy River, intending to operate in Central Kentucky through McCormick's Gap. General Nelson early in the month started with all the troops of his command to drive the rebels out of their encampment. Nelson ordered the Second Ohio under Colonel L. A. Harris to move from Paris, and the Twenty-first Ohio under Colonel Norton to advance from Nicholasville to Olympia Springs, where the entire command was concentrated. From here he advanced to McCormick's Gap, and then divided his command, sending the Second Ohio, a section of Captain Konkle's battery, and a company of Ohio cavalry under Captain McLaughlin—all under the command of Colonel Harris—through West Liberty to unite with the command at Salyersville. Nelson then moved forward with three regiments of infantry, two detachments of Kentucky troops, and two sections of Konkle's battery, with a battalion of cavalry, on the road to Hazel Green. On the 23d Harris occupied West Liberty, after a brisk skirmish. The command united at Salyersville and followed the enemy to Prestonburg. At this point Nelson sent the Thirty-third Ohio, with the Kentucky troops and a section of Konkle's battery under Colonel Sill, by a detour to the right to flank the rebel position at Ivy Mountain. Nelson on the next day then advanced with his command on the direct road to Piketon, and encountered the enemy in ambush on the mountain at Ivy Creek. Pushing forward at once with the force under his immediate command, Nelson attacked the enemy, and after a brisk engagement, lasting over an hour, routed them from their cover and drove them in full retreat.

Sill occupied Piketon on the 9th without much opposition. General Nelson arrived there on the 10th, when the rebels leaving the State and retreating through Pound Gap, he was ordered to report with his command to General Buell at Louisville.

On the retirement of General Anderson, as the ranking officer in the department, General Sherman assumed the command. On the 9th of November, by general order from the headquarters of the army, No. 97, the Department of the Ohio was created, "to consist of the States of Ohio, Michigan, Indiana, that portion of Kentucky east of the Cumberland River, and the State of Tennessee, and to be commanded by Brigadier-General D. C. Buell, headquarters at Louisville;" and General Sherman was relieved from command at his own request.

Nelson's command being ordered out of East Kentucky, the rebel forces again entered, and in small bands were depredating on Union people in the Big Sandy Valley. The Fourteenth Kentucky under Colonel L. P. Moore was ordered to move from Catlettsburg and advance up the valley. General Buell finding that the rebel force had been largely reinforced by the advance of General Humphrey Marshall, one of the ablest rebel generals in that part of the country, ordered the Twenty-second Kentucky under Colonel Lindsay from Maysville to join the Fourteenth, and Lindsay was placed in command of the two regiments. Marshall was a graduate of West Point; he had served in the Black Hawk war and had seen service in Mexico as a colonel of Kentucky cavalry, winning distinction at Buena Vista. He had now entered the State from Virginia through Pound Gap, and had reached a strong natural position near Paintville, where he was rapidly increasing his army, with the intention of raising a sufficient force—already some five thousand—to operate on General Buell's flank and to retard his advance into Tennessee. The Forty-second Ohio, just organized, was in a camp of instruction near Columbus, Ohio, under its colonel, James A. Garfield. While there, in December, he was ordered by General Buell to move his regiment at once to Catlettsburg, at the mouth of the Big Sandy River, and to report in person to Louisville for orders.

Starting his regiment eastward, from Cincinnati, Garfield, on the 19th of December, reported to General Buell, who informed him that he had been selected to command an expedition to drive Marshall and his forces from Kentucky. That evening Garfield received his orders, which organized the Eighteenth Brigade of the Army of the Ohio, and placed him in command. General Buell with these orders sent a letter of instruction, giving general directions as to the campaign, leaving all matters of detail and the fate of the expedition, however, largely to the discretion of the brigade commander. The latter reached his command on the 24th of December, at Louisa, some twenty-eight miles up the Big Sandy. He then proceeded to concentrate his troops, the main body consisting of his own regiment—the Forty-second Ohio—the Fourteenth Kentucky, and a battalion of Ohio cavalry under Major McLaughlin, which was with him; but these gave only some fifteen hundred men for duty.

The next largest portion of his command was stationed at Paris, Kentucky, under Colonel Cranor, with his regiment, the Fortieth Ohio, 800 strong. Cranor was ordered to join the main body as expeditiously as possible, and to bring with him that portion of Colonel Wolford's Kentucky cavalry stationed at Stanford, consisting of three small battalions under Lieutenant-Colonel Letcher, and to report at Prestonburg. The Twenty-second Kentucky was ordered from Maysville, and some three hundred men of that command reported before Garfield reached Paintville. He was also joined by a battalion of West Virginia cavalry under Colonel Bolles. After a toilsome march in mid-winter, Garfield's command, on the 7th of January, drove Marshall's forces from the mouth of Jenny's Creek, and occupied Paintville. On the morning of the 9th, Cranor reported with his command, footsore and exhausted, after a march of over one hundred miles through the mountains of Eastern Kentucky. At noon of the 9th Garfield advanced his command to attack Marshall with his cavalry, pressing the rebels as they fell back. Reaching Prestonburg some fifteen miles from Paintville, he learned that Marshall was encamped and fortified on Abbott's Creek. Pushing on to the mouth of the creek, some three miles below Prestonburg, he there encamped for the night, a sleety rain adding to the discomfort of the men. Intending to force the enemy to battle, he ordered up his reserves under Colonel Sheldon from Paintville, with every available man. As soon as the morning light enabled the command to move, Garfield advanced, and soon engaged the rebel cavalry, which was driven in after a slight skirmish, falling back on the main body some two miles in the rear, strongly posted on high ground, between Abbott's Creek and Middle Creek, at the mouth of the latter stream. It was impossible to tell what disposition Marshall had made for his defence, owing to the formation of the ground at this point concealing his troops until our forces drew his fire. Throwing several detachments forward, the entire command was soon actively engaged. The engagement lasted for some four hours, commencing at about twelve o'clock. At 4 P.M., the reserves under Sheldon reached the field of battle, and the enemy was driven from his position. Night coming on prevented pursuit.

Marshall's command fled down the valley, set fire to their stores, and pressed forward in rapid retreat to Abington, Va. Garfield with his command returned to Paintville, where it could receive supplies. In February he received orders from Buell, directing him to advance to Piketon, and drive the rebels from that place, which he did, and later from Pound Gap. This freed Eastern Kentucky of rebel troops, and relieved the Union men of that section of the depredations that had been committed on them by the roving bands of the enemy. The services of Garfield's command were recognized by Buell, and the thanks of the Commanding General extended to Garfield and his troops. Shortly after this Garfield received his commission as Brigadier-General of Volunteers, to date from the "Battle of Middle Creek."

In the latter part of March General Garfield was ordered to leave a small force in the Big Sandy Valley, and to report with the rest of his brigade to General Buell at Louisville.

CHAPTER II.

MILL SPRINGS.

On September 10, 1861, General Albert Sidney Johnston, who had resigned the colonelcy of the Second United States Cavalry to engage in the service of the Confederacy, was assigned to the command of the Department of the West, embracing, with a large number of the Western States, the States of Kentucky and Tennessee. On the 18th Johnston directed Buckner to occupy Bowling Green, and ordered Zollicoffer to advance from Knoxville to Cumberland Gap. The rebels, under General Polk, occupied Columbus, Ky., September 7th, and the line of operations of the Confederates, under General Johnston, as then formed, had the Mississippi River at its extreme left, Cumberland Gap at its extreme right, with Bowling Green as the centre. No point in advance of Bowling Green could have been safely taken by the Confederate general with the force at his command, owing to the disposition of the Union troops in Kentucky at that time.

As we have seen, Zollicoffer with his command was driven from Rock Castle Hills and Wildcat, and taking a new position nearer Bowling Green, encamped at Beech Grove, where he fortified his position.

General Zollicoffer was a civilian appointment, without military training of any kind. He had been editor of a Nashville paper, had held a number of minor State offices,

1*

and served two terms in Congress prior to the war. Johnston, in ordering Zollicoffer to the Cumberland River at
Mill Springs, intended that he should occupy a position of
observation merely until he should be reinforced, or his
troops be incorporated in the main command. He could
not have been located farther west without inviting the
advance of the Federal forces into East Tennessee or to
Nashville, flanking Bowling Green. Zollicoffer had no ability as a soldier to handle troops, and General George B.
Crittenden, of Kentucky, a graduate of West Point, who had
seen service in the Mexican War, and who held, at the out-
break of the rebellion, a commission as Lieutenant-Colonel
in the regiment of Mounted Riflemen, was, in November,
assigned to the command of the district as Major-General,
with headquarters at Knoxville. Great expectations were
entertained in regard to Crittenden's military abilities ; and
about the first of the year 1862 he assumed command in person
of the rebel forces at Beech Grove. The fact that Zollicoffer had established his camp on the north side of the Cumberland, "with the enemy in front and the river behind,"
was known to Johnston, and information given by him to
Crittenden. General Johnston had written Zollicoffer that
the interests of the service required him simply to watch
the river, and that he could do this better from Mill Springs
without crossing it.

Zollicoffer, however, had crossed the river before he heard
from Johnston, and replied that, while from this letter he
inferred that he should not have done so, it was now too
late, as his means of recrossing were so limited that he
could hardly accomplish it in the face of the enemy. On
his reaching the Cumberland with his command, he had
sent forward his cavalry to seize the ferryboats at Mill
Springs. In this they failed, and the crossing was effected

on one ferry-boat, seized lower down, and barges built by his troops.

General Thomas was ordered in November to concentrate his command in order to be prepared for any movement Zollicoffer might make, and, if necessary, to attack him in his camp. General Carter with his brigade was stationed at London, Colonel Hoskins was near Somerset, and Colonel Bramlette at Columbia, all watching Zollicoffer's movements, and reporting them to General Thomas, who endeavored to stop his advance at the Cumberland River. Five hundred of Wolford's Cavalry were ordered from Columbia to reinforce Colonel Hoskins; and General Schoepff, with the Seventeenth Ohio, the Thirty-eighth Ohio, and Standart's battery, to take position on the Cumberland River at Waitsborough, where he could command the crossing. Here he was to fortify and guard the river at this point and above and below, to prevent the enemy from crossing, or from obtaining the means for doing so.

On December 2d, Zollicoffer, while building his ferries, sent some troops to shell General Schoepff's camp. A brisk cannonading was kept up for some time, when the rebels withdrew. Schoepff regarding this as a feint, and anticipating a movement of Zollicoffer's troops to cross the river, ordered two companies of cavalry under Captain Dillon to guard the ford and to give timely notice of any attempt to effect a crossing. He also ordered the Seventeenth Ohio with three pieces of artillery and another company of cavalry, all under the command of Colonel Connell, to support the cavalry under Dillon. The latter proved wholly incompetent, and failed to comply with his orders in any particular. He went into camp two miles in the rear from where he was ordered, and neglected even to post his men to guard the ford, whereby Zollicoffer was enabled to occupy the north bank of the Cumberland without opposition and without Dillon's even knowing that the movement had been made. This was only discovered on the 4th, when the rebels drove back the Federal cavalry and attacked Connell, who was advancing on a reconnoissance. Connell, in ignorance of the movement of the enemy, had reached the vicinity of the ford and found himself confronted by a strong force of rebels, who had crossed the river, and who being rapidly reinforced rendered his situation one of extreme peril. He withdrew under cover of the night beyond Fishing Creek, without being molested. Schoepff, finding that the advance of the rebels was supported by reinforcements and that Zollicoffer's entire force was slowly crossing, which would make the enemy's force in his front largely exceed his own, asked General Carter at London to reinforce him. He also ordered Colonel Coburn with the Thirty-third Indiana to move from Crab Orchard to his support ; and on the 6th established his camp in a strong position three miles north of Somerset, where he was able to command both the Stanford and the Crab Orchard roads. Here Carter reported with two regiments on the 9th, Colonel Vandeveer's regiment, the Thirty-fifth Ohio, with Captain Hewitt's battery having already arrived. On the 8th, the rebel cavalry crossed Fishing Creek and reconnoitred the Federal camps. They were fired on by Wolford's cavalry, which then fell back ; and after a brisk skirmish with the Thirty-fifth Ohio they were driven back with a loss of two or three men on each side.

General Buell had ordered Thomas to keep his immediate command at Columbia, and had directed him not to send any more troops to Schoepff at Somerset, considering that the latter had sufficient force to drive the rebels across the Cumberland. Thomas was also directed to hold himself in readiness to make an immediate movement, when ordered, from Columbia on the rebel General Hindman, who with some seven thousand troops was operating in that vicinity, throwing out his cavalry far in advance of his main column, and feeling the position of the Federal forces. Hindman had been ordered by General Johnston to make a diversion in favor of Zollicoffer; and when Thomas from Columbia checked Hindman's advance, the latter reported that the force under Thomas had not been weakened to reinforce Schoepff, or to strengthen the main command at Bowling Green, and that Zollicoffer was in no immediate danger.

Schoepff with his entire command on the 18th made a reconnoissance to determine the location and purposes of the rebel force. Pushing his command forward he drove their cavalry pickets in and found that Zollicoffer had been intrenching his camp, his line of fortifications extending from the river to Fishing Creek and his camp being in the angle formed by the junction of this stream with the Cumberland. Having accomplished this, and not intending to bring on an engagement, Schoepff returned with his command to their encampment north of Somerset.

Buell now finding that the only rebel force encamped in Eastern Kentucky was that under Zollicoffer, and deeming it important that he be driven from the State, modified his previous order to Thomas, and on December 29th directed him to advance against Zollicoffer from Columbia and attack on his left flank. He also ordered Schoepff to attack him in front. Two days later Thomas started from Lebanon with the Second Brigade, under command of Colonel Manson, and two regiments of Colonel McCook's brigade, Kinney's battery of artillery, and a battalion of Wolford's cavalry. Heavy rains, swollen streams, and almost impassable roads impeded the movement of the command so that it was not until the 17th of January that they reached Logan's Cross Roads, ten miles from the rebel encampment. At this point Thomas halted his command and awaited the arrival of the Fourth and Tenth Kentucky, the Fourteenth Ohio, and the Eighteenth United States Infantry, detained in the rear by the condition of the road. He communicated at once with Schoepff, and the same day the latter reported in person. General Thomas directed Schoepff to send him Standart's battery, the Twelfth Kentucky and the First and Second Tennessee regiments, which were to strengthen the command on the immediate front until the arrival of the regiments in the rear. Thomas placed the Tenth Indiana, Wolford's cavalry, and Kinney's battery on the main road leading to the enemy's camp. The Ninth Ohio and the Second Minnesota were posted three-quarters of a mile to the right on the Robertsport road. Strong pickets were thrown out on the main road in the direction of the enemy, with cavalry pickets beyond. Our pickets were fired on and had a skirmish with the rebel pickets on the night of the 17th. On the 18th, the Fourth Kentucky, a battalion of the Michigan Engineers and Wetmore's Battery also reported to Thomas.

Crittenden, on learning that Zollicoffer had crossed the Cumberland, had sent at once an order by courier, post haste, directing him to recross; but on his arrival at Mill Springs he found Zollicoffer still on the north bank, waiting his arrival before retiring. Crittenden gave orders at once for the construction of boats to take his command across the river; but they were not ready when he heard of the approach of General Thomas on January 17th.

On the 18th, Crittenden reported to General Johnston that he was threatened by a superior force of the enemy in his front, and that as he found it impossible to cross the river, he should have to make the fight on the ground he then occupied.

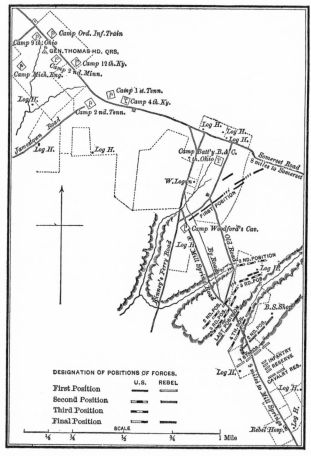

Mill Springs.

His weekly reports showed eight infantry regiments, four battalions (seventeen companies) of cavalry, and two companies of artillery, making an aggregate of 9,417 men. His circular order of the 18th, directing the order of march in his advance to attack, shows that his army was on the day of battle composed of the same companies, and that his force was about the same.

At midnight, on January 18th, in a heavy winter rain, the Confederate army marched out to battle with Bledsoe's and Saunders's independent cavalry companies in advance. Zollicoffer's brigade of four regiments, with Rutledge's battery of artillery, followed. Then came General Carroll's brigade of four regiments, one in reserve, with McClung's battery of artillery, Brauner's battalion of cavalry on the right, and McClellan's battalion of cavalry on the left, with Cary's battalions in the rear. After a six hours' march through the rain and mud, the advance struck our cavalry pickets at six o'clock, in the early gray of a winter morning, two miles in front of the Federal camp. Wolford's cavalry slowly fell back, reporting the enemy's advance to Manson, who immediately formed his regiment—the Tenth Indiana—and took position on the road to await the attack. Manson then ordered the Fourth Kentucky, Colonel Speed S. Fry, to support him; and reported to Thomas, in person, the advance of the rebels in force, and the disposition he had made of his troops to meet the attack. General Thomas directed him to return to his brigade immediately, with orders to hold the enemy in check until the other troops could be brought up. Orders were given to the other commanders to form immediately, and in ten minutes they were all marching to the battle-field, except the battalion of Michigan Engineers and a company of the Thirty-eighth Ohio, detained to guard the camp.

The rebels, in their advance, opened the attack with Walt-. hall's Mississippi and Battle's Tennessee regiments, which as they moved forward, forming the right of the rebel line, encountered the Fourth Kentucky and the Tenth Indiana, formed on the first line to resist their attack in the edge of the woods to their front.   The Tennessee regiment endeavored to flank the Fourth Kentucky on the left, while the latter regiment was resisting the rebel attack on the front, in a most obstinate manner.   Carter's Tennessee brigade was ordered up in position to meet this flanking movement with a section of Kinney's battery ; and the attempt of Battle's regiment was checked.

Orders were sent to Colonel McCook to advance with the Ninth Ohio and the Second Minnesota regiments.   These regiments coming up occupied the position of the Fourth Kentucky and Tenth Indiana, who by that time were out of ammunition.   As soon as this disposition of these troops had been made the enemy opened a most determined and galling fire, pressing our troops at all points.   General Thomas's command returned the fire with spirit, and holding their position the contest was maintained for half an hour on both sides most obstinately.

At this time, General Zollicoffer, being in the rear of the Nineteenth Tennessee regiment of his command, became convinced that the Fourth Kentucky (Federal) regiment was a part of his brigade, ordered the Tennessee regiment to cease firing, as they were shooting their own troops. He then rode to the front, where he met Colonel Fry, the commanding officer of the Fourth Kentucky.   Zollicoffer stated to Fry that both commands belonged to the same side, and that firing should stop.   To this Fry assented and started to order the Fourth Kentucky to cease firing, when one of Zollicoffer's aids coming up, seeing that Fry was a Federal officer, opened fire upon him with a revolver, wounding his horse. Fry returned the fire, shooting Zollicoffer through the heart.

Shortly after, the First and Second East Tennessee regiments of Carter's brigade and Hoskins's Kentucky regiment were placed on the left of the Second Minnesota regiment, and opening a heavy fire on the right flank of the rebel line caused it to give way. The Second Minnesota regiment kept up a galling fire in the centre, while the Ninth Ohio charged the enemy with fixed bayonets on the left, turned that flank, and drove them from the field. The whole rebel line then gave way, retreating in the utmost confusion and disorder to their intrenchments at Beech Grove. Thomas ordered an immediate advance, after supplying his troops with ammunition, driving the rebels into their intrenchments. As these were approached they were invested by the division deployed in line of battle. Cannonading was kept up until dark, firing being in the direction of the ferry to defeat a crossing. During the night preparations were made for an assault on the intrenchments on the following morning. The Fourteenth Ohio, Colonel Steedman, and the Tenth Kentucky, Colonel Harlan, reported after the fight, were placed in the front of the advance, and were the first to enter the intrenchments. Schoepff's brigade joined the command during the evening, and was placed in position for the attack.

At midnight Crittenden abandoned everything, and between that hour and daylight escaped across the river by means of a steamer and some barges at the landing, which he burned, leaving behind him his badly wounded, all of his cannon—twelve pieces—with their caissons packed with ammunition, a large amount of small arms, with ammunition for the same, over one hundred and fifty wagons, and more than one thousand horses and mules, with a large amount of tools, stores, camp and garrison equipage.

As all the boats were destroyed, it was impossible for Thomas to cross his command in pursuit. General Thomas in his official report of the engagement says : " Their command was completely demoralized and retreated with great haste and in all directions, making their capture in any number quite doubtful if pursued. There is no doubt but that the moral effect produced by their complete dispersion will have a more decided effect in re-establishing Union sentiments than though they had been captured."

The rebels suffered terribly by heavy marching through the rain, mud, and cold, with insufficient food ; frequently with nothing but parched corn to sustain life. Crittenden finally took position at Chestnut Mound, within reach of relief from Nashville.

In the life of Albert Sidney Johnston, speaking of Crittenden's retreat, the author says : " During his retreat his army became much demoralized, and two regiments, whose homes were in that neighborhood, almost entirely abandoned their organization and went every man to his own house. A multitude deserted, and the tide of fugitives filled the country with dismay."

The battle fought at Logan's Cross Roads, called by the rebels the Battle of Fishing Creek, and by the Federals the Battle of Mill Springs, was most disastrous to the enemy, and inflicted the most severe blow they had up to that time experienced. The victory for the Federal forces was the first complete success of the war, and was hailed everywhere with joy and hope. An order was issued by the President congratulating the troops on their success, and the general in command conveyed his thanks to General Thomas and troops for their brilliant victory.

Thomas's command lost in the engagement 39 killed, and 207 wounded. He reported the rebel loss at 122 killed, and the total loss at 349. The large proportion of killed to the wounded indicates heavy fighting at close quarters, and also a superiority of either the arms of the Federal troops or their firing.

The body of General Zollicoffer was treated with great respect. General Thomas had it embalmed and carried around by Lebanon. It was then sent by General Buell through his lines under a flag of truce. Zollicoffer's death was a very depressing event to the Tennesseeans. He was their most popular leader, and his death was felt by the people of Tennessee as a personal bereavement.

Crittenden's attack and defeat were a great surprise to Johnston. This force had been ordered to Mill Springs to maintain that point of the general military line as a corps of observation merely. With the attack and defeat Johnston found his line broken, his position at Bowling Green liable to be turned on that flank, and an army on which he counted demolished. This with his losses on his left in Western Kentucky and at Fort Henry compelled his main command at Bowling Green to abandon that place, and retire into Tennessee. Thomas, after the battle of Mill Springs, concentrated his command at Somerset, awaiting orders. He was ordered to Mumfordsville, February 15th, to take part in the general advance against Bowling Green. These orders were countermanded by reason of the evacuation of that place, on the 14th; and on the 22d, Thomas was ordered with his division to proceed by forced marches to Louisville, and there embark for Nashville. The command arrived at Nashville on the 2d, 3d, and 4th days of March.

CHAPTER III.

CONCENTRATION AT NASHVILLE.

Don Carlos Buell, who was placed in command of the Department of the Ohio on Sherman's request to be relieved, had been serving from the early summer of 1861 as Assistant Adjutant-General on the staff of Brigadier-General E. V. Sumner, U.S.A., in command of the Department of the Pacific. He had been promoted to the rank of lieutenant-colonel in the adjutant-general's department, May 11, 1861. His appointment as brigadier-general in the volunteer force was made May 17, 1861. General Buell was a graduate of West Point, and had been in the army all his life. He was a thoroughly trained soldier, with great pride in his profession, a man of great integrity, with abilities of the first order, animated by high principle. His long training in the adjutant-general's department, added to his natural faculty, made him a first-class organizer of an army. Under his direction the soldiers of the Army of the Ohio received their training in the drill of the camp, the discipline of the march, and learned endurance under fire in the skirmishes and engagements during his command. For all the soldierly qualities that the troops of the later organization— the Army of the Cumberland—possessed, they were indebted in large measure to their first commander in the field, General Buell. He was constant in his endeavors for the care of the troops, and insisted on their camps being carefully selected and well drained. His highest aim was to make good soldiers of his command, and everything that detracted from this, as straggling, pillaging, disobedience of orders, he regarded as unworthy of a soldier, and meriting prompt and stern punishment at his hands. In the earlier days of the war, with the lack of the knowledge that the stricter the obedience to orders the better for the soldier, General Buell seemed at times harsh and severe. But as time brought hard campaigns and heavy fighting to the Army of the Cumberland, the older soldiers who were under Buell saw that he was actuated solely for their good and the good of the service in all he did.

The organization of the troops into brigades and divisions first engaged Buell's attention on assuming command. On December 2d, an order was issued creating this organization and designating it the "Army of the Ohio," consisting of six divisions. The brigades were numbered consecutively throughout the army, and not as they were formed in the divisions. General G. H. Thomas was assigned to the command of the First Division, consisting of four brigades. The entire force of the First Division was at Nashville on March 4th.

The Second Division was organized at Camp Nevin, a camp established by General Rousseau, when left by Sherman in command after the latter assumed the command of the department. General Alexander McD. McCook, who had relieved Rousseau October 14, by order of Sherman, was assigned to the command of this division, which consisted also of four brigades.

The Third Division was placed under the command of General O. M. Mitchell, who had been in Cincinnati in command of the "Military Department of Ohio," and who was relieved November 19th, after two months' service there, superintending the forwarding of troops to the armies in the field. This division consisted of three brigades.

General William Nelson, on reporting at Louisville after his Eastern Kentucky campaign, was placed in command of the Fourth Division, consisting of three brigades.

The Fifth Division, consisting of three brigades, was placed under the command of General Thomas L. Crittenden, a son of John J. Crittenden.

In January, 1862, General Buell organized the Sixth Division, and relieving General T. J. Wood from the command of the Fifth Brigade, assigned him as commander of this division, which consisted of three brigades.

To each brigade was attached a battery of artillery.

In this organization of the "Army of the Ohio," as the new regiments from the North reported, additional brigades and divisions were formed from time to time. Thus organized, the army under Buell, in the early spring entered upon its first campaign. There had been some slight skirmishing during the winter with portions of the command. A detachment of the Thirty-ninth Indiana, under Lieutenant-Colonel Jones, met a body of the rebel cavalry a few miles beyond Camp Nevin, and routed it with slight loss to the enemy.

On December 10th, General R. W. Johnson moved onward his brigade, and occupied Mumfordsville, sending a detachment of the Thirty-second Indiana to Green River, where a temporary bridge was constructed. On the 17th, four companies of this regiment, under Lieutenant-Colonel Von Trebra, crossed and took position at Rowlett's Station. General A. S. Johnston had sent Hindman with his brigade from Bowling Green, with instructions to destroy the railroad as far north as Green River. On the same day that the Thirty-second Indiana crossed the river, Hindman reached Woodsonville. On the approach of Hindman, Von Trebra threw out two companies as skirmishers. The enemy fell back with the purpose of decoying the Federals to the point where his main command of infantry and artillery was posted. The cavalry—a squadron of the "Texas Rangers" under Colonel Terry—made a spirited attack. The skirmishers rallied by fours. to receive this charge. After repeated charges from the cavalry, which were resisted by the Thirty-second—in one of which Colonel Terry was killed—Colonel Willich reinforced Von Trebra with four additional companies. After maintaining their position under fire for an hour and a half, the Indiana troops repulsed the enemy in every charge, and Hindman's force then withdrew. Colonel Willich had in the engagement only the eight companies of his command, with Cotter's battery. The enemy attacked with a force of 1,100 infantry, 250 cavalry, and 4 pieces of artillery. The Thirty-second Indiana lost 8 men killed and ten wounded. After the fall of Bowling Green, the Second Division reached Nashville on March 3d.

The Third Division in February was ordered to make a demonstration, moving by forced marches against the enemy's position at Bowling Green, to prevent troops being sent from there to reinforce Fort Donelson. The rebels had commenced their retreat from this place to Nashville prior to the arrival of Mitchell's command, but the shells thrown by his artillery on the 14th into the city hastened the movements of the rear guard of Johnston's army. Before their retreat, the enemy burned both bridges over Barren River, and set fire to a large quantity of military stores, railroad cars, and other property. Turchin's brigade, capturing a small ferryboat, crossed over the river, swollen above high-water mark by the heavy rains, entered the city at five o'clock the next morning, and succeeded in extinguishing the fire and saving a portion of the railroad cars. During the succeeding week Mitchell crossed the greater part of his command over the river, and, without his wagons, reached Edgefield opposite Nashville on the evening of the 24th, at the same time that General Buell arrived by rail, the latter using some of the cars captured at Bowling Green. At Edgefield Mitchell found both of the bridges into Nashville destroyed, and his crossing was effected on the steamers that brought Nelson's division to that place.

The Fourth Division was ordered in February to reinforce the Federal troops at Fort Donelson. Nelson, with two brigades, moved from Camp Wickliffe to the Ohio River on February 13th, and there took steamer for the Cumberland River. On his arrival at Fort Donelson, he found it in possession of the Federal troops, and he then proceeded by the boats with his command to Nashville, arriving there on the 25th. Nelson's Third Brigade reported a few days later, having marched direct from Bowling Green.

General Thomas L. Crittenden's command, organizing at Owensboro, had a skirmish with a force of 500 rebels at Woodland. Colonel Burbridge was sent with some three hundred troops of his own command and a small force from Colonel McHenry's regiment. Attacking the enemy, they routed him, inflicting a loss of some fifty killed, wounded, and prisoners. On the 24th, the rebel General Breckinridge made a demonstration with 4,000 men at Rochester, occupying Greenville with his cavalry. Crittenden made such disposition of his troops that the enemy, without risking an attack, returned to Bowling Green. Early in February General Buell ordered Crittenden to send Colonel Cruft with his brigade to report to General Grant. Cruft, however, reached Fort Henry after the surrender, but his brigade was incorporated into Grant's army, and rendered effective ser-

VII.—2

vice in the reduction of Fort Donelson. Later, the brigade was transferred to General Halleck. Crittenden, soon after this, proceeded by boat with the balance of his division, and reported at Nashville, arriving there at the same time as Nelson's division.

The Sixth division, after aiding in the repair of the railroad, arrived at Nashville March 6, 1862.

General A. S. Johnston, at no time prior to his retreat had sufficient force to meet or to resist the advance of the Federal forces. His long line, extending from Columbus to Knoxville, invited attack, and wherever the attack was made his troops were not able to successfully resist it. Concentrating his command at Bowling Green, after Mill Springs and the fall of Fort Henry, he found that, to save Nashville, it was necessary to make a determined stand at Fort Donelson, and this he reinforced with all his available troops. The fall of Donelson compelled the evacuation of Nashville. To the Southern people these reverses were a bitter blow to their high hopes and boasting threats that the war was to be carried into the North, and peace was to follow the first victories to their arms. Duke, in his "History of Morgan's Cavalry," says: "No subsequent reverse, although fraught with far more real calamity, ever created the shame, sorrow, and wild consternation that swept over the South with the news of the surrender of Fort Donelson. To some in the South these reverses were harbingers of the final defeat and overthrow of the Confederacy."

With the fall of Donelson, after detaching the troops at Columbus, Johnston's force was reduced to a little over one-half of his total effective strength as reported by him at Bowling Green. In a report to Richmond, he gave the total of his command as barely forty-three thousand men.

General Buell's army amounted to over seventy-five thousand men, not all of these available for field duty, as a very large proportion of the command was needed to maintain his line of supplies, and the farther his advance the greater the drain on his command for railroad guards.

With the fall of Donelson, Johnston modified his plans of operations, and then determined to relinquish the defensive, and to concentrate all available forces of the Confederacy in the southwest for offensive operations. He had, as early as January, 1862, contemplated the possibility of the disasters that had taken place, and the retreat consequent upon them, and at that time indicated Corinth, Miss., as being the proper place to concentrate the troops.

On January 3d General Buell wrote at length to General Halleck, proposing a joint campaign against the enemy in "a combined attack on its centre and flanks," moving the troops by water under protection of the gunboats, striking for the railroad communications of the enemy, and destroying his bridges over the Cumberland and Tennessee Rivers, both of which were protected by batteries, the first at Dover—Fort Donelson—and the other at Fort Henry, respectively thirty-one and eighteen miles below the bridges. To this, on the 6th, General Halleck replied that, situated as he was, he could render no assistance to Buell's forward movement on Bowling Green, and advised the delay of the movement, if such co-operation by troops sent to Cairo and Paducah should be deemed necessary to the plan of the campaign, of which he knew nothing, and then adds: "But it strikes me that to operate from Louisville and Paducah or Cairo, against an enemy at Bowling Green, is a plain case of exterior lines, like that of McDowell and Patterson, which, unless each of the columns is superior to the enemy, leads to disaster ninety-nine times in a hundred."

On the 30th of January, Buell received a despatch from

Halleck, without particulars, saying that he had ordered an expedition against Fort Henry. On the 15th of February Halleck telegraphed Buell " to move from Bowling Green to Nashville is not good strategy. Come and help me take and hold Fort Donelson and Clarksville, then move to Florence, cutting the railroad at Decatur, and Nashville must be abandoned precisely as Bowling Green has been." After the fall of Fort Donelson, and the occupation of Nashville, General Halleck directed a column of the troops under General C. F. Smith to proceed up the Tennessee River by steamer, and to operate as occasion presented, either on Corinth, Jackson, or Humboldt, destroying the railroad communications at these points. At this time Halleck had no thought of the subsequent movement of the command, that Johnston would concentrate at Corinth, or that the Armies of the Ohio and Tennessee should unite at Pittsburg Landing. On the 15th General Smith dropped down the river to Pittsburg Landing, and there placed his troops in camp. On the 11th of March, President Lincoln, by War Order No. 3, created the Department of the Mississippi, consolidating the three departments under Generals Halleck, Hunter, and Buell, and placed General Halleck in command. Halleck at once ordered Buell to march his army to Savannah, and to execute the movements that had already been agreed on by them.

Buell immediately gave his attention to the preparation of his command to carry out these orders. He directed O. M. Mitchell to march south, strike, and hold the Memphis and Charleston Railroad. Organizing the seventh division of his army, Buell assigned General George W. Morgan to this command. This division was formed of four brigades, out of a number of regiments gathered up from different points in Kentucky. General Morgan concentrated his entire command at Cumberland Ford, being directed to take Cumberland Gap if possible and to occupy East Tennessee if able to enter. If not, then to resist any advance of the rebels.

General E. Dumont was placed in command of Nashville. The Twenty-third Brigade under Colonel Duffield, composed of four regiments, was ordered from Kentucky to garrison Murfreesboro, and protect the road from Shelbyville to Lavergne.

Buell designated the First Division under Thomas, the Second under Nelson, the Fifth under Crittenden, and the Sixth under Wood, to constitute the army under his personal command, which was to join Halleck in the operations against the enemy's position at Corinth. These divisions, with cavalry and artillery attached, made a force of 37,000 effective troops. In addition to these, Buell had under his command 36,000 effective men to defend his communications, maintain his line of supply, enforce order within his lines, and to perform any special duty assigned to them. The muster-rolls of his army showed that he had at this time 92 regiments of infantry—not including those sent to Halleck under Cruft. These regiments aggregated 79,334 men. He had 11 regiments, 1 battalion, and 7 detached companies of cavalry, making a total of 11,496 men, and 28 field, and 2 siege batteries, with 3,935 men. The grand total was 94,765 men. His effective force, however, was 73,487 men, comprising 60,882 infantry, 9,237 cavalry, and 3,368 artillery.

Buell's army, after crossing Duck River, pressed rapidly forward. The day before Nelson's arrival at the Tennessee River he was informed by General Grant, to whom he had reported his movements by courier, that he need not hasten his marches, as he could not cross the river before the follow-

ing Tuesday, the 8th.   Nelson's entire division, with forced
marches, reached Savannah April 5th, the other division
closely following.   Ammen's brigade of Nelson's division
crossed the river on the afternoon of the 6th, and reported to
Buell, and was engaged in the battle of that day, aiding in
resisting the final attack of Chalmers on the left of Grant's
command.   Crittenden's and McCook's divisions arrived on
the field during the night of the 6th, and took an active part
in the fighting of the next day.   The rest of the command
arrived on the field after the battle.

The movements of the troops of the "Army of the Ohio"
in the battle of Shiloh and in the operations against
Corinth are treated in Volume II. of this series, and it is
not within the purview of this volume to enter further into
the narrative of their service than to give a few brief facts as
to the disposition of the troops, in order to follow the subsequent events in which the Army of the Ohio was the main
actor.

CHAPTER IV.

MORGAN'S AND FORREST'S RAIDS.

On April 11th, Halleck arrived at Pittsburg Landing and at once reorganized the troops in his command, designating the divisions of his army as the right wing, centre, left wing, reserves, and cavalry under Major-Generals George H. Thomas, D. C. Buell, John Pope, and J. A. McClernand and Brigadier-General A. J. Smith respectively. Thomas's command comprised four divisions of the " Army of the Tennessee," and his old division of the "Army of the Ohio." The remainder of that army was under the command of Buell. After the fall of Corinth, the enemy breaking his large force into several smaller commands rendered necessary a similar disposition of the Federal forces. Buell was ordered with his command to enter into a campaign looking to the occupation of East Tennessee. One division of his army under O. M. Mitchell left Nashville about the middle of March under orders to proceed to Murfreesboro and repair the railroad bridges burned by Johnston on his retreat. On Colonel Duffield's reporting with the Twenty-third brigade, Mitchell pressed forward to Shelbyville and from there by a rapid movement on the 7th of April he occupied Huntsville, Ala., with Turchin's brigade, Kennett's Ohio cavalry, and Simonson's battery, capturing 170 prisoners, 15 locomotives, and 150 passenger and freight cars, and a large amount of army stores. On the 8th, Mitchell ordered Sill with his brigade to proceed east along the line of the railroad to seize Stevenson, the junction of the Nashville and Chattanooga, and Memphis and Charleston Railroads, and directed Turchin with his command to move west and take possession of Decatur and Tuscumbia. This was successfully done, and Mitchell was in possession of over one hundred miles of this important link connecting Corinth with Richmond in the heart of the enemy's territory. He then posted his troops at the more prominent points, ready to move to any place threatened by the enemy.

On April 29th, Mitchell, hearing of the advance of the force under Kirby Smith from Bridgeport against the command beyond Stevenson, moved as rapidly as possible by rail from Huntsville to resist him. He found the enemy had attacked the detachment posted five miles west of Bridgeport, and that his troops had driven the enemy's advance back across Widow's Creek. The bridge over this creek had been burned by the enemy on their retreat. Mitchell strengthened the detachment and engaged the attention of the enemy by an apparent effort to cross this creek, while with his main force he advanced on Bridgeport by a detour by the left and drove that portion of the enemy in the town across the Tennessee River. In their retreat the enemy set fire to the bridge reaching from the west bank of the river to the Island. This bridge Mitchell succeeded in saving, but the bridge east of the Island was completely destroyed. General Mitchell then turned his attention to that part of the enemy's force at Widow's Creek, which he succeeded in capturing, taking in all some three hundred and fifty prisoners. Early in May, Mitchell, who had been placed in command of all the troops between Nashville and Huntsville, ordered General Negley with the Seventh Brigade, belonging to McCook's division—who had been left at Columbia on the advance of the main army upon Savannah—to make an advance against General Adams with a brigade of troops at Rogersville, Ala. At the same time Mitchell sent Colonel Lytle from Athens, Ala., to co-operate with Negley. On the 13th, the enemy learning of the approach of the Federal forces, retreated across the Tennessee River. This placed Mitchell in complete possession of that portion of Alabama north of that river. On May 29th, Mitchell concentrated Negley's command from Columbia, Turchin's brigade from Huntsville, and the Eighteenth Ohio under T. R. Stanley from Athens at Fayetteville for an expedition against Chattanooga under the command of Negley. These troops passed through Winchester, Cowen, and University Place to Jasper. Advancing upon the latter place, the head of his column, under Colonel Hambright, encountered a brigade of the enemy's troops under General Adams. The enemy was driven from the place after a sharp engagement, leaving his supply and ammunition trains. His loss was 18 killed, 20 wounded, and 12 prisoners. Leaving Jasper, Negley arrived on the north bank of the Tennessee, opposite Chattanooga, on the 7th. Negley, on the evening of that day and the morning of the next, bombarded Chattanooga, and made a demonstration of crossing the river and attacking the town. General Duke says: "The commandant of the place, General Leadbetter, had two or three guns in battery and replied, when the gunners, who were the most independent fellows I ever saw, chose to work the guns. The defence of the place was left entirely to the individual efforts of those who chose to defend it, and nothing prevented its capture but the fact that the enemy could not cross the river."

Negley then withdrew and encamped his command at Shelbyville.

General G. W. Morgan, under orders from Buell, assumed command of the forces in Eastern Kentucky early in April. Acting under his orders he proceeded to Cumberland Ford and commenced operations at once against Cumberland Gap. This gap is situated in the Cumberland range on the boundary line between Kentucky and Tennessee, near the Western Virginia line, is a deep depression in the mountain range, making a natural roadway through it, and is the centre of all the roads in that section of country. It is a stronghold protected by nature with abrupt slopes on the mountains, frequently so steep as to be almost perpendicular, with the ranges much broken by spurs, knobs, and ravines, protected by parallel ranges of less height in close proximity on the east and west. Morgan, after encountering the enemy in several skirmishes, determined either to compel him to fight or retreat. He sent General Spears with three brigades to Pine Mountain, on the road to Big Creek Gap. General Kirby Smith, commanding the enemy's forces in East Tennessee, placed General Barton's command of two brigades of infantry in Big Creek Gap, and then advanced with some eight thousand men under his immediate command to cut Spears off, and to threaten the Federal forces at Cumberland Ford. Morgan, under orders, withdrew Spears, but learning a few days later from Buell of the operations of Negley's command before Chattanooga, and that Kirby Smith had proceeded with a part of his command to the relief of that place, resumed the advance. Negley's movements had caused Smith to suspend his operations, but when he heard of Negley's withdrawal he proceeded at once to execute his plans against Morgan. On June 18th, the latter, finding that Kirby Smith had taken his entire command away from Cumberland Gap, marched his troops up Powell's Valley and late in the evening of that day reached the fortifications, found the Gap empty, and took possession. This natural stronghold had been extensively fortified by the rebels, who regarded the position of their troops such as to prevent the success of any attempt on the part of the Federal forces to obtain possession without a battle. The enemy were completely out-manœuvred, and General Morgan had the satisfaction of occupying this fortress without the loss of any of his command.

In the early part of May, the rebel Colonel John H. Morgan's command of some five hundred men, in the neighborhood of Pulaski, Tenn., captured a wagon train with about four hundred Federal troops, mostly convalescents going to Columbia. On the night of the 5th, Morgan reached Lebanon and quartered his entire force in houses in the town. On the evening of the 6th, Dumont with his command from Nashville, joined by that of Duffield from Murfreesboro, surprised and attacked Morgan's troopers, completely routing them after a severe engagement. Morgan with a few men under his immediate command escaped after a chase of twenty-one miles from Lebanon, crossing the Cumberland River on a ferry. Dumont had with him detachments of Wynkoop's Seventh Pennsylvania cavalry, of Wolford's First Kentucky cavalry and of Green Clay Smith's regiment of Kentucky cavalry. Morgan's loss was 150 men captured, with the same number of horses. The balance of his command was dispersed. Wolford and Smith were both wounded, and the Federals lost 6 killed and 25 wounded. On the 11th, Morgan with his men that had escaped, and two new companies, made a raid on the Louisville and Nashville Railroad at Cave City, captured a freight train of forty-eight cars and burned it. He also captured a passenger train, which had a few Federal officers on it. His object was to rescue the men of his command taken prisoners at Lebanon, but in this he failed, as they had been sent North by boat.

From this place Morgan reported with his command at Chattanooga to refit, preparatory to his first extended raid into Kentucky. Here he was joined by two full companies of Texan cavalry under Captains R. M. Gano and John Huffman, both native Kentuckians, who, on reporting at Corinth, had asked to be ordered on duty with Morgan and his command, enlarged from a squadron to a full regiment. After he had obtained all the recruits he could at Chattanooga he set out for Knoxville, to further increase his command and to re-arm. It was at this place that he received the two mountain howitzers which were used so effectively in the first raid into Kentucky, and which just before his command started on the Ohio raid were taken from it by Bragg's ordnance officers. This came near raising a mutiny, and the only consolation that Morgan's men had was that Bragg lost the guns within two weeks after they were taken away from them. In the latter part of June, Colonel Hunt, of Georgia, reported at Knoxville with a regiment of "Partisan Rangers," nearly four hundred strong, ordered to accompany Morgan on his contemplated raid, making the strength of his entire command 876 effective men.

Morgan set out from Knoxville on the morning of July 4, 1862, taking the road to Sparta, one hundred and four miles due west from Knoxville, which was reached on the evening of the third day of this march. The Union men of East Tennessee frequently gave these raiders medicine of their own prescription, lying in wait for them and firing upon them from the bushes. This was a new experience for these freebooting troopers, who wherever they went in the South were generally made welcome to the best of everything, being regarded as the beau-ideals of Southern chivalry. On the 8th, Morgan's command reached the Cumberland River at the ford near the small village of Celina, eighteen miles from Tompkinsville, where a detachment of the Ninth Pennsylvania, 250 strong, was encamped under command of Major Jordan. Morgan learned at Knoxville the fact that a Federal force was at this point, and was told the particulars of it on his arrival at Celina, and he now wished to surprise and capture the entire command. Sending a detachment under Gano by the right to cut off Jordan's retreat, at five o'clock on the morning of the 9th Morgan moved to the attack. Jordan posted himself on a thickly wooded hill and fired several volleys at the rebels as they advanced over an open field, but being outnumbered was routed with a loss of four killed, six wounded, and nineteen prisoners. The enemy's loss was several wounded, among them Colonel Hunt, who died a few days later from the effects of his wound. Morgan paroled the prisoners and then left for Glasgow, reaching there at one o'clock that night, where they were received with open arms by the citizens, breakfast cooked for the entire command, and three days' rations prepared for them. From here the command marched all night, and at eleven o'clock next morning was within a short distance of Lebanon. Morgan, preparatory to an attack, despatched one of his companies to destroy the railroad north of the town to prevent the arrival of reinforcements. The company struck the railroad at New Hope Church, and had just commenced their work of destruction when a train came up with a number of Federal troops on it, who drove the rebels off in confusion, but for some un known cause the train then returned to Louisville, leaving Morgan unmolested at Lebanon, who advanced to the attack and drove in the pickets. After a slight skirmish the place was surrendered by Lieutenant-Colonel Johnson of the Twenty-eighth Kentucky, with a small detachment of that command. Morgan destroyed some fifty thousand dollars' worth of Government stores. He left Lebanon at two o'clock in the afternoon, passed through Springfield, without halting the command, and pushed on for Harrodsburg, reaching there at nine o'clock on Sunday morning. Here he sent Gano with his squadron around Lexington to burn the railroad bridges on the Kentucky Central Railroad, in order to prevent troops being sent there from Cincinnati. Another detachment was sent to destroy the bridge on the Louisville and Lexington Railroad, cutting off reinforcements from Louisville. Morgan's design was to make it appear that he intended to attack Frankfort, then turn suddenly to the right and attempt the capture of Lexington. He had given out everywhere in Kentucky that he was marching on the State Capital with a force five thousand strong, and had succeeded in spreading the utmost alarm. On the 15th Morgan reached Midway, captured the telegraph operator and installed his own operator at the instrument, sent despatches in the name of Federal Generals, and changed the orders for the movement of troops. He telegraphed in all directions, without the slightest regard for truth, and succeeded in creating the utmost confusion and alarm at Cincinnati, Louisville, Lexington, and Frankfort. The command left Midway late in the afternoon and started for Georgetown, which place they reached at sundown, where they met a small force of Home Guards, who were driven out of town. From here Morgan sent a force to burn the bridges on the Kentucky Railroad between Lexington and Paris. Then learning how strongly Lexington was garrisoned, he gave up all thought of attacking it, and finding that the Federal forces were closing in on him commenced his return south. On the

18th, Morgan attacked Cynthiana, which was garrisoned by some five hundred men, under the command of Lieutenant-Colonel John J. Landrum, of the Eighteenth Kentucky. The fighting continued for two hours, when the Federal force was driven from the town and nearly all captured. Landrum and a few of his command escaped. The Federals lost 16 killed and 40 wounded, and 14 of the enemy were killed and 42 wounded. The rebels claimed to have captured 420 prisoners, who were at once paroled. The depôt, with a large amount of Government stores, was burned. Morgan then left for Paris, where he arrived late in the evening and rested there that night. About eight o'clock in the morning his command was driven out of this place by the troops under General Green Clay Smith, numbering some twelve hundred men, who killed 2, wounded six, and captured several prisoners. Morgan pushed through Winchester, reaching that point about twelve o'clock, crossed the Kentucky River just at dark, and arrived at Richmond at four o'clock in the morning. Here he rested his command twelve hours, then marched toward Crab Orchard, arriving about daybreak the next morning. It had been his intention to make a stand at Richmond, but there were too many troops marching to attack him. Besides General Smith's command, which was following him closely, Colonel Wolford was collecting forces in the southern part of Kentucky to intercept him, and troops were *en route* from Louisville to aid in the pursuit. Morgan left Crab Orchard at eleven o'clock the same morning, and reached Somerset about sunset. At these two places he captured 130 wagons, with large quantities of Government stores, of which he loaded as much into wagons for the use of his command as he wanted, and burned the rest. From Somerset he marched to Stagall's Ferry on the Cumberland River, and there

crossed, reaching Monticello, twenty-one miles from the
river, that night, when all pursuit ended.

Morgan's object in making this raid was to obtain recruits
and horses, to equip and arm his men, and to prepare for his
fall raiding trip. In his official report he says : "I left
Knoxville on the 4th day of this month with about nine
hundred men, and returned to Livingston on the 28th inst.
with nearly twelve hundred, having been absent just twenty-
four days, during which time I have travelled over a thousand miles, captured seventeen towns, destroyed all the
Government supplies and arms in them, dispersed about fifteen hundred Home Guards, and paroled nearly twelve
hundred regular troops. I lost in killed, wounded, and
missing, of the number that I carried into Kentucky, about
ninety."

When Buell received his orders to open the campaign
in East Tennessee, the key to that part of the State was
Chattanooga, and this was the objective point of his campaign. With the concentration of the Southern forces in
Mississippi, both Halleck and Buell thought that a favorable
time had arrived for this movement, anticipating that no
advance of the enemy's forces would be made to dispute
the occupancy of those portions of Kentucky and Tennessee already held by the Federal forces. The great problem with Buell was to furnish supplies to his army, now
some three hundred miles away from its base at Louisville,
dependent during the greater part of the year on one line of
road, which was subject to being raided at any time, bridges
burned, the roadbed destroyed, and the entire road rendered useless for months. To continue this line the many
miles through the enemy's country, subject to increased
risks before Chattanooga could be reached, was a matter
that required a great amount of careful thought and delib-

eration. Buell had tried infantry in stockades at bridges, and was satisfied that this was not the proper solution of the problem. He then made earnest and repeated application for more cavalry, to protect his communications and to meet and repulse the enemy's raiding parties before they could reach his line of communication. If he was to move with his command into East Tennessee, he regarded the line from Nashville to Chattanooga as the proper road on which he should depend for his supplies, and to which he should give his care and attention for this purpose.

Halleck considered the line from Memphis to Chattanooga the one over which the supplies for Buell's army should pass. The latter objected to this, by reason of that road crossing the Tennessee River twice, thus giving two long bridges to rebuild and protect, instead of one, and for the additional reason that this road ran for a considerable distance parallel with the front of the enemy, and thus invited raiding parties. While the risks attending the other road were great enough, Buell regarded the Memphis and Charleston road far the more objectionable. Besides, he wished to move through Middle Tennessee to McMinnville, and thence to Chattanooga, with Nashville as his depot of supplies. In this Halleck overruled him and directed that he march his command on the line of the Memphis road, repairing the track as he advanced.

While this matter was under consideration by the Federal commanders, Bragg, who had been appointed to the position of General made vacant by the death of General Johnston, and who had succeeded Beauregard in the command in the West, put his columns in motion eastward to occupy Chattanooga. Johnston, on the retreat from Nashville, sent all surplus army stores to Chattanooga, and Bragg now regarded that point as the proper place to refit his command, and from which to assume the offensive, and open the campaign he had planned to free, for a time at least, Tennessee from the control of the Federal forces.

With the start thus made by both commands for Chattanooga, everything was in favor of Bragg, whose movements were unimpeded, as his route was south of the Tennessee, through his own territory, with his lines of communication open when he arrived at that place. With Buell, the repairs of the railroad retarded his progress, and the advance weakened his command by the increased number of detachments required to guard his line as it lengthened.

McCook's and Crittenden's commands were started eastward, the first from Corinth, and the latter from Booneville. McCook reached Florence on the 15th of June, where ferryboats had been provided by Mitchell for the crossing of his division. A delay was occasioned here by the report that Nelson had been attacked, but this was found to be false; and, on the 26th, the divisions of McCook, Crittenden, and Nelson crossed, and started at once for Athens, which place they reached on the 29th. On the same day Buell established his headquarters at Huntsville, Ala., and gave personal supervision to the repair of the railroads, now extremely urgent. He placed his troops by division upon the different sections of the line, under orders to push repairs with all possible expedition. These troops, as repairs were made, advanced from time to time, concentrating on the line of the Nashville and Chattanooga road. The repairs to this railroad were completed on July 28th, and on the Nashville and Decatur road on August 3d. During the latter part of July the last division of Buell's army, under Thomas, crossed the Tennessee River, being relieved—on the line of the Memphis and Charleston Railroad—by troops from Grant's army. Thomas established his head-

quarters at Dechard: It was on this march with his brigade
that General Robert L. McCook was murdered by guerillas.
He was riding in an ambulance, ill at the time, and unarmed.

Nelson's division had been sent to Murfreesboro about
the middle of July, to drive Forrest, who, with his cavalry,
on the 13th, attacked the Federal garrison in the town.
The post was under the command of General T. T. Crittenden, and the troops composing the Twenty-third Brigade
were under the command of Colonel Duffield. There was,
unfortunately, a disagreement between the ranking officers
at the post that led to the most unfortunate results. Colonel Lester, of the Third Minnesota, during the absence of
Duffield, commanding the brigade, had, by reason of the
unpleasant relations existing between portions of the command, widely distributed them in different parts of the
town. On the return of Crittenden and Duffield on July
11th, neither of them assumed command, and their action
made it appear as if they were standing on their dignity,
thinking more of their own personal importance than the
good of the service. With no one in command, there was
no unity or proper *esprit de corps* among the troops, and
no disposition for defence when Forrest made his attack. The latter had advanced through McMinnville from
Chattanooga, with about two thousand men, and arrived
at Murfreesboro about five o'clock on the morning of the
13th, captured the pickets, and made disposition of his
forces for immediate attack. Forming his entire command
into columns of fours, with the Eighth Texas in front, Forrest moved forward on a trot until he reached the Federal
encampments, which Colonel Wharton, with two regiments,
charged. The Second Georgia dashed into the town, captured the provost guard and all Federal officers and men
on the streets, seized and secured the supplies.

Major Smith with the Kentucky troops was sent to the rear of the Federal command to cut off the retreat. The Texans charged into the camp of the Ninth Michigan, and reaching the tents, roused some of the men from sleep. A portion of that regiment, however, rallied by the officers, made a handsome stand and drove the Texans off. Duffield was wounded while rallying his men. The Second Georgia charged into the public square and surrounded the Court House, occupied by a company of the Ninth Michigan, who twice repulsed the attacking force. Reinforcements being brought forward, the doors of the building were battered down and the company was forced to surrender. Forrest now attacked the Third Minnesota on the east bank of Stone's River, about a mile and a half from town, which had just left their camp to join the force in the town, when Forrest with three regiments moved to the attack.

Colonel Lester formed his command in line of battle, with nine companies of infantry and four pieces of artillery, and opened fire on the rebels as they advanced. Forrest attempting to get to the rear of this force, encountered the camp guard of some hundred men left by Lester to protect his camp, posted behind a strong barricade of wagons and some large ledges of rocks, difficult to carry. Forrest at once ordered a charge which was twice made and repulsed. Leading his men the third time, he succeeded in driving the guard from their position to the main command, posted some six hundred yards away. It was now one o'clock, and beyond the skirmishes between the commands but little had been accomplished.

Forrest's officers urged him to withdraw with the results obtained up to that time. This he refused to do, and made disposition of his command for further attack on the Federal forces occupying the camp of the Ninth Michigan, which consisted of this regiment and a company of the Second Kentucky cavalry. He dismounted two of his regiments and threw forward skirmishers, directed them to open brisk firing, and sent the Second Georgia dismounted to attack on the left. After this he brought up the Eighth Texas and placed them in position to charge on the left.

Having made this disposition of his forces, he sent forward, under a flag of truce, a written demand for the surrender of Duffield's command, which was complied with at once. After this, Forrest demanded the surrender of the Third Minnesota, which Lester, after an interview with Duffield and a consultation with his own officers, made, surrendering some five hundred infantry of his regiment and two sections of Hewitt's battery of artillery. The entire forces surrendered were seventeen hundred troops with four pieces of artillery. Forrest captured about six hundred horses and mules, and a very large quantity of stores and Government supplies, part of which he carried away and the rest he destroyed, to the value of nearly a million of dollars.

This loss occurred the day after the opening of the road from Nashville south, and very seriously interfered with the movements at the front. Nelson endeavored to intercept Forrest, but could not successfully "chase cavalry with infantry." Forrest on Nelson's approach withdrew to McMinnville, and from there made a dash on Lebanon, some fifty miles distant, where he expected to find a force of five hundred Federal cavalry. This force escaped him, and he then swept around to the south of Nashville, captured 150 bridge guards and burned four bridges. Learning that Nelson was again in pursuit of him, Forrest returned to McMinnville.

From this point he made repeated raids on the line of road south of Nashville, leaving Morgan to operate against the Louisville and Nashville Railroad. These raiders were able to move almost without opposition, as Buell was without sufficient cavalry to cope with them. The latter had been compelled to divide his cavalry into small bands to run down the guerillas that had been operating on his line of railroad. Now that Forrest's and Morgan's commands had become so formidable, he was compelled to organize his cavalry into united bodies for better defensive movements against these raiders. The Second Indiana, Fourth and Fifth Kentucky, and Seventh Pennsylvania cavalry regiments he formed into one brigade, and on August 11th, he sent it under General R. W. Johnson against Morgan, who had been ordered by Bragg to break the railroad between Louisville and Nashville, in order to retard Buell's movement north to Louisville as much as possible, and who was operating about Gallatin, Tennessee, which he had captured with 200 prisoners. Colonel Boone was in command of the Federal forces at this point. Morgan hearing that Boone slept in the town away from the camp, sent a small force to capture him, which was done, just as he had dressed and was starting to camp. Morgan then destroyed a railroad bridge south of Gallatin, and the tunnel six miles north, the roof of which was supported with large beams on upright timbers. Running some freight cars into the tunnel, they were set on fire and some eight hundred feet of it destroyed, the roof caving in.

Johnson sought to attack Morgan before he could unite with Forrest, who was on his Lebanon raid at that time, but Morgan hearing that Johnson had infantry and artillery supports, endeavored to avoid an engagement. Johnson forced the fight, engaged Morgan with spirit, and although repulsed three times, after the first and second repulse formed promptly and renewed the attack. After the third repulse the Federal forces commenced retreating, when Morgan followed, attacked Johnson's retreating forces and drove the Federals some three miles. Johnson reformed his lines twice, but the enemy broke, and drove them each time. He then reformed the remnant of his command and fought the enemy dismounted, when the latter charged again, and Johnson, seeing that the greater part of his command had scattered, surrendered. The force that was with him at this time was only a small band of some twenty-five soldiers and a few officers. His loss was 20 killed and 42 wounded. Duke, in his "History of Morgan's Cavalry," says: "A great deal of censure was at the time cast upon these men"—Johnson's command—"and they were accused of arrant cowardice by the Northern press. Nothing could have been more unjust. They attacked with spirit and without hesitation, and were unable to close with us on account of their heavy loss in men and horses. I have seen troops much more highly boasted than these were before their defeat, behave not nearly so well." And of Johnson, Duke says: "His attack was made promptly and in splendid style; his dispositions throughout the first fight were good, and he exhibited fine personal courage and energy."

CHAPTER V.

BRAGG'S ADVANCE INTO KENTUCKY.

AFTER Nelson's pursuit of Forrest on his raid around Nashville, he was ordered by General Buell to McMinnville. Crittenden and McCook with their divisions were at Battle Creek, Thomas and Wood were on the line of the Nashville and Chattanooga Railroad, and Mitchell's division, under the command of Rousseau, on the line of railroad from Decatur to Columbia. Bragg had so well concealed his intention as to his advance, that Buell was compelled to be in readiness to meet him in the event of one of three movements, which it was supposed he would make if he moved before Buell was ready to advance upon him.

The latter thought Bragg would either move by the left, pass around into Northern Alabama, cross at Decatur, and press north for Nashville. This he regarded as the most likely movement. Or, second, move direct, crossing the mountains, pass through McMinnville, and so on to Nashville. Or, third, to move by way of Knoxville into Eastern Kentucky. The latter, up to the first of September, Buell regarded as hardly a possibility, supposing Bragg's movements all indicated an advance on Nashville. Thomas was ordered to assume command of the troops at McMinnville, to repair the railroad from Tullahoma to that point as he went, and to establish posts of observation with signal stations on the mountains to watch Bragg's movements. Thomas assumed command at McMinnville on the 19th of August, on the same day that Bragg sent a column of three or four thousand troops across the river at Chattanooga. Buell, in anticipation of this being the advance of Bragg's entire army *en route* for Nashville, despatched Wood to the vicinity of McMinnville, to aid in resisting his advance. He then ordered McCook to move from Battle Creek to the Therman road, where he was to hold the enemy in check until reinforced by Thomas. Crittenden's division was sent up the valley through Tracy City, by the Altamont road, to be within supporting distance of McCook, and to watch the road from there to Chattanooga. Thomas was directed to hold his command in readiness to move at a moment's notice, either on the Therman or Dunlop road. On the 22d, Buell learned that Bragg's whole army was north of the Tennessee, and he then, further to concentrate his command, moved his supplies from the depôt at Stevenson to Dechard. Thomas on the same day telegraphed from McMinnville to Buell that he believed Bragg's movements meant an advance of his entire army into Kentucky. Thomas reconnoitred thoroughly the front of his position, and ascertained that the enemy was not there and not as yet even in Sequatchie Valley. This he reported to Buell, and suggested that Wood's division be posted at Sparta, to intercept Bragg's advance, if made through that place ; that another division be left at Dechard, to watch any movement in that direction, and that the remaining portions of the command be concentrated at McMinnville, ready to offer battle to Bragg's army if it should advance on that front. Thomas regarded Bragg's advance either on Nashville or Louisville as possible only through McMinnville or Sparta, and he proposed to attack before Bragg could reach either. On the next day Buell, under advices that he regarded as reliable, ordered

VII.—3

the First, Second, Fourth, Fifth, and Sixth Divisions to concentrate at Altamont, intending there to offer battle. He
sent detailed instructions to Thomas, in charge of the movement, as to the disposition of his command, with orders in
the event of defeat to fall back, keeping his force between
the enemy and Nashville. On the 25th, Thomas reached
Altamont, and finding no enemy nearer than the Sequatchie
Valley, and regarding Bragg's advance by way of Altamont
improbable, owing to the bad condition of the roads, and
lack of forage and water, returned to McMinnville with the
Fourth and Sixth Divisions. On the 30th, Buell gave orders
concentrating his entire command at Murfreesboro, still
under the impression that Bragg expected to strike for
Nashville. The latter's movements were so well guarded,
and Buell had as yet so little reliable information in regard
to them, that he hesitated even after the order was issued,
and the next day asked Thomas's advice in regard to it, in
the light of any further information as to the movements
of the enemy. Thomas advised that the movement proceed,
having been commenced, and gave a plan of battle in the
movement from Murfreesboro. Thomas, on the 30th, captured a despatch that Bragg, on the 27th, had sent to Van
Dorn, in command in Mississippi, conveying to him in full his
plans in regard to his advance into Kentucky, and informed
him that Kirby Smith, reinforced with two divisions from
his army, had turned Cumberland Gap, and was marching
on Lexington, Ky.

Buell's army at Murfreesboro consisted of five divisions
under his immediate command, the troops being then on
the line of the railroad. In addition he had two divisions
sent to him from the Army of the Tennessee—General J. C.
Davis's division, under General R. B. Mitchell, which arrived at Murfreesboro on the 2d of September, and Gen-

eral E. A. Paine's division, under the command of General
J. M. Palmer, which reached Nashville on the 10th. This
concentration of the army at Murfreesboro of course withdrew all troops from the mountains, leaving Bragg unham-
pered in the selection of his route, either west to Nashville,
or north to Louisville. He made choice of the latter, and
pushed down the valley of the Cumberland to Carthage,
where he crossed, moving through Scottsboro and Glasgow,
to strike the Louisville and Nashville Railroad. Bragg entered Kentucky with five divisions, making an army of some
thirty-five thousand men, divided between Generals Polk
and Hardee. While at Murfreesboro Buell first learned
definitely of Bragg's movements, and of his intended advance into Kentucky. The news of the movements of Kirby
Smith and of Nelson's defeat also reached him here.

On August 16th, Buell had ordered Nelson to assume command in Kentucky, and to make such dispositions of his
troops as would resist any movement by Kirby Smith, then
threatening Cumberland Gap. The plan of the rebels in
their campaign, which was intended to free the soil of the
South from the Northern armies by carrying the war into the
North, was for Kirby Smith to move through Eastern Kentucky to Lexington and thence to Cincinnati, and for Bragg
to push through Central Kentucky to Louisville. With these
two cities in the possession of their armies it would be a
short step to enter upon the rich fields of the Northern
States, and with the large number of new recruits gained
en route their armies could resist any Northern troops that
would be brought against them. This had been Sidney
Johnston's plan to be worked out after he had achieved the
victory he contemplated at Shiloh, and Bragg as his successor
endeavored to carry out Johnston's plan of campaign. One
was as much a success as the other, and in both the hour of

defeat trod so quickly on their apparent victory that the campaign in each instance ultimately resulted in failure. So far as the advance of Bragg and Kirby Smith into Kentucky was concerned, by it the South suffered a loss instead of a gain, and was compelled from that time on to act upon a steadily lessening line of defence. Bragg's report shows that he took a smaller command out than he took into the State.

On the same day that Nelson's orders were dated, Stevenson appeared with his division before Cumberland Gap. George W. Morgan in command there immediately sent out cavalry to the adjoining gaps to watch for further movements of the enemy. When a short distance from Roger's Gap the cavalry struck the head of Kirby Smith's army on its advance to Kentucky. Smith's forces were those of his own command in East Tennessee, re-enforced by the divisions of McCown from Mississippi, sent him by Bragg, and also the two fine brigades of Cleburne and Preston Smith, ordered to report to him from Chattanooga. Kirby Smith moved with his main command to Barboursville, and ordered McCown to Cumberland Ford with a large force, which cut off Morgan, in the Gap, from his base of supplies in that direction. Leaving Stevenson in Morgan's front to engage his attention, Kirby Smith with his entire force advanced into Kentucky, thus entirely cutting off re-enforcements and supplies to Morgan's command. The latter failing in his efforts to bring on an engagement, placed his command on half rations, and after a council of war abandoned the Gap, dismounting his siege guns and destroying what stores and ammunition he could not remove, marched out with his entire command, to the east of Kirby Smith's force, to the Ohio River. John Morgan's cavalry annoyed the command for some days, without inflicting any material loss.

When Nelson reached Kentucky he found that a new department had been created, with General H. G. Wright in command, embracing that part of the State east of Louisville and the line of the Nashville Railroad, taken from under Buell's command. Wright ordered Nelson to proceed to Lexington and assume command of all the troops in that locality, nearly all of them new regiments, principally from Ohio and Kentucky, hastily gathered together, without drill or discipline. Nelson concentrated these troops at Lexington, and organized them into a division with Generals M. D. Manson, J. S. Jackson, and Charles Cruft as brigade commanders. On August 23d, Nelson sent a detachment of the Seventh Kentucky cavalry and Colonel Child's battalion of Tennessee cavalry, under Colonel Metcalfe's command, to Big Hill to resist the advance of the enemy. These troops being attacked by a greatly superior force the Seventh Kentucky broke and fled, leaving, however, about one-fourth of the command with the Tennessee battalion, which, after fighting bravely, was compelled to retire. Metcalfe rallied his men, but on the approach of the enemy they again broke and ran, leaving the Tennesseeans to resist the attack, which they so far succeeded in doing as to secure a safe retreat to Richmond. The enemy pushed forward and demanded the surrender of the town, but learning that re-enforcements had arrived, retired. Nelson then ordered Manson's and Cruft's brigades, under the command of the former, to proceed to Richmond. On arriving there Manson went into camp south of the town and threw out his pickets. The cavalry, on the 29th, reported an advance of the enemy in large numbers, and that a heavy force of infantry was driving in the pickets. Manson advanced to their support with his own brigade, leaving Cruft with his command at Richmond. Moving forward with his troops he drove the attacking party back and formed his line of battle on each side of the road some two miles from the town. The enemy attacked with infantry, artillery, and cavalry, but was driven back with the loss of one field piece and several men captured. Manson then occupied Rogersville, where he remained in camp all night. 'In the morning he ordered Cruft to join him, and moved out beyond the town to meet the enemy's advance. After heavy fighting for over an hour the left of Manson's command was fiercely assaulted, which being reinforced, the right began to give way in confusion.

The troops were rallied on a new line a mile to the rear, but as this was badly posted for defence, the command was withdrawn from this position to the line occupied the day before, and from this—the enemy attacking in heavy force —the Federal troops were again routed and driven back to their camps, where the last stand was made and the heaviest fighting took place. Nelson, arriving on the ground, assumed command and endeavored to stem the tide of defeat. The enemy advanced in such overwhelming numbers upon the position of the Federal forces that they were driven in complete disorder at all points from the field. Nelson was twice wounded, but was able to reach Louisville with several detachments of his routed troops. Here he assumed command and bent every energy to the organization of new troops, forming the citizens in commands for the defence of that city. Nelson's losses in the engagement at Richmond were two hundred and twenty-five killed, six hundred wounded, and over two thousand captured. He also lost nine guns. His entire command consisted of some seven thousand troops. The enemy's force was twelve thousand men and thirty-six pieces of artillery, and he lost over nine hundred killed and wounded. Kirby Smith then pushed his command north, occupying Lexington, and sent out detachments threatening

Louisville and Cincinnati. On the 6th of September, General Heth with some six thousand troops advanced and took position a few miles south of Covington. He was ordered by Kirby Smith not to attack, but to hold his command in readiness to move at a moment's notice to form a junction with Bragg, then marching north through Kentucky.

Smith, while waiting to form a junction with Bragg, was actively employed in gathering supplies for his army in the richest part of the State. He also sought to obtain recruits for his command, but recruiting for the infantry service did not prove a success. During the entire period the rebel army was in Kentucky not one entire infantry regiment was raised. Individual enlistment was constantly going on, but the leading officers of that army estimated their entire gain was not over five thousand men, including three regiments of cavalry recruited under Buford. Heth's advance alarmed the three cities of Covington, Newport, and Cincinnati, spreading consternation among all classes. Martial law was proclaimed, and all able-bodied citizens were ordered to report for work on the fortifications south of Covington. These works were manned by the population of the surrounding country, coming to Cincinnati to defend that city from pillage. Regiments of "Squirrel Hunters" were formed, and a show of force was kept up until veteran troops could be brought forward to take their place. Heth wished to attack, but Kirby Smith would not permit this, as he anticipated a battle with Buell, and that Bragg would have to fight his entire army, in which event he would need every available man. Heth fell back in a few days and on October 4th Smith reported with his command to Bragg at Frankfort.

Bragg's movements became clearly apparent to Buell while the latter was concentrating at Murfreesboro. On

September 7th, Buell started with Ammen's, Crittenden's, McCook's, Wood's, Rousseau's, and Mitchell's divisions in the race between the opposing armies for Louisville. If Bragg moved energetically and with the intent of taking Louisville without fighting a battle in Kentucky before he reached that city, his start in the race and the shorter line he was moving on gave him the decided advantage in the movement. Buell's object was to overtake Bragg, and, if necessary, force the fighting. This would compel the latter to move his army so closely on the one road open to him that his movements would be necessarily slow. Failing in this, Buell's plans were to press Bragg so hard that if he refused to fight in Kentucky he must leave the State in possession of the Federal forces before he could gain anything by his advance.

Buell, after reaching Nashville, crossed the river there at once and pushed on with all possible speed. He left Thomas's, Palmer's, and Negley's divisions, with Thomas in command, as the garrison at this place. So important did Buell regard the holding of Nashville, that he determined to weaken his immediate command and leave this strong force under his most trusted subordinate, to retain possession of that point. He considered his army in pursuit of Bragg of sufficient strength to make the fight for the possession of Kentucky, and in the event Bragg was driven from that State he would then concentrate in the vicinity of Nashville, where the battle for that important position with Middle Tennessee would yet have to be fought. In the happening of the latter event it was an absolute necessity that the Federal army should hold Nashville as a point at which to concentrate and move to the attack. If the result of the movement in Kentucky should be the defeat of Buell, then it was important that the general in command of the forces at Nashville should be an officer of experience, to save the troops left there, in their retreat to rejoin the main army. Buell regarded the holding of Nashville by our forces as second only to the safety of Kentucky, and made the disposition of his command accordingly. With this view, on the 12th, he ordered R. B. Mitchell's division to return to Nashville and form part of the garrison of that place. Bragg, on the 8th, had reached the railroad, where he burned the bridge at Salt River, and for some days in his northward march was engaged in tearing up the railroad as he advanced. On the 13th, his cavalry reached Munfordsville beyond Green River.

Buell, on the 10th, learning that additional forces of Bragg's command were crossing the Cumberland at Gainesville, at once countermanded the order to Mitchell, and directed Thomas to place Negley in command of Nashville, and if he regarded it best to do so, to leave Paine's division with Negley's to hold that place. If Paine could be spared, then Thomas was to move forward by forced marches with his division and Paine's, and unite his command with the main army. Thomas, knowing that Bragg had left a large force to threaten Nashville, ordered Paine's division to remain there, and started at once with the first division to report to Buell.

Bragg, to reach Munfordsville, had only sixty-eight miles to march from his crossing of the Cumberland River, while Buell had one hundred and five miles to travel before he could intercept him at that place. Bragg's advance had reached and attacked Munfordsville before Buell's army had arrived at Bowling Green. On Bragg's advance under General Chalmers, arriving at Munfordsville, his cavalry engaged the attention of the garrison there under Colonel John T. Wilder, while the artillery and infantry were being placed

3*

in position. On the 13th, demand was made of Wilder to surrender. This he refused to do. With the early light of the next day an assault was made by the enemy, which was repulsed with heavy loss. Two detachments reported during the day, reinforcing Wilder's command. One of them was under Colonel Dunham from Louisville, who, being Wilder's senior in rank, assumed command. On the following day a second demand for surrender was made by Chalmers, who represented his command sufficiently large to capture the place. Dunham refused to comply with this demand, and the enemy then withdrew, going north. Two days later the rebels made another attack on the works and were again repulsed. In the afternoon Bragg appeared in person before the town, and sent, under a flag of truce, another demand for the surrender of the command, as the garrison of the place was surrounded by his entire army, and to assault would only be a needless sacrifice of human life. This was declined, but with the request from Colonel Dunham that Bragg suspend hostilities to give time for consultation. This Bragg agreed to do until nine o'clock in the evening. Dunham, who had succeeded in opening communication with General Gilbert at Louisville, telegraphed him the facts, and added that he feared he would have to surrender. Gilbert telegraphed back an order placing Dunham in arrest, and ordering Wilder to assume command. At the Council of War that was held by Wilder it was determined that the place should not be surrendered without personal inspection by the commanding officer that Bragg's statements as to his force and situation were true. Wilder, under Gilbert's orders, assumed command at seven o'clock in the evening, and notified Bragg of the result of the consultation, proposing, with Bragg's permission, to satisfy himself of the truth of his statements. Remarkable as it appears, this proposition wás agreed to by Bragg, and Wilder, under escort, investigated the enemy's lines prepared for assault, and counting forty-five cannon in position, supported by 25,000 men, he concluded it was impossible to further successfully defend the place. He reported the facts to the Council of War, and the demand for the surrender was acceded to at two o'clock in the morning of the 17th. Under the terms of the capitulation the troops marched out with the honors of war at daylight, retained their sidearms and private property, and were at once paroled. This attack on Munfordsville by Bragg established the fact that it was not his intention to press on to Louisville, and the advantage Buell derived from the delay attending this attack was in a measure some compensation for the loss of the place.

Bragg then took position at Prewitt's Knob, where Buell moved with his entire army, Thomas having reported on the 20th. The two armies confronted each other at this point for three days, and disposition was made for battle. On the 21st, while the troops were being placed in position by Thomas, under order of Buell, the enemy retreated, marching for a short distance toward Louisville, then turned to the right, and took position at Bardstown. Bragg claimed in his official report that after manœuvring unsuccessfully for four days to draw General Buell into an engagement, he found himself with only three days' rations on hand for his troops "and in a hostile country," that even a successful engagement would materially cripple him, and as Buell had another route to the Ohio, to the left, he concluded to turn to the right, send to Lexington for supplies to meet him in Bardstown, and commenced the movement to that place. This gave Buell an open road to Louisville, of which he immediately availed himself, and on the 29th, the last division of the Army of the Ohio reached that city.

The place was under the command of Gilbert, who had nothing but new levies of inexperienced troops. These Buell incorporated with the brigades of his Army of the Ohio, and on the morning of the 30th, after furnishing his command with needed supplies, moved his army out of Louisville against the enemy. The movement was delayed a day, by Halleck's order relieving Buell and placing Thomas in command. The latter remonstrated against this order, and at his request it was withdrawn. The next day Buell again assumed command, with Thomas announced in General Orders as second in command, and commenced the advance movement of his army in five columns.

CHAPTER VI.

BATTLE OF PERRYVILLE.

THE main portion of the army had been organized into three corps, designated the First, Second, and Third, under McCook, Crittenden, and Gilbert, respectively. General Sill, in command of two divisions, was ordered to move on the left toward Frankfort, to hold in check the force of the enemy under Kirby Smith at that place. The other columns marched by different routes upon roads converging upon Bardstown, through Shepardsville, Mount Washington, Fairfield, and Bloomfield. Each column engaged the enemy's cavalry and artillery in a series of skirmishes from within a short distance of Louisville. As the army approached Bardstown the resistance constantly increased, retarding Buell's advance, and enabling Bragg to effect his withdrawal from that place, which was accomplished eight hours before the arrival of Buell's army. A sharp cavalry engagement occurred at this place between Buell's advance and Bragg's rear-guard, when the whole of Bragg's command retired, taking the road to Springfield. At Bardstown Buell received information that a junction of Bragg's and Kirby Smith's commands would be made at Danville. He ordered McCook to advance from Bloomfield on the Harrodsburg road, and directed Thomas to move with Crittenden's corps on the Lebanon road, which passes four miles south of Perryville, with a branch to the latter place, while he accompanied Gilbert's corps, which moved on the direct road to Perryville. After leaving Bardstown, Buell learned that Kirby Smith's force had crossed to the west side of the Kentucky River, near Salvisa, and that Bragg was concentrating either at Harrodsburg or Perryville. He at once ordered McCook to change his line of march from the former road, and to proceed direct to Perryville. On the afternoon of October 7th, Buell, with Gilbert's corps, arrived in front of the rebels in strong force three miles from Perryville, where he immediately drew his troops up in line of battle. Advancing the cavalry and artillery, supported by two regiments of infantry, the rear guard of the enemy was pressed to within two miles of the town, when it was discovered that the rebels were concentrating for battle. Orders were sent by Buell to Crittenden and McCook to march at 3 o'clock on the morning of the 8th, and for them to take position as early as possible on the left and right of the centre corps respectively, the commanders themselves to report in person their arrival, for orders, the intention being to make the attack that day if possible.

McCook did not receive this order until 2.30 o'clock, and was on the march at five. Owing to the difficulty of finding water for his command where the troops were expected to encamp, Thomas, on the night of the 7th, moved off the direct line of march some six miles and was delayed several hours in reaching his position on the field. During the night some pools of water were discovered in a small creek about two miles and a half from Perryville. Colonel Dan McCook with the Thirty-sixth Brigade was ordered forward, and, after a sharp engagement, secured possession of the pools, and a supply of bad water for Gilbert's troops was obtained.

On October 1st, Bragg, leaving Polk in command at Bardstown, under orders to slowly retire to Bryantsville, started for Lexington. Here he ordered Kirby Smith with all his forces to Frankfort, to assist in the installation services of the rebel Provisional Governor of Kentucky at the capital of the State. At Lexington, on the 2d, learning of Buell's movements from Louisville, Bragg ordered Polk in writing—sending two copies to him—to advance at once, "with his whole available force, by way of Bloomfield, toward Frankfort, to strike the enemy in flank and rear." Polk was informed in the order that Kirby Smith would at the same time attack in front.

On the 3d, Polk received the orders, and, submitting them to a council of war, decided not to obey them, but to move as originally ordered. Of this Bragg was notified in time to prevent the attack on Buell's front with Smith's command alone. Giving orders for the supplies that had been accumulated at Lexington to be sent to Bryantsville, Bragg, on the 6th, proceeded to Harrodsburg, where he met Polk at the head of his column that had left Bardstown on the 3d. On the 7th, Bragg ordered Polk to move Cheatham's division back to Perryville, and to proceed to that point himself, to attack the Federal force, immediately rout them, and move rapidly to join Kirby Smith. These orders were given under the impression that Buell's command was so separated that his right and left were sixty miles apart. Bragg also sent Wither's division to Kirby Smith at Frankfort, who reported himself threatened by a large force on his front—the troops under Sill.

Early on the morning of the 8th an attempt was made by the enemy to drive Colonel McCook from his position at the creek. He was supported by Mitchell's and Sheridan's divisions, which were ordered up and directed to hold the posi-

tion until the entire army was prepared to attack.   The
assault was made with great spirit on Colonel McCook, but
the enemy was handsomely repulsed.   Buell anticipated an
attack on Gilbert's corps in its isolated position in the early

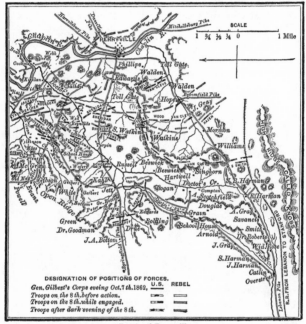

Battle of Perryville.

morning, but nothing occurred until after the arrival of
McCook's corps on the Maxville road, between 10 and 11
o'clock, when he at once formed his command, of Rousseau's and Jackson's divisions, in line of battle on the left of
Gilbert, Rousseau on the right, and sent his cavalry to the
front to make a reconnoissance toward Perryville.   Thomas

arrived and took position with Crittenden's corps about twelve o'clock.

On McCook getting his command into position, he reported to General Buell in person, who ordered him to send out a force to the Chaplin River, and find out the position of the enemy in his front. During McCook's absence Rousseau had advanced the right of his line a half mile to obtain a supply of water, for which the troops were suffering. On seeing this, the rebels opened a heavy fire with some twenty pieces of artillery. Rousseau moved his other troops to support his right, and, posting Simonson's and Loomis's batteries, returned the enemy's artillery fire.

When McCook returned to his command, seeing that a good position on high ground could be occupied by our troops on the left and front of Rousseau's new line and near the river, he at once sent skirmishers into the woods at that point, to find out if the enemy held the position. He also directed Jackson to form a new line of battle with his division nearer the stream, and sent the skirmishers forward to the river as soon as this was done, where they obtained the needed supply of water. On the formation of the new line, as no heavy force of the enemy had been encountered, McCook, at about half-past one o'clock, rode to the right of his line. About half an hour later, Hardee, in command of three divisions, under Cheatham, Buckner, and Anderson, some sixteen thousand strong, advanced to the attack on McCook, driving back the skirmishers, first striking those posted in the woods. McCook had formed his line of battle, with Rousseau's right near a barn on the right of the Maxville road, extending to the left and across that road on a ridge through a cornfield to the woods where the skirmishers were. The right of Jackson's line was holding a wooded elevation, running off to the left in rear of Chaplin

River, while his left, north of Maxville road, was thrown back in a northwesterly direction, forming an obtuse angle, deflected about thirty degrees along broken heights from their centre and right, the point of the angle being near where the Maxville road crosses Doctor's Creek. The enemy considered the key of McCook's position to be at this crossing, and directed their main attack on that point. McCook had posted Starkweather's brigade in the rear of the left as support to Jackson, with Stone's and Bush's batteries of Rousseau's division, and had placed Webster's brigade of Jackson's division in rear of Rousseau's line. The enemy opened the attack on the extreme left of the Federal force posted in the angle. This was a very strong position, by reason of the character of the ground, which enabled these troops to sweep their front with a heavy fire. The troops here were protected by being posted behind stone fences, and were supported by batteries in the rear. In the attack on the left Jackson was killed by the first fire. Terrill's troops—nearly all new—were driven back, and McCook's left turned. In falling back, Terrill endeavored to rally his command near the batteries posted in his rear. While gallantly doing so, he fell, mortally wounded, and died in a few hours. McCook sent to Sheridan, asking him to protect his right, and sent to Gilbert for reinforcements.

The advance of the enemy was checked by Starkweather's brigade, with Stone's and Bush's batteries, all well posted to meet the assault after Terrill's brigade had been driven back. The enemy made repeated assaults with fresh troops at this point, but was driven back each time with heavy loss until the troops and batteries were out of ammunition, when they fell back to the original line, and obtaining a supply renewed the fight.

On the right in Rousseau's front the enemy under Anderson made a vigorous charge on Lytle's and Harris's brigades, attacking in greatly superior numbers. They were however handsomely repulsed. After fighting until their ammunition was exhausted, these troops retired on the line with Starkweather's command. The rebels then pushing forward under a heavy fire from their batteries drove Lytle's brigade from the new line. Sloan's battery getting into position opened on the rebels with canister and checked their advance. Colonel Gooding's brigade from Mitchell's division of Gilbert's corps, with Penney's Fifth Wisconsin Battery, was ordered up, and after a brisk engagement the enemy was driven back and the original line of battle reoccupied. Stedman's brigade of Schoepff's division also came up, and attacking the enemy aided in the final repulse.

When the heaviest attack was made on Rousseau the enemy assaulted Sheridan's division in the advanced position which he occupied after forcing back their line earlier in the day. He now withdrew his troops, and posting them in more favorable position on the original line, opened on the rebels with heavy musketry fire and canister. The enemy pressing him very hard at this point, he called on Gilbert for support, who reinforced him with Carlin's brigade from Mitchell's division. As the enemy moved forward in strong force to the attack, Carlin immediately ordered his troops to charge, which they did, and drove the rebels before them through Perryville, capturing in the town two caissons, fifteen wagons loaded with ammunition, and a guard of 138 men under command of three officers. Sheridan also drove the enemy for some distance, but did not consider it prudent to advance too far, leaving McCook's right exposed. He then directed his artillery fire on the enemy at his left, and aided in checking the advance in that quarter. Wagner's brigade of Wood's division became engaged, and did good service on the right of Mitchell's division. The rest of Crittenden's corps was not engaged in the action. Thomas, on arriving on the battlefield with this corps, was directed to take position in the line of battle on the right and wait for orders. Here he waited during the entire day, and received none. Only part of Gilbert's corps was engaged in the fight, the heavy blow striking McCook's, which he failed to report to Buell until after two hours' fighting. The battle was closed by night coming on, and a general engagement was anticipated the next day. Thomas was directed to move Crittenden's and Gilbert's corps forward in the morning at six o'clock, and attack the enemy's front and left flank.

Buell ordered McCook during the night to close the opening between his right and Gilbert's left. His orders for the following day were to hold his position and take advantage of any opportunity that the events of the·day might present, the main attack to be made by the other corps. On the following morning, the advance being made in accordance with these orders, it was discovered that the enemy's main body had retired during the night, and was falling back on Harrodsburg, with indications that he would there make a stand. Bragg left his dead and wounded on the field, but retired leisurely and in good order.

Buell reported the strength of his command before the engagement at 58,000 effective men. Of these he claimed 22,000 were raw troops, not drilled, and undisciplined. Less than one-half of this entire force was in the action. His reports show a loss of 4,348, being 916 killed, 2,943 wounded, and 489 missing. Nearly all the losses were from McCook's command, which bore the brunt of the heavy fighting.

Bragg referring to his loss in his official report says : " In such a conflict our own loss was necessarily severe, probably not less than 2,500 killed, wounded, and missing." During the campaign General Buell captured nearly five thousand prisoners.

The enemy's troops engaged in the battle were under the immediate command of General Polk. Bragg had been with Kirby Smith at Frankfort, where these active operations found him engaged in superintending " the ceremony of installing the Provisional Governor into office."

In his official report of the battle of Perryville, made from Bryantsville, October 12, 1862, Bragg says : " After consulting with the General (Polk) and reconnoitring the ground and examining his dispositions, I declined to assume the command, but suggested some changes and modifications of his arrangements, which he promptly made." In a subsequent report of Perryville, made while he was at Shelbyville, of date May 20, 1863, he reflects very severely upon Polk's movements at Perryville. He says that he ordered the attack to be made by Polk on Gilbert early in the morning of the 8th, that he waited until 10 A.M., and hearing no firing started to see Polk and have an explanation of the delay. Here he was "informed that it was determined not to attack, but to assume the ' defensive offensive.' " Bragg gave orders for some changes in the line of battle, restoring certain portions of the command that had been withdrawn, and again ordered Polk to bring on the engagement. The execution of this order was delayed by Polk, and Bragg, becoming "impatient at the delay after this order," "despatched a staff officer to repeat it to the General, and soon thereafter followed in person and put the troops in motion."

Bragg's intention was not to fight a general engagement at Perryville, but merely to check the advance of Buell's army, thereby gaining time to gather his supplies and men together and leave the State. Bragg had been urged, by leading Kentuckians in his command and others, to undertake the campaign in Kentucky with the promise of immense numbers of recruits and large quantities of supplies. He anticipated that his coming would be hailed as that of a deliverer, and that the young men of the State would flock to his banners and fill up his army, so that he could attack Buell at any point. Bragg's entire command in Kentucky was estimated at thirty-five to forty thousand. He anticipated enlisting twenty thousand recruits, and took arms to Kentucky for that number of new troops. Buell's command, with his losses and the garrison at Nashville was less than this, but at Louisville he received some twenty two thousand new troops. The number of infantry recruits for Bragg's army was very small, for he says in his first official report of the battle of Perryville—when he at that time was preparing to leave the State—" with ample means to arm twenty thousand men and a force with that to fully redeem the State, we have not yet issued half the arms left us by casualties incident to the campaign."

General Buell waited for Sill to join him with his division, leaving Dumont at Frankfort. On the march Sill's advance was attacked by a portion of Kirby Smith's command, which he repulsed and arrived at Perryville on the 11th. Buell then moved forward, expecting Bragg to give battle at Harrodsburg, and throwing out a strong force to reconnoitre, discovered the enemy in force some three miles south of that place. During the day Bragg continued his march south, his rear guard being driven out of the place with the loss of considerable stores and about twelve hundred prisoners, in the main sick and wounded. On the next day Buell made a strong reconnoissance to the crossing of

Dick's River, and there ascertained that Bragg had crossed his entire army.

Learning on the 13th that the enemy was retreating south, Buell ordered pursuit to be made immediately, for the purpose of overtaking Bragg, or of intercepting him if he should attempt to pass toward Somerset. Wood's division marched at midnight, and engaged the enemy at Stanford at daylight next morning. The rest of Crittenden's and McCook's corps followed on the same road; Gilbert marching on the Lancaster road. The enemy was steadily pressed on the road to Cumberland Gap, but could not be brought to an engagement. McCook's and Gilbert's corps were halted at Crab Orchard, while Crittenden, with W. S. Smith's division, was sent in pursuit as far as London on the direct road to the Gap. It now appearing that Bragg did not intend to fight in the State, and the country beyond Crab Orchard being extremely barren and rough—no supplies existing in it—the pursuit was discontinued, and the Army of the Ohio was turned toward Bowling Green and Glasgow, preparatory to the advance to Nashville. McCook's and Gilbert's corps were concentrated at the former place, and Crittenden's at the latter. This movement of the troops was made by Buell, who was confident that Bragg would concentrate in the vicinity of Nashville, and seek to recover that place, and to fight his great battle for the possession of Kentucky.

The military affairs of the nation at this time were unfortunately in charge of General Halleck, who had been called to Washington as Commander-in-Chief. On the retreat of Bragg from Kentucky, Halleck insisted that Buell should make a campaign into East Tennessee, a distance of two hundred and forty miles, over mountain and river, without any communication to the rear, except by wagon train, over

almost impassable roads, the advance to be made in the face
of the enemy, who, operating on his line of communications
could move his entire command to defeat our advance in
detail. Buell reported to the War Department that it was
impossible to make the campaign as ordered, and knowing
the necessity of protecting Nashville, he directed the concentration of his troops on the line of the railroad to that
place. That road had been repaired up to Bowling Green,
after the destruction of two months before, and here the
troops received their needed supplies. On the 30th of October, Buell was relieved of the command of the Department
of the Ohio, and Major-General William S. Rosecrans was,
by the direction of the General-in-Chief, assigned to the
command of the troops. The designation of the command
being changed to that of the Department of the Cumberland.

It is a somewhat singular fact, that the campaign in Kentucky should have caused the most intense feeling in the
opposing armies against their respective commanders. In
the Federal army, after Buell allowed Bragg to move north
from Munfordsville without an engagement, the expressions
of the troops against their commanding general were open,
bitter, and almost universal, from the lowest to the highest.
However, there was one who never for a moment lost faith,
soldierly trust, and esteem for his commander, and he was
of all persons in the command most competent to judge.
This was General Thomas. He knew the great difficulties
of Buell's position, how his plans had been interfered with
by Halleck, under whose command it was his misfortune
early in the year to be; and later, how he was made to feel
the power of this same man as a personal matter. Halleck,
invested by the Administration with supreme powers,
planned a campaign into East Tennessee, on paper in Wash-

ington, and ordered Buell to execute it. This, the latter, with full knowledge of the situation, refused to do, and quietly ordering his troops to the line of the railroad from whence they could be moved with the least delay, as needed, waited for the order he knew was pending for his removal.

General Buell was right in refusing to attack Bragg at Munfordsville, or in fact at any time until he had placed his army north of the enemy, and received his own reinforcements from Louisville. Then this point was safe, and Nashville could not be imperilled by the defeat of our army. Buell made three dispositions for an engagement during the Kentucky campaign, but each time Bragg drew off except at Perryville, and here there was no design of the latter to fight, beyond checking Buell's advance, and gaining time for his troops to make their retreat from the State with all stores and material. Bragg, from his closing remarks in his first report of the battle of Perryville, certainly did not consider—so far as the Confederacy was concerned—that the State was worth fighting for. Had he received the 20,000 new troops he was promised, instead of General Buell having his army increased by that number, then he would have struck quick and sharp. He left the State deeply disgusted with Kentucky, and took every occasion after that to show it. The account was even, however, as Bragg was not a favorite in that State.

At Perryville Buell labored under the same disadvantage in the organization of his command that made itself felt on the first two great battlefields of the Army of the Cumberland. That was the inefficiency of his corps commanders. Of Gilbert it is only necessary to say, that a worse appointment as a corps commander was not made during the war. Fortunately, the battle of Perryville was his first and only

appearance in that position.   Buell, after expressing his
thanks for McCook's services on that field and in the campaign, in his official report says: "It is true that only one
serious battle has been fought, and that was incomplete, and
less decisive than it might have been.   That this was so is
due partly to unavoidable difficulties which prevented the
troops, marching on different roads, from getting on the
ground simultaneously, but more to the fact that I was not
apprised early enough of the condition of affairs on my left.
I can find no fault with the former, nor am I disposed at this
time to censure the latter, though it must be admitted to
have been a grave error.   I ascribe it to the too great confidence of the general commanding the left corps (Major-General McCook), which made him believe that he could manage
the difficulty without the aid or control of his commander."
Buell was not notified of any attack by the enemy on his
left until over two hours after the engagement was begun.
He then hurried to the field, and sent the necessary supports forward, at once checking the enemy, and made disposition of his troops for battle.

With a willingness to lay down command that character-
ized all the commanders of the Army of the Cumberland
when the authorities in Washington regarded the good of
the service as requiring it, Buell placed the new commander in full possession of all plans and information that
he possessed, and without a word left the troops that were
to win undying fame on other battle-fields, largely by reason
of the training he had given them during the period of his
command, half a month less than one year.

The Comte de Paris, in his "History of the Civil War in
America," in writing on the battle of Shiloh, where he re-
fers to the massing of the artillery by Grant's Chief of Staff,
Colonel Webster, says: "The fate of the day depends upon

the preservation of these heights, whence the enemy could have commanded Pittsburg Landing," and on the following page adds, "Nevertheless, at the sight of the enemy's battalions advancing in good order, the soldiers that have been grouped together in haste, to give an air of support to Webster's battery, become frightened and scatter. It is about to be carried, when a new body of troops deploying in the rear of the guns, with as much regularity as if they were on the parade-ground, receives the Confederates with a fire that drives them back in disorder into the ravine. This was the brigade of Ammen, belonging to Nelson's division, that rushed forward so opportunely." In speaking of the second day's fight he says : " At a signal given by Buell, his three divisions, under Nelson, Crittenden, and McCook, put themselves in motion at the same time. The soldiers of the Army of the Ohio, constantly drilled for the year past by a rigid disciplinarian, and trained by their long marches across three States, are distinguished by their discipline and their fine bearing. The readiness with which they march against the enemy wins the admiration of generals who, like Sherman, have had to fight a whole day at the head of raw and inexperienced troops."

The greatest service that General Buell rendered to his country was as the organizer and disciplinarian of the mass of the raw, undrilled troops that were hurried to the front under the need of the hour, and who, unaccustomed to military or other restraint, had all the freedom that characterizes the American sovereign both in speech and action. To take these troops by the thousands and make an army of fifty to seventy-five thousand trained skilled soldiers, who, in later days, were to do as splendid fighting as the world ever saw, was a stupendous undertaking. General Buell not only did this, but accomplished his task in time to bring

some of these soldiers that he was justly proud of to the
field of Shiloh, where, under his eye, they met the enemy
like veterans. Buell's military training and habits of life
led him, however, into one error. He was so good a soldier
himself, and so anxious that his army should be thorough
soldiers, that he failed to recognize the distinction between
the regular soldier in garrison during times of peace and the
thinking volunteer during the active campaigns of the rebellion. The latter could not and would not be made the
mere machine the former becomes, and Buell's failure to
appreciate this caused great ill-feeling against him at the
time in his army. Then, again, Buell's earlier military
training in the bureau office he held so many years unfitted
him for the handling, on the battle-field, of the large number of troops which composed his command. But very few
generals during the rebellion were able to successfully handle on the battle-field as large an army as was under Buell.
In fact, the general who has sufficient talent as a good organizer and drill-master to enter into the details necessary
to bring an army out of raw troops, has not the military
genius required to handle a large army in fighting and winning great battles. But Buell rendered many valuable services, in the camp and on the field, to his country. It was
Buell who planned the Fort Henry, Fort Donelson, and
Nashville campaign, which Halleck put under his hat, and
proceeded to carry out as *his* original idea, being careful to
say nothing in regard to his plans until they were so far
executed as to render any action on the part of Buell and
his command simply that of a supporting column. Then to
Buell is due the credit of the second day's fight at Shiloh.
That day's battle was the fight of the Army of the Ohio with
Lewis Wallace's division, General Grant giving Buell largely
his discretion in the movements of the troops. Whitelaw

Reid says of him, in "Ohio in the War," "He came into that action when, without him, all was lost. He redeemed the fortunes of the field, and justly won the title of the 'Hero of Pittsburg Landing.'"

The order placing Rosecrans in command—General Order No. 168, War Department, of date October 24, 1862—created the Department of the Cumberland, embracing that portion of the State of Tennessee lying east of the Tennessee River, and such portion of Georgia and Alabama as should be occupied by the Federal troops. The troops in the field were designated in the same order as the "Fourteenth Army Corps."

General Rosecrans assumed command on October 30th at Louisville. On November 2d he arrived at Bowling Green, and on the 7th he announced, in General Orders, the division of his army organization into "the Right Wing," "the Centre," and "the Left Wing," under the command respectively of McCook, Thomas, and Crittenden, with five divisions in the centre and three in each wing. He instructed Thomas to advance Fry and Dumont's divisions to Gallatin, and to push rapidly forward the repairs of the railroad to Nashville.

Up to this time the movements of Bragg's army remained undeveloped, and no disposition of the Federal forces could be safely made without the knowledge of what Bragg's plan of operations would be. That he would ultimately attempt the capture of Nashville or force a battle for it there could be but little doubt. Not to fight for Nashville was the abandonment of Tennessee. Kentucky surrendered without a blow produced such demoralization in Bragg's command that to have given up Tennessee without a struggle would have either compelled a change in the commanding officer of that army or a disbandment of it, so far as the Kentucky and Tennessee troops were concerned.

General Halleck's brilliant paper campaign into East Tennessee again was produced and aired with a show of the most profound wisdom, based on the extreme of ignorance of the situation and surroundings.   Buell's forethought in concentrating the army within supporting distance of Nashville ·became apparent on the appearance of the advance of Bragg's army at Murfreesboro, reinforcing Breckinridge's command, which had been left in Tennessee to enforce the "blockade of Nashville."   This was another grievance the Kentucky troops had against Bragg.   All the Kentucky infantry troops under Bragg were in Breckinridge's command, and they were exceedingly anxious to return to the State with Bragg's army to visit their friends and relatives and aid in recruiting that army.   Bragg's distrust of these troops was such that he refused to allow them this privilege, and his action in holding them in Tennessee, just out of Kentucky, did not materially increase his popularity with them.   Breckinridge had established his headquarters at Murfreesboro and assumed chief command, with about ten thousand troops under him, over one-third of which were cavalry under Wheeler and Forrest.   With this force Breckinridge endeavored to enforce the siege of Nashville, using his cavalry to prevent the gathering of forage and supplies by our troops from the surrounding country.   These foraging parties were constantly sent out, going as far at times as ten miles on these expeditions.   The main deprivation the garrison suffered during the six weeks of the siege was in having nearly all communication cut off from their friends at the North, and while they received nothing, they embraced every opportunity of sending letters by citizens returning north.   The garrison was not willing to remain entirely on the defensive. Besides the numerous raiding parties sent out for forage which were uniformly successful, on the night of the 6th

of October, Negley sent Palmer with some twenty-eight
hundred troops to attack General S. R. Anderson, who had
established his camp at Lavergne with some three thousand
men, principally new recruits. Palmer with the artillery and
about four hundred infantry to support it, moved directly
on Lavergne, some fifteen miles from Nashville, while Colonel John F. Miller with about twenty-four hundred men
in his command moved on the road to the right to make the
attack on the rear of the enemy. Miller marched his command during the night, captured the enemy's pickets at daylight and moved on the encampment. Palmer opened with
artillery as soon as he heard Miller's musketry firing and the
latter, pushing his troops rapidly forward, after an engagement lasting half an hour, had the enemy in full retreat on
the road to Murfreesboro with a loss of 80 killed and
wounded, and 175 prisoners. He also captured three pieces
of artillery, and the regimental colors of the Thirty-second
Alabama. Palmer's command then returned to Nashville.

During the siege of Nashville skirmishing between our
pickets and the scouting parties of the enemy was constantly
occurring, and the garrison of Nashville was indebted for its
safety to the services of Lieutenant-Colonel Von Schrader of
the Seventy-fourth Ohio, Inspector of Negley's division, as
much as any one thing. Von Schrader was an educated
Prussian officer and a thorough soldier. He established a
system of pickets, strongly posted, with block houses for
their protection, and then gave his personal attention to it
that the pickets performed their entire duty. There was
no determined assaults on the place at any time during the
siege. The only appearance of an attack in force was on the
6th of November, by a body of some eight thousand troops,
equally divided between cavalry and infantry, under General
Roger Hanson. Forrest, knowing that the Federal force at

Nashville was not a very strong one and that by the pursuit of Bragg by Buell's army, Nashville was completely cut off from any immediate support or relief, obtained General Breckinridge's permission to make an attack with his cavalry, numbering over four thousand men, in concert with the infantry under Hanson, numbering a little less than Forrest's command. The enemy's cavalry moved in columns on the Charlotte, Franklin, and Nolinsville turnpikes from the south, while Forrest in person with 1,000 cavalry and Hanson's infantry, pushed rapidly forward on the Murfreesboro pike, arriving at the Lunatic Asylum, six miles from Nashville, by daylight. Our pickets and cavalry were driven in, and Hanson was in readiness to make the attack with the infantry when a peremptory order from Breckinridge was received, directing further operations to cease, under express orders from Bragg. After skirmishing with his cavalry around the city at the different outposts, Forrest withdrew, greatly incensed at being ordered to desist from the attack when confident of success.

Bragg in leaving a large number of men in middle Tennessee merely to watch the post of Nashville—thus crippling his army to that extent—committed a great mistake. He needed every available man in his army to make the Kentucky campaign a success. With these 10,000 troops, if Buell had left Negley's and Paine's divisions as garrisons at Nashville, Bragg's force would have outnumbered Buell's command before he reached Louisville three to two. With the defeat of Buell, Nashville would have been worse than worthless, proving an incumbrance instead of a benefit. On the other hand, with Bragg driven out of Kentucky, and opening the struggle for that State in Tennessee, the possession of Nashville as a second base of supplies for our army was an absolute necessity. Bragg, however, was cor-

rect in refusing to allow the place to be attacked by Forrest, for even in the event of success the non-combatants
and sympathizing friends of the South would have suffered
in person and property to an extent far beyond what the
temporary occupation of the city by the Southern forces
would have compensated.

Nashville was reinforced by the arrival of the advance of
the army concentrating there on the 17th of November, and
a few days after Rosecrans arrived and established his
headquarters in that city. The first thing that demanded
the attention of the new commander was that which had
given the most serious trouble to General Buell, viz. : the
safety of his communications in the rear to his base of supplies. The repairs to the tunnel just south of Mitchellville
occupied a large force several weeks to complete. During
this time all supplies for troops at Nashville were with the
greatest labor hauled thirty-five miles by wagon train. The
railroad from Louisville to Nashville was re-opened on the
26th of November, and for one month every effort was made
to forward supplies, so the troops could have new clothing
issued to them, and that they could be provided with ammunition. The depôts at Nashville were filled with needful
supplies to provide against the interruption of communication arising from raids on the railroad by rebel cavalry.
Since the middle of November Bragg had been concentrating his forces at Murfreesboro, and anticipating that the
Federal forces would go into winter quarters at Nashville, had
placed his troops in quarters for the winter in the vicinity of
the former place. He had sent nearly all of his cavalry to raid
on the lines of the Federal communication—Morgan into Kentucky and Wheeler into West Tennessee. With this knowledge, Rosecrans, on the 26th of December, ordered his army
to move out of Nashville to attack the enemy on his front.

4*

While the army was being refitted at Nashville, Morgan's cavalry was raiding the surrounding country. On the 7th Morgan's command captured the Thirty-ninth Brigade under Colonel A. B. Moore, at Hartsville, where he had been posted by Thomas to guard the ford of the Cumberland River, and to watch the enemy on the Lebanon road. The brigade consisted of three infantry regiments, a battalion of cavalry, and a section of artillery, making a force of about two thousand effective men. The command was badly posted, and the commanding officers of the infantry regiments failed to co-operate, or to obey orders. It was, in the main, a repetition of the disgraceful affair at Murfreesboro, when Forrest captured that place during the previous summer. Moore was surprised in his camp early in the morning. No warning was given by the pickets, and before any disposition could be made of the troops, Morgan's men were upon them. Morgan's command consisted of his cavalry, and two regiments of infantry. Moore threw out a skirmish line to resist the advance of Morgan's infantry and dismounted cavalry in line. The rebels pressed steadily forward to a ravine at the foot of the hill on which Moore had formed his line, and under shelter of this poured such a destructive fire upon the Federal troops, that he ordered a new line to be formed in the rear. In this movement the whole line was thrown into confusion, and being attacked on their right and rear by the rebel cavalry, who had, up to this time not been engaged, Moore's command was crowded one on the other into a narrow space where the fire of the enemy proved terribly effective. Moore's troops being unable to return the fire, and he not being able to make another disposition of them, the white flag was raised, and the entire command surrendered. Colonel Tafel, in command of the One Hundred and Sixth Ohio, becoming separated from the

other troops, made some further resistance, but, being overpowered, he also surrendered.   The contest only lasted a little over an hour.   Moore's loss was 150 killed and wounded,
his entire command captured, with all army and camp equip-
ment, trains, and two pieces of artillery.   Morgan's loss was
125 killed and wounded.

General D. S. Stanley, on reporting to Rosecrans from the
Army of the Tennessee, had been assigned to the position
of Chief of Cavalry to the Commanding General.   On the
12th he attacked and drove the enemy out of the town of
Franklin, killing five and capturing twelve men, with a large
number of horses and stores.   He destroyed the mills at
that place, with a great quantity of valuable property.

After the capture of Hartsville by Morgan, his services
were recognized by his superiors to the extent that Mr.
Davis, who was on a visit to Murfreesboro shortly after this
engagement, signed and handed him his commission as
Brigadier-General.   General Hardee urged that the appointment be made as Major-General, but this was refused.
Morgan's command had increased so that it was unwieldy as
one body, and he decided to form it into two brigades.   His
command consisted now of seven regiments, with an aggregate force of over four thousand men.   This he divided,
placing three regiments under Colonel Basil W. Duke, in
the first brigade, with a battery of four guns.   The second
brigade was placed in command of Colonel W. C. P. Breckenridge, and was composed of four regiments, with one
three-inch Parrot gun and the two mountain howitzers.
This force, trained as it had been, had no superior for the
work it was ordered to do—raiding in the rear, destroying
bridges, trestleworks, and capturing bridge-guards.   So accustomed had they become to hardships of every nature,
that it was almost incredible the amount of rough riding,

scant fare, and loss of sleep these men endured. Proud of their past success, and emboldened by it to the belief that they were able to defeat any force that could overtake them, they at last found the country south of the Ohio too confined for them, and, aiming at grander feats, they passed north of that river, and, entering upon an entirely different kind of warfare, met with complete disaster.

On the morning of the 22d the command of Morgan took the road again for Kentucky. Bragg ordered the railroad in Rosecrans's rear to be broken, and his communication with Louisville destroyed. Morgan and his men were in most excellent spirits at the prospect of another raid into that State. He had with him the pick of the youth of the State of Kentucky. On the 24th Morgan's command had their first skirmish with a battalion of Michigan troops, which resulted in the loss to Morgan of seventeen of his men and two of his officers. On the 25th Colonel Hobson had an engagement with Johnson's regiment near Munfordsville, in which the rebels suffered a loss of some fifty men killed and wounded. Morgan then attacked the stockade at Bacon Creek, held by a force of 100 men, who made a most stubborn and determined resistance, inflicting severe loss upon the attacking party, and demonstrating the worth of a stockade properly built and efficiently manned. These stockades were built with heavy upright timber ten or twelve feet high. They were surrounded by ditches and pierced for musketry. Assailants, when right at the base, were still far from taking them. It was supposed that they would not resist artillery, and, in fact, they were not built with the expectation of doing so. If the garrison of the stockade succeeded in driving off the guerilla parties that swarmed through the country, it fully accomplished its purpose. This stockade successfully resisted the heavy artillery firing brought to bear upon it, even when a number of shells exploded within the work. After making such a brave defence, it is to be regretted that they did not hold out to the last, and refuse to surrender at all. The commanding officer had rejected a number of demands made on him to surrender; when Morgan came up in person, and in his own name offering them liberal terms, they surrendered. Morgan then burnt the bridge across Bacon Creek, and pressed on to Nolin, fourteen miles beyond, where the stockade was surrendered without a fight. The bridge here also was destroyed. Morgan's division, on the 27th, captured Elizabethtown, after a severe engagement with the command of Lieutenant-Colonel Smith—a detachment of some six hundred infantry. Smith sent Morgan a demand for him to surrender, which Morgan declined, and returned the compliment by making the same demand on Smith, who also declined. After an engagement lasting some six hours, Morgan's artillery rendered the building Smith's command was fighting in untenable, and he then surrendered. The next day Morgan, moving along the railroad, destroyed it thoroughly. The principal object of the expedition was the great trestleworks at Muldraugh's Hill, only a short distance apart. The garrison defending the lower trestle, 600 strong, was captured by the Second Brigade. The First Brigade captured the garrison at the upper trestle—200 strong. These trestles were respectively 80 and 90 feet high, and each of them 500 feet long. They were thoroughly destroyed. Thus was accomplished the objects of the raid, but the destruction of these bridges—trestle and railroad— did not accomplish the design contemplated by Bragg. Rosecrans's prompt movement from Nashville on the rebels encamped at Murfreesboro, and the result of that campaign, rendered Morgan's raid a failure in the main, as Bragg intended the road should be so thoroughly destroyed as to prevent the further occupation of Nashville by our army. The loss to the Federals was an exceedingly severe one, and had Rosecrans remained at Nashville inactive all the winter of 1862, Bragg's designs would have met with a greater degree of success.

On the 29th, Colonel Harlan with his brigade attacked and routed Morgan's troopers at Rolling Fork of Salt River, and drove them to Bardstown. While Morgan was moving around Lebanon, Colonel Hoskins's command attacked him and captured 150 men. Morgan passed between the forces sent against him, showing again that it is impossible to catch cavalry with infantry. Morgan then commenced his retreat from the State. On the morning of January 1, 1863, as his command was passing Columbia, 115 miles in an airline from Murfreesboro, his men reported hearing distinctly the roar of heavy cannonading in that direction. On the 2d Morgan crossed the Cumberland, and felt safe once more from all pursuit.

On December 21st, General Carter moved with three regiments of cavalry toward East Tennessee, from Lebanon, Ky., to raid on the rebel line of communication. Crossing the Cumberland mountains forty miles northeast of Cumberland Gap, he passed through Southwestern Virginia and Tennessee to Carter's station, destroying the Holston and Watauga bridges and several miles of railroad. He then leisurely returned to Kentucky by the same route he had advanced.

CHAPTER VII.

THE ADVANCE TO MURFREESBORO.

On December 22d, General Thomas moved his headquarters from Gallatin to Nashville, and there concentrated the divisions of Rousseau and Negley, and Walker's brigade of Fry's division. Of the five divisions composing the Centre, that of J. J. Reynolds was guarding the Louisville and Nashville Railroad; and on the same duty were the remaining two brigades of Fry's division. R. B. Mitchell was assigned to the command of Nashville with his division as the garrison. This left, under the immediate command of Thomas, the two divisions and the brigade as above, as his only available force. McCook with three divisions under Johnson, Davis, and Sheridan, and Crittenden, also with three divisions under Wood, Palmer, and Van Cleve, were in camp in front of Nashville, on the Franklin, Nolinsville, and Murfreesboro turnpikes.

The position of the enemy under Bragg was fully known to Rosecrans. Two corps under Polk and Kirby Smith were at Murfreesboro with strong outposts at Stewart's Creek and Lavergne. The corps under Hardee was on the Shelbyville and Nolinsville pike, between Triune and Eaglesville, with an advance guard at Nolinsville. Rosecrans, on the morning of the 26th, directed the advance movement to commence in the following order. McCook was to move his command of three divisions direct on the Nolinsville pike to Triune. Thomas was to advance his command of two divisions and a brigade on McCook's right by the Franklin and Wilson pikes, threatening Hardee's left, and on his falling back was then to cross over on country roads and occupy Nolinsville. Crittenden was ordered to move his command direct on the Murfreesboro pike. On the arrival of Thomas at Nolinsville, and being in a position to support, McCook was to attack Hardee at Triune, and if the latter was reinforced and McCook's advance resisted, Thomas was to go to his aid. If Hardee fell back to Stewart's Creek, five miles south of Lavergne, and the enemy made a stand there, then Crittenden was to attack him at once, and Thomas was to come in on his left flank, while McCook was to bring his forces in supporting distance of Thomas and Crittenden as needed, after sending a division to watch Hardee and to pursue him if retreating.

Davis took the advance of the Right Wing with the First Division. He moved from camp at 6 A.M. on the Edmonson pike, on which he was ordered to move to Prim's blacksmith shop, from whence he was to march direct on a country road to Nolinsville. The Third Division under Sheridan moved on the Nolinsville pike, followed by the Second under Johnson. The advance of both these columns encountered the cavalry pickets of the enemy, within two miles of the Federal picket line. As these commands advanced, there was constant skirmishing until the heads of each of these columns reached Nolinsville. About one mile south of the town the enemy made a determined stand in a defile, and upon the hills through which the pike ran at this place, known as Knob's Gap. This was a favorable position for the rebels, well guarded by their artillery, which opened fire at long range upon Carlin's lines. Davis then brought up two batteries and opened fire upon the enemy, while Carlin charged their position, capturing two guns and several prisoners. Davis's other brigades carried the enemy's position on the right and left. His division then bivouacked for the night. McCook's loss that day was about seventy-five killed and wounded.

Early on the morning of the 27th, McCook's command pressing forward, encountered the enemy in force. A dense fog prevailed at the time, rendering it hazardous in the extreme to open an engagement at that time, as McCook's troops could not distinguish friend from foe at one hundred and fifty yards, and his cavalry had been fired on by his infantry. On learning that Hardee was in position and had been in line of battle since the night before, McCook ordered a halt until the fog lifted. This it did about noon, when Johnson's division was pushed rapidly forward, followed by that of Sheridan. As the command approached Triune they found the enemy had burned the bridge across Wilson's Creek and retired, leaving a battery of six pieces with cavalry supports to hold the crossing. As the skirmishers of Johnson's command advanced, the battery withdrew, and with the cavalry moved off rapidly on the Eaglesville road. Johnson's division then repaired the bridge, crossed and went into camp beyond Wilson's Creek.

On Sunday the 28th, there was no general movement of the troops. McCook, however, sent Willich's brigade out on a reconnoissance, to learn whether the enemy had retired to Murfreesboro or Shelbyville. Willich went several miles on the Shelbyville road and found that the force in his front had turned to the left and moved toward the former place. Stanley with the cavalry also made a reconnoissance, and reported that Hardee had retreated to Murfreesboro.

On the 29th, McCook, leaving Baldwin's brigade at Triune to cover the extreme right, moved forward with the remainder of his command on a country road known as the

Bole Jack road toward Murfreesboro. The command did
not reach their encampment until late in the evening, when
from the movements of the enemy it was concluded that
he intended to give battle at Murfreesboro, and every disposition of the troops was made with reference to this.
That night McCook's command was encamped in line of
battle with two brigades of Johnson's division watching the
right, Woodruff's brigade guarding the bridge at Overall's
Creek, Davis on the right of the Wilkinson pike, with
Sheridan on the left of that road. The brigade that Mc-
Cook had left at Triune was ordered up and assumed its
position with the troops on the 30th. McCook's entire command on the morning of that day advanced down the Wilkinson turnpike until the head of the column encountered
the enemy's pickets. The line of battle was at once formed
with the divisions deployed in a line running to the right in
a southeast direction with the left of Sheridan upon the Wilkinson pike immediately on Negley's right. Davis's division
was at once thrown into line of battle with his left resting on
Sheridan's right, and Johnson's held in reserve. Covering
the front with a strong line of skirmishers, McCook moved
his line slowly forward, the enemy stubbornly contesting
every foot of ground. McCook's skirmishers soon became
sharply engaged with those of the rebels. The ground was
very favorable to the enemy, they being under cover of heavy
woods and cedar thickets. At 12 o'clock part of the enemy's
line of battle was determined, McCook's skirmishers being
then about five hundred yards from it. The resistance to
Davis's advance was especially stubborn, and the losses of
the day footed up seventy-five in Sheridan's division and
some two hundred in Davis's. Shortly before sunset the
rebel position was plainly discernible from Davis's front, and
was formed running diagonally across the old Murfreesboro

and Franklin road. In the afternoon, McCook learned from
a citizen who had seen the enemy's line of battle and the
position of his troops, that they were posted with the right
of Cheatham's division resting on the Wilkinson pike;
Withers's division on Cheatham's left, with his left resting
on the Franklin road; the entire of Hardee's corps to the left
of that road extending toward the Salem pike. This formation of the enemy's line placed the right of McCook's line as
then formed directly in front of the enemy's centre. Information was at once sent to Rosecrans, and McCook informed his three division commanders of this fact and then
placed two brigades of the reserve division under Willich
and Kirk—two of the best and most experienced brigade
commanders in the army—on the right of Davis, to protect the
right flank and guard against surprise—that of Kirk with
his left resting on Davis's right, with his right refused, Willich on Kirk's right and in a line nearly perpendicular to the
main line, thus covering the right flank. The third brigade
of Johnson's division was held as reserve. McCook's line of
battle as thus formed was broken in several points. The
general direction of Sheridan's line was to the east and south,
facing nearly at right angles with Negley, that of Davis was
to the west, facing south, nearly at right angles to Sheridan,
Kirk's brigade to Davis's right faced more to the east, while
Willich's faced due south. The general direction of Mc-
Cook's line, however, conformed to the line of the enemy in
its front, except the latter had no breaks in the line and that
its left division under McCown had its left extended due
south. The main portion of the enemy's battle-line faced
northwest. Breckinridge on the right of the line was facing
nearly north while McCown on the left faced due west. The
enemy awaiting attack—acting on the defensive—had as far
as practicable located its line in the cedars, with open ground

in the front. McCook considered his line a strong one, with "open ground in the front for a short distance." Rosecrans, on being informed by McCook of the location of his line of battle, expressed himself against it, saying: "I don't like the facing so much to the east, but must confide that to you, who know the ground. If you don't think your present the best position, change it." At six o'clock in the evening McCook received an order from Rosecrans to have large and extended camp-fires made on the right, extending far beyond the right of the line, to deceive the enemy and make him believe that troops were being massed there. Fires were built extending nearly a mile beyond the right of McCook's line. In this position the right wing rested in the cedars the night before the battle. The troops, cutting cedar boughs for beds, and officers and men, wrapping themselves in their blankets, slept in the frosty night air with the silent stars looking down.

On the 26th, Thomas's command, "the Centre," with Negley's division in the advance, moved out promptly to Brentwood on the Franklin pike, and from there turned to the left and advanced on the Wilson pike to Owen's store, where the troops were to encamp for the night. But on arriving here, Negley left his train and pushed on at once with his troops to Nolinsville, from whence the sound of Davis's guns had reached him, to his support. Negley encamped at Nolinsville, Rousseau at Owen's store, and Walker's brigade at Brentwood. A very heavy rain during the night rendered the country roads almost impassable, and it was not until the night of the 27th that Rousseau's command reached Nolinsville. On the morning of the 27th, Negley's train coming up, his division moved to the east, over an extremely rough by-road, to the right of Crittenden on the Murfreesboro pike, taking position at

Stewartsboro. Walker was sent back by Thomas from Brentwood, to take the direct Nolinsville pike. On the 28th, Rousseau, under orders, marched to Stewartsboro, where he joined Negley's division. On the 29th Negley crossed Stewart's Creek at the ford southwest of, and two miles above the turnpike bridge, and marched in supporting distance of the head of Crittenden's command on the Murfreesboro pike. Rousseau was ordered to remain in camp at Stewartsboro, detaching Starkweather's brigades with a section of artillery to the Jefferson pike, to watch the movements of the enemy. Negley's division moved eight miles that day and took position within three miles of Murfreesboro. Walker reached Stewartsboro from the Nolinsville pike about dark. Early in the morning, Crittenden's command moved into line of battle on the left, under a brisk fire, while Negley's division, by an oblique movement to the right, took position on the right of Palmer's division, and was then advanced through a dense cedar thicket several hundred yards in width to the Wilkinson cross roads, driving the enemy's skirmishers steadily, and with considerable loss. Rousseau's division, with the exception of Starkweather's brigade, was ordered up from Stewartsboro, reached the front, and bivouacked on the Murfreesboro pike in the rear of the centre. Thomas during the night ordered Walker's brigade to take a strong position near the bridge over Stewart's Creek, and to defend it against any attempt of the enemy's cavalry to destroy it. Rousseau was ordered to take position in rear of Negley's division, with his left on the Murfreesboro pike, and his right extending into the cedar thicket through which Negley had marched to take position. The troops held every foot of ground that had been won from the enemy, and remained in line of battle during the night.

The "Left Wing" under Crittenden advanced on the 26th to Lavergne, Palmer's division in the front. He was engaged in a short time with heavy skirmishing, which increased as the command moved south. The advance of this column was over a rough country, intersected with forests and cedar thickets. Crittenden was ordered to delay his movements until McCook reached Triune, in order to determine the direction in which Thomas should move as support; Crittenden's command encamped that night four miles north of Lavergne. On the 27th Wood's division was placed in the advance of Crittenden's column. Hascall's brigade drove the enemy from Lavergne with a loss of twenty men wounded, and pushing rapidly on, forced them south of Stewart's Creek, five miles beyond. At this place the enemy set fire to the bridge, which Hascall's advance reached in time to save. Hazen's brigade of Palmer's division was sent down the Jefferson pike to seize the bridge over Stewart's Creek at the crossing of that road. That night the "Left Wing" went into camp at Stewartsboro, and remained there over the next day, Sunday. On the 29th, Crittenden's command crossed Stewart's Creek by the Smyrna bridge, and the main Murfreesboro pike, and advanced that day—Palmer's division leading—to within two miles of Murfreesboro, driving back the enemy after several severe skirmishes, saving two bridges on the route, and forcing the enemy into his intrenchments.

Rosecrans, about three o'clock in the afternoon, received a signal message from Palmer at the front, that he was in sight of Murfreesboro, and that the enemy was running. Rosecrans then sent an order to Crittenden to send a division to occupy Murfreesboro, camping the other two outside. Crittenden received this order as he reached the head of his command, where Wood and Palmer were gathering up their troops preparatory to encamping for the night. These divisions were in line of battle,—Wood on the left and Palmer on the right,—with the rebels in sight in such heavy force that it was evident that they intended to dispute the passage of the river, and to fight a battle at or near Murfreesboro. On receipt of the order, Crittenden gave the command to advance. Wood was ordered to occupy the place, and Palmer to advance in line of battle until the passage of the river had been forced. Wood on receiving the order objected greatly to carrying it out, saying that it was hazarding a great deal for very little, to move over unknown ground in the night, instead of waiting for daylight, and that Crittenden ought to take the responsibility of disobeying the order. This the latter refused to do. After Wood and Palmer had issued their orders to advance, they both insisted that the order should not be carried out. The order was then suspended for an hour, so that Rosecrans could be heard from. During this interval the general himself came to this portion of the front, and approved of the action of Crittenden, as the order had been issued on the report that the enemy had evacuated Murfreesboro. Under the order, before it was suspended, Harker with his brigade had crossed the river at a ford on his left, where he surprised a regiment of Breckinridge's division, and drove it back on its main lines, not more than five hundred yards distant, in considerable confusion. He held this position until it was dark, with Breckinridge in force on his front, when Crittenden ordered his return. Hascall's command was fording the river, advancing, when the order was suspended. Harker succeeded in recrossing the river in the face of this strong force of the enemy without any serious loss. Crittenden placed Van Cleve's division, which had reported marching from the Jefferson turnpike to the Murfrees-

boro road, in reserve behind Wood. During the 30th there
was but little change in the position of the Left Wing, while
the other troops were moving into position on the line of
battle. Palmer's division was advanced a short distance, the
enemy contesting stubbornly.

The pioneer brigade had prepared the banks at three
places for the fording of the river. Wood's division covered two, and the pioneer brigade, under Captain St. Clair
Morton, covered the lower one. At night Crittenden's corps
with Negley's division bivouacked in order of battle, being
only seven hundred yards from the enemy's intrenchments.
The left of Crittenden's command extended down the river
some five hundred yards.

The first movement of Rosecrans's advance was made
known to Bragg as soon as it had reached a point two miles
beyond the Federal picket-line, where the heads of the several columns encountered the rebel cavalry pickets. For
all Bragg had placed his army in winter quarters, and pre-
sumed that Rosecrans had done the same, his experience in
the matter of a surprise to an army led him to be well prepared to know and take advantage of the slightest change
in his immediate front. By the night of the 26th Bragg
knew that Rosecrans's entire army was moving out to force
him to fight or compel his retreat. He at once selected his
line of battle at Stone's River, and directed his three cavalry
brigades, under Wheeler, Wharton, and Pegram, supported
by three brigades of infantry with artillery, to check the
advance of the several columns until he could unite his
army. He then gave the necessary orders for the concentration of his command and the formation of his line of
battle.

Murfreesboro is situated on the railroad to Chattanooga,
thirty miles southeast of Nashville, in the midst of the great

plain stretching from the base of the Cumberland Mountains toward the Cumberland River, and is surrounded by a
gently undulating country, exceedingly fertile and highly
cultivated. Leading in every direction from the town are
numerous excellent turnpikes. Stone's River—named after
an early settler—is formed here by the middle and south
branches of the stream uniting, and flows in a northerly
direction between low banks of limestone, generally steep
and difficult to cross, emptying into the Cumberland. At the
time of the battle the stream was so low that it could be
crossed by infantry everywhere. The Nashville Railroad
crosses the river about two hundred yards above the turnpike bridge. At some five hundred yards beyond, it intersects
the Nashville turnpike at a sharp angle, then runs some
eight hundred yards between the pike and the river, when
the stream turns abruptly to the east and passes to the north.
Open fields surrounded the town, fringed with dense cedar
brakes. These afforded excellent cover for approaching infantry, but were almost impervious to artillery.

The centre of Bragg's army was at Murfreesboro, under
Polk. The right was at Readyville, under McCown, and
the left at Triune and Eaglesville, under Hardee. Polk's
command consisted of Cheatham's and Withers's divisions.
These divisions and three brigades of Breckinridge's division of Hardee's corps were at Murfreesboro. Cleburne's
division and Adams's brigade of Breckinridge's division
were under the immediate command of Hardee, near Eaglesville, about twenty miles west of Murfreesboro. McCown's
division of Kirby Smith's corps was at Readyville, twelve
miles east of Murfreesboro. Each of the two divisions
of Hardee's corps consisted of four brigades of infantry.
To this corps Wheeler's brigade of cavalry was attached.
The brigade of T. R. Jackson—which was in the rear, guard-

VII.—5

ing the railroad from Bridgeport to the mountains—Bragg
also ordered up. On Sunday, the 28th, Bragg formed his
line of battle, placing Breckinridge's division on his extreme right, across Stone's River, to protect that flank and
cover the town. Adams's brigade rested on the Lebanon
road, about a mile and a half from town. Breckinridge's
division formed the first line, facing north, and was posted
in the edge of the forest, with Cleburne's division in the
second line, 800 yards to the rear. To the left of Adams the
line was broken by an intervening field, about three hundred yards in width, which was apparently left unoccupied,
but was covered by the Twentieth Tennessee and Wright's
battery, of Preston's brigade, which swept it and the fields
in front. The remainder of Preston's brigade rested with
its right in the woods, and extended along the edge with its
left toward the river. On the left of Preston, Palmer's brigade was formed, and on his left Hanson's completed that
portion of the line. Jackson's brigade reported to Breckinridge, and was placed on the east side of the Lebanon road,
on commanding ground, a little in the advance of the right
of Adams. On the other side of the river the right of
Withers's division rested at the bank, near the intersection
of the turnpike with the railroad, and was slightly in advance of Hanson's right. It extended southwardly across
the Wilkinson pike to the Triune or Franklin road, in an
irregular line adapted to the topography of the country.
In the rear of Withers's division that of Cheatham was posted
as a supporting force. McCown's division was placed in the
rear of these divisions as the reserve. This was Bragg's
first disposition of his troops for battle. On Monday, the
29th, no change of importance was made, the troops remaining in line of battle. In the evening, when Harker's brigade crossed the river, Bragg thought this was a movement

to occupy a hill situated about six hundred yards in front of
Hanson's centre. This commanded the ground sloping to
the river south and west, and from it the right of Withers's
division across the river could be enfiladed. Hanson's brigade was sent out, and, on Harker's return, the hill was occupied by the batteries of the enemy. On Monday Bragg,
finding that Rosecrans was extending his line on his right,
—as Bragg supposed to operate on that flank—threw his reserve division under McCown on Withers's left. Hardee was
ordered to take command of McCown's division, and to move
Cleburne from the second line in the rear of Breckinridge,
and place him on the left as support to McCown. Cleburne
was brought forward and placed five hundred yards in
rear of the latter. Bragg's main line of battle was in the
edge of the woods, with open ground to the front. His
troops were formed in two lines, the first line protected
by intrenchments, and his second line formed some six hundred yards to the rear. He awaited the attack of Rosecrans
on the 30th, and not receiving it, on Tuesday made his arrangements for an advance and attack in force on the morning of the 31st. His troops remained in line of battle, ready
to move with the early dawn of the coming day. The two
armies were now arrayed only some five hundred yards apart,
facing each other, and eager for the conflict of the morrow.

At nine o'clock on the evening of the 30th, the corps commanders met at Rosecrans's headquarters, in the cedars near
the Murfreesboro pike, to receive their final instructions
and to learn the details of the plan of battle for the next
day. McCook was directed with his three divisions to occupy the most advantageous position, refusing his right as
much as practicable and necessary to secure it, to await the
attack of the enemy, and in the event of that not being
made, to himself engage and hold the force on his front.

Johnson's division held the extreme right of his line; on Johnson's left was Davis's division, and on Davis's left Sheridan's was posted. Thomas was instructed to open with skirmishing and engage the enemy's centre with Negley's division of his command and Palmer's of Crittenden's corps, Negley's right resting on Sheridan's left, and Palmer's right on the left of Negley, Rousseau being in reserve. Crittenden was ordered to move Van Cleve's division across the river at the lower ford, covered and supported by the pioneer brigade and at once advance on Breckinridge. Wood's division was to follow—crossing at the upper ford and joining Van Cleve's right—when they were to press everything before them into Murfreesboro. This gave a strong attack from two divisions of Federal troops on the one of Breckinridge's, which was known to be the only one of the enemy's on the east of the river. As soon as Breckinridge had been dislodged from his position, the artillery of Wood's division was to take position on the heights east of the river and open fire on the enemy's lines on the other side, which could here be seen in reverse, and dislodge them, when Palmer was to drive them southward across the river or through the wood. Sustained by the advance of the Centre under Thomas crushing their right, Crittenden was to keep advancing, take Murfreesboro, move rapidly westward on the Franklin pike, get on their flank and rear and drive them into the country toward Salem, with the prospect of cutting off their retreat and probably destroying their army. Rosecrans called the attention of the corps commanders to the fact that this combination, which gave to him such a superiority on the left, depended for its success upon McCook's maintaining his position on the right for at least three hours, and if compelled to fall back that he should do so in the same manner he had advanced the day before, slowly and steadily, refusing his right. McCook was asked if he could hold his position for three hours, and replied that he thought he could. The importance of doing so was again impressed upon him, and the officers then separated.

As will be seen, the plan of battle as formed by Rosecrans contemplated a feint attack by his right, which in the event of a repulse was to fall back slowly, contesting the ground stubbornly, while the main attack was to be made by the forces on the left, followed up by the advance of the centre, the right to be temporarily sacrificed for the success of the general plan. Rosecrans knew that Bragg had weakened his right to support his left, looking to offensive movements on his part, and that the vital point in his own plan was the ability of McCook to hold the enemy in check on his front.

During the 30th, Bragg formed his plan of battle, which, singular as it appears, was the exact counterpart of that of the Federal commander. Hardee on the left, with McCown's and Cleburne's divisions, was to advance against the Federal right, which being forced back, Polk with Withers's and Cheatham's divisions were then to push the centre. The movement to be made by a steady wheel to the right on the right of Polk's command as a pivot. Bragg's plan was to drive our right and centre back against our left on Stone's River, seize our line of communication with Nashville, thus cutting us off from our base of operations and supplies, and ultimately securing the objective of his campaign, Nashville. Bragg's plan was equally as bold as that of his opponent— whose command was slightly inferior in strength to the rebel force—and the success of either depended very largely on the degree of diligence in opening the engagement. Rosecrans's orders were for the troops to breakfast before daylight and attack at seven o'clock. Bragg issued orders to attack at daylight.

CHAPTER VIII.

THE BATTLE OF STONE'S RIVER.

WITH early light, on the morning of the 31st, the movement in each army began. Rosecrans had established his headquarters in the rear of the left, in order to direct in person the forward movement of that portion of his army which was to cross Stone's River, sweep all resistance before it, and swing into Murfreesboro. The command was given, and at once Van Cleve advanced two brigades, making the crossing of the river at the lower ford without opposition. Wood's division had reached the river bank prepared to make the crossing and support Van Cleve. Everything on the left appeared to be working satisfactorily, when the opening sounds of the enemy's attack on the right reached the left. This was as intended, and went to show that if Bragg's left was fully occupied he then could give the less attention to his right, engaged by our army. With high hopes the troops then pressing forward continued to cross the river. Within an hour after the opening of the battle, one of McCook's staff officers reported to Rosecrans that the Right Wing was heavily pressed and needed assistance. Rosecrans was not told of the rout of Johnson's division, nor of the rapid withdrawal of Davis, made necessary thereby. Rosecrans, sending word to McCook to make a stubborn fight, continued his own offensive movement. Everything was working well as far as he knew. His strong force on the

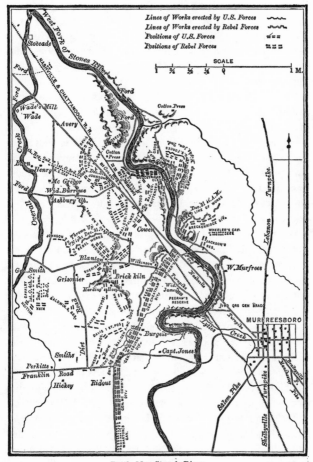

Battle-Map Stone's River.

left was not yet engaged. This he could hurl at the enemy's line of communications and strike on the flank Bragg's army that was flanking him. Soon after another staff officer from McCook arrived and reported that the entire Right Wing was being driven, a fact that manifested itself by the troops from the broken divisions pouring forth from the cedars in alarming numbers, and by the rapid movement of the noise of battle to the north. Then Rosecrans saw the necessity of abandoning his own movement, of recalling the left, and of proceeding at once to the right to save what was left of that corps as speedily as possible. He ordered back his left from across the river, and calling on his staff to mount, rode full gallop over to the right to reform that command on a new line and save his army. Now that he was on the defensive, after McCook's disaster, it was impossible to carry out his original plan of battle.

On the 30th, McCown in posting his division placed Ector's and Rains's brigades in the first line, and McNair's brigade in the second. Hardee ordered McCown at once to change this so as to bring McNair on the front line. This order was not obeyed until the morning of the 31st, when the movement was made, causing, however, some delay in the advance of Hardee's command on our right. At half past six o'clock, McCown's division in the front line with Cleburne's division in the second swinging around by a continuous change of direction to the right, advanced on to the right of McCook. McCown did not properly execute the movement as intended, and was carried so far to the west as to leave a large gap in the rebel front between Withers's left and McCown's right. Into this gap Cleburne immediately threw his division, and advanced, filling the interval in the front line between McCown and Polk. This gave Hardee double the length of front originally contemplated, and made it a single line instead of a double with division front. These two divisions thus formed then struck McCook's right flank—Johnson's division. McCook's line was very weak and poorly posted. It was thin and light, without reserves, with neither the troops nor the commanding officers in their places, as they should have been, under Rosecrans's orders of the evening before.

Every soldier on that field knew when the sun went down on the 30th that on the following day he would be engaged in a struggle unto death, and the air was full of tokens that one of the most desperate of battles was to be fought. In the face of all this, Johnson, the commander of the First Division on the right, was not on the line nor near enough to his troops to give orders to them, his headquarters being a mile and a half in the rear. General Willich, the commander of the Second Brigade, which had been posted for the express purpose of protecting the extreme right of our army, was absent from his command at division headquarters. His brigade was not even in line, as they had been ordered to get their breakfast. The batteries of the division were not properly posted, and in some cases the horses were away from the guns to the rear for water. All this was criminal negligence—a failure in the performance of duty—for which some one should have suffered. To the faulty position of the line and to the unprepared condition of the troops is to be attributed the almost overwhelming disaster that overtook our army on that day. As the two divisions of the enemy advanced, Kirk threw forward the Thirty-fourth Illinois to support the skirmish line, and called on Willich's brigade for help. This brigade being without an immediate commander, no effort was made to support Kirk. The contest was too unequal to be maintained for any great length of time, and Johnson's division, after a sharp

5*

and spirited but fruitless contest, crumbling to pieces, was driven back with a loss of eleven guns. Kirk was mortally wounded and Willich was captured, returning to his command as it was driven back. Kirk's brigade lost 473 killed and wounded, and had 342 captured. Willich's brigade had a few less killed and wounded, but more than twice that number captured.

Baldwin in reserve near headquarters was too far from the front to aid in supporting either of the other brigades of Johnson's division. Stragglers from Kirk's and Willich's brigades gave the first information to Baldwin of the disaster on the right. Hastily forming his troops, he had barely time to post them in line of battle before the enemy in immense masses appeared on his front at short range, their left extending far beyond the extreme right of his line. Opening at once a destructive fire upon their dense masses with his infantry and artillery, Baldwin succeeded in checking their advance in his front, but their left continued to swing around on his right. Here four pieces of Simonson's battery posted near the woods in the rear of the first position opened with terrible effect. The enemy came on in such overwhelming numbers, that after half an hour's stubborn resistance Baldwin was compelled to retire, not however until the enemy had flanked his right and were pouring in an enfilading fire. As it was he barely made his escape, since in a moment longer his entire command would have been surrounded and captured. At the edge of the woods Baldwin endeavored to make another stand, but before he could form his line he was again forced back. Retiring slowly, with several halts in the cedars, Baldwin with his brigade reached the railroad where the rest of the division was being reformed.

The right flank being driven from its position by the left

of the enemy, Davis's division then felt the full force of
the victorious sweep of the rebel troops, flushed with success and aided by the forces immediately in his front.
Davis, as soon as the disaster on his right had fully developed, at once changed front and formed a new line, with
his right brigade under Post nearly at right angles to its
former position, and made all necessary disposition of his
troops to receive the attack. Baldwin's brigade had hastily
taken position and had already felt the force of the enemy's
concentrated attack. Still the advancing lines of the enemy
greatly overlapped the extreme right of Baldwin. Hardly
had the troops been placed in this position before the
enemy swept down in heavy masses upon both the flank and
front, charging with the rebel yell. The two divisions of
McCown's and Cleburne's troops which had driven Johnson, hurled themselves upon Baldwin's and Post's brigades,
while the fresh troops of Withers's division, composed of
Maningault's and Loomis's brigades, rushed upon those of
Davis, under Carlin and Woodruff, and upon that on the
right of Sheridan's line under Sill. The change of position of Post's brigade gave to the two remaining brigades
of Davis's division, and Sill's brigade of Sheridan's command, the length of division front, and on this the enemy
made a united attack. After Baldwin had been compelled
to retire, Post repulsed the attack on his brigade, and Carlin, Woodruff, and Sill in the front drove back the assaulting
column of the rebels with heavy loss. The enemy then reformed his lines, strengthened them with his reserves under
Vaughn and Maney of Cheatham's division and once more
pressed forward. Again these heavy lines struck Carlin,
Woodruff, and Sill, and were again handsomely repulsed ;
Sill gallantly charging the rebels and driving them into their
line of intrenchments. In this charge, General Sill was

killed. His brigade then slowly retired and formed anew
in line of battle. Cleburne at the same time charged down
on Post's brigade, and he too was a second time repulsed.

The formation of the battle-front of Davis's two left brigades under Carlin and Woodruff was almost perpendicular
to that of Sheridan's division, and the left of Woodruff's
with the right of Sill's brigade formed the apex of a right
angle. This position was at once observed by the enemy,
who saw that if he could take this extreme point of the
angle he would then be in position to enfilade both lines at
once. For the possession of this point every effort was
made, and a third attack was ordered upon it with four
brigades, under the immediate command of Cheatham, in
double lines. Hardee had gathered his command together
again for another attack on Post's position. Pressing forward with the victorious troops of McCown's and Cleburne's
divisions—the troops that had swept Johnson from the field
—he enveloped both flanks of Post's brigade, and compelled
him to fall back, with the loss of one gun, to the Nashville
pike, where he also reformed his command.

On the withdrawal of Post's brigade, Carlin's right was
left exposed to the enemy, who with renewed vigor pressed
forward in overwhelming numbers on converging lines,
massing as they advanced. Circling around on their right
the rebels swept down on the remaining brigades of Davis's
division in dense columns. In the previous charge the attack had been so heavy upon the angle formed by Woodruff's left and Sill's right, that in the new formation—after
the second repulse—the line at this point was somewhat
broken, and after Sill's death the right of the brigade was
reformed somewhat to the rear of the former line, the better
to support the battery attached to it. In the heavy fighting of the morning the position of all the brigades had

been more or less changed, and in several instances the commanding officer of each brigade considered his command as being without support on either flank. On the third assault both Carlin and Woodruff thought this to be the case with their commands, and in the attack then made upon their brigades they became almost surrounded. Carlin stubbornly resisted every effort to drive him from his position until by his remaining longer the loss of his entire brigade became imminent. His regiment on the left gave way and he then retreated across open fields in the rear to the edge of the woods, where Davis was attempting to reform his line, having placed Hotchkiss's battery just within the timber. Woodruff then fell back, but being closely pressed, turned and with a determined charge sent the enemy beyond his original position. Being unsupported he was compelled to retire into the cedars. Before Woodruff reached the new lines that Davis was trying to form, Carlin's troops opened fire on the advancing enemy, when he was informed that Davis had ordered a farther withdrawal. He then fell back across the Wilkinson pike, where he rallied his men, who however, on the advance of the enemy, fired one volley and broke to the rear without orders. Carlin then went with them through the lines of reserves, halting at the railroad, where he reformed his command. After reaching the cedars Woodruff charged a second time, and compelled the enemy to fall back, but his ammunition giving out, his troops passed to the rear, resisting every effort to rally them until they reached the Murfreesboro pike.

Davis's division had up to this time protected Sheridan's right, and these divisions unitedly had resisted two assaults. After the charge of the enemy that broke Davis's division and sent it through the cedars, Sheridan was compelled to change his line and to protect the right flank of his command from the enemy, now pressing that part of his position, as well as his front, in increasing numbers, as the line became shortened. Hastily withdrawing Sill's brigade, with the reserves sent it as support, he directed Roberts, with the left brigade, which had changed front and formed in column of regiments, to charge the enemy in the cedars from which he had withdrawn Sill's brigade and the reserves. This charge was at once made by Roberts, and the enemy's advance checked sufficiently to give Sheridan time to form his troops on the new line, which he at once did by placing Sill's and Shafer's brigades on a line at right angles to his first one, and ordered Roberts to return and form his command on this same line. Sheridan now attempted to form the broken troops of the other division on the right of his new line, but in this he was not successful. After making a gallant fight with his division, finding the right of his new line turned, Sheridan was directed by McCook to advance to the front and reform his troops to the right of Negley's division of the Centre under Thomas. Throwing forward his left to join Negley's right, he placed Roberts's brigade in position at right angles to Negley's line, facing south, and then placed his two other brigades in the rear, and at right angles to Roberts, so as to face westward and to cover the rear of Negley's lines. In the angle of these lines on the right of Negley, he placed his artillery. Here he was again fiercely assaulted by the enemy, and one of the fiercest and most sanguinary contests of the day ensued. Massing the four divisions of Hardee's and Polk's corps— each of four brigades—Bragg hurled them against the divisions of Sheridan and Negley, and at the same time the enemy opened fire from the intrenchments in the direction of Murfreesboro. Here the fighting was terrific. Five batteries were posted with these two divisions, the artil-

lery range of the respective forces being not to exceed two
hundred yards.   Three times in dense masses the enemy
charged on these divisions, and three times were they repulsed.   Here Colonel Roberts was killed.   Sheridan's
troops having now exhausted their ammunition—Shafer's
brigade being entirely out and nearly all his horses killed—
then gave way, after over four hours of some of the hottest
fighting of the day.   Sheridan lost in falling back from this
position eight guns.   Nearly all the remainder of his artillery was drawn by his men through the cedars.   On arriving
at the Murfreesboro pike, Sheridan reformed his command
in an open space near the right of Palmer.

Before assisting in the gallant fight on the right of the
centre with Sheridan in his new position, Negley's division,
after repelling all assaults made on it, had been engaged in
heavy fighting on its front since the middle of the morning.
On the withdrawal of Sheridan, Negley's division found
themselves surrounded by the enemy in swarms.   Rousseau's division in reserve, and Palmer's on the left, had retired to the rear of the cedars, to form a new line.   Falling
back through the cedar brakes in the rear of the division,
under a concentrated fire of musketry and artillery at short
range, the rebels were driven back in front and checked in
the rear.   Miller's and Stanley's brigades on reaching the
woods reformed their lines, faced to the rear and fired several volleys into the enemy, then advanced over the open
fields across which these brigades had just retired.   In passing through the cedars the enemy pressed so closely on
the division that in some parts of Miller's brigade the lines
of the opposing armies seemed commingled.   The division
then reformed on the new line, as directed by Thomas, near
the Nashville pike.

Early in the day, with the breaking up and retreat of the

two fine divisions of McCook's corps, the extent of the disaster to the right was forced upon Rosecrans with terrible
earnestness. Realizing at once that upon him devolved the
task of making such disposition of his command as would
ensure the safety of his army, he immediately gave the necessary orders for the movement of the troops. Hurriedly
galloping to the centre, where he found Thomas, he at once
ordered Rousseau's division—held as reserve heretofore—to
be sent to the support of what was left of McCook's line into
the cedar-brakes to the right and rear of Sheridan. Rosecrans then ordered Crittenden to suspend Van Cleve's movement across the river on the left, to cover the crossing with
one brigade, and to move the other two brigades westward
across the fields toward the railroad for a reserve. He also
directed Wood to suspend his preparations for his crossing,
and for him to move at once to the new line on the right
and hold Hascall in reserve. Up to this time Rosecrans
had hoped that McCook, notwithstanding the disaster to the
right, might stay the onset with his own troops. With the
volume of stragglers and the detachments from the broken
commands swarming to the rear through the cedars Rosecrans soon became satisfied that McCook was routed. He
then ordered Van Cleve to be sent in to the right of Rousseau, and Wood to send Colonel Harker's brigade farther
down the Murfreesboro pike with orders to go in and attack
the enemy on the right of Van Cleve. The pioneer brigade
had been posted on the knoll of ground west of the Nashville pike and about four or five hundred yards in the rear of
Palmer's centre, supporting Stokes's battery. On Negley's
division being compelled to retire, Thomas ordered him with
Rousseau to form their divisions along a depression in the
open ground in rear of the cedars, as a temporary line, until
the artillery could be posted on the high ground near to and

west of the Murfreesboro pike. Rousseau's division, cutting
its way through the enemy in falling back from the cedars,
took position on this temporary line with all its batteries
posted on the knoll a short distance to the rear. Here the
severest engagement of this day of heavy fighting was had,
almost hand to hand. At this point the new line had open
ground in front of it for some four or five hundred yards.
Rousseau, while his batteries were unlimbering, requested
Van Cleve to move with Colonel Samuel Beatty's brigade of
his division to form on his right, check the rebel advance and
drive it back. Van Cleve instantly moved his troops on the
double quick and reached the desired position in good season. Upon these troops in this new line the rebels charged
in dense masses, flushed with the victory of the early morning and elate with the hope of continued success to the end.
They had swept everything before them thus far, and felt
that with renewed effort the successful issue of the battle
was within their grasp. Emerging from the cedars with
yell after yell, firing as they came, they rushed forward four
lines deep in the attempt to cross the open field and drive
back this new line that stood in their pathway to final
victory. At once Rousseau's division and Beatty's brigade
opened fire upon the advancing columns, while Guenther's
and Loomis's batteries added effect to it by sending double
shotted canister into their thick ranks. The rebels moved
on for a time, but the fire proved too terrible and they were
driven back with great slaughter. On reaching the cedars
these troops were rallied by their officers, and with fresh
troops as supports they advanced once more, with a determined effort to carry our position at this point. But again
they were, after a most desperate struggle, driven back.
Again and again they returned to the assault, in four deliber-
ate and fiercely sustained efforts, each time to meet with a

repulse. The brigade of regulars under the command of Colonel Sheppard sustained the heaviest blows of this assault. They had the efficient support of Scribner's and John Beatty's brigades, of Loomis's and Guenther's batteries, and of the pioneer brigade under Captain St. Clair Morton, with Stokes's battery. Sheppard's command lost in killed and wounded in this short and severe contest, 26 officers and 611 enlisted men, making a total loss of 637 out of 1,566 effectives. The centre succeeded in driving back the enemy from its front, gallantly holding its ground against overwhelming odds, while the artillery concentrating its fire on the cedar thickets on their right drove the enemy far back under cover of the woods.

While the right and centre had been thus actively engaged, the left had also borne its full share of the heavy fighting of the day. Palmer's division was posted in line of battle with his right resting on Negley's left. His line was formed with Cruft's brigade on the right, connecting with Negley, and his left extending across a point of woods to the right of Hazen's brigade, which was formed in two lines with his left resting on the Nashville pike, while Grose's brigade was in reserve some two hundred yards to the rear, formed in two lines nearly opposite the interval between the brigades in line of battle. On the withdrawal of the troops of the left from across the river, Wood ordered Wagner with his brigade to hold his position in the woods on the left of the Murfreesboro pike at all hazards, this being an exceedingly important point, protecting our left front and flanks and securing command of the road leading to the rear. Hascall's and Harker's brigades were withdrawn, and the latter, under an order from Rosecrans, was moved to the right and rear. In the heavy fighting of the general movement on the right and centre, the left gradually became engaged, and with this Hascall was ordered by Wood to take position between Wagner and Hazen on Wagner's right. With the general advance of the enemy, moving on the right of Polk's corps as a pivot, Palmer and the two brigades of Wood's division on the left became engaged. Cruft early in the morning had been ordered by Palmer to advance, keeping in line with Negley, the latter having sent word to Palmer that he intended to advance his division to attack the enemy. Cruft was advanced in two lines, two regiments in each line with Miller's brigade of Negley's division on the right and Hazen's brigade on his left. After Cruft had advanced about a hundred yards, Palmer discovered that Negley had thrown back his right so that his line was almost perpendicular to Cruft's and to his rear. After Cruft had driven the enemy's skirmishers in, the rebels advanced in great force in four ranks with double lines, Chalmers in the front line with Donelson's brigade following. This charge Cruft repulsed, inflicting severe loss on the enemy. Chalmers was so severely wounded by the bursting of a shell as to disqualify him for further duty on the field. Advancing once more, the rebels again attacked Cruft's line, when a very severe engagement ensued, and after some thirty minutes' firing the enemy was again repulsed. When Negley's division went back through the cedars, Cruft was left without support on his right and he then withdrew to the wood, the enemy following him closely and pressing him hard. While Cruft was thus engaged on the front, Palmer found that the right and centre had been driven from the first line, and that the enemy in Negley's front was forcing his way into the open ground to his rear. He then changed Grose from front to rear, retired his new left so as to bring the rebels under the direct fire of his line, and opened on them with great effect, holding his ground until the enemy was driven back. Hazen was ordered to fall back from the advanced position he then held, and to occupy the crest of a low wooded hill between the pike and the railroad, and there resist the attack. This was about eleven o'clock, and all of Palmer's command was engaged with the enemy—Hazen on the railroad, one or two detached regiments to the right, Cruft still farther to the right, actively engaged, while Grose to the rear was fighting heavy odds. Grose shortly after this changed to the front again, the enemy being driven back from his rear, and moved to the left to co-operate with Hazen. After aiding in the repulse of the troops that struck Cruft's lines, Hazen with constant firing maintained his position on his left at the railroad, retiring his right to place his troops behind the embankment at that place. General Palmer had ordered Grose to co-operate with Hazen, and part of Grose's troops reporting to him, they were placed in position on the front. Here was held what was considered by the enemy to be the key to our position, known as the "Round Forest." This was attacked by the right of Donelson's brigade, but the attack was met with a fire that mowed down half its number, one regiment losing 207 out of 402. In another regiment the loss was 306 out of 425. Polk finding that his troops had been so severely punished that they were not able to renew the attack on the extreme left of our line, and that the new line on the right as formed by Rosecrans resisted every attack, applied for an order from Bragg directing four brigades from Breckinridge's command to be sent to him to drive our left from its line, and especially to dislodge us from our position in the "Round Forest." These brigades were sent to him, arriving in two detachments of two brigades each. Adams and Jackson's brigades first reported, under Breckinridge in person. Those of Preston and Palmer re-

ported about two hours later. About two o'clock in the afternoon Adams and Jackson's brigades assailed our left
with determined energy, but after a severe contest they
were compelled to yield and fall back. They were rallied
by Breckinridge, but were too badly cut up to renew the
attack. About four o'clock, on the arrival of the brigades
of Preston and Palmer, the assault on the left was renewed
and again repulsed, when the enemy withdrew and made no
further attack upon that position. When this last attack
was made, Rosecrans, anxious as to this vital point of his
lines, hurried there with his staff to assist in the repulse.
It was here that a shell grazing the person of Rosecrans
carried off the head of his chief of staff, the lamented
Garesche.

The new line formed by Rosecrans to protect his communication extended from Hazen on the Murfreesboro pike
in a northwesterly direction, Hascall supporting Hazen,
Rousseau filling the interval to the pioneer brigade, Negley
in reserve, Van Cleve west of the pioneer brigade, McCook's
corps refused on his right and slightly to the rear on the
Nashville pike, with the cavalry at and beyond Overall's
Creek. After the formation had been completed later in
the afternoon, with a wild yell the enemy debouched from
the cedar thickets, and forming into line, advanced as if to
charge once more. At once a terrific fire of artillery and
infantry opened on them, and their broken ranks went back
over the fields driven in great confusion; the batteries Rosecrans had placed on the commanding ground near the railroad inflicting a heavier loss on Polk's brigade than it had
suffered in all the previous fighting of the day. This attack
was in the main repulsed by Van Cleve's division, aided by
Harker's brigade, and the cavalry under General Stanley.
This was the last assault on the right and centre, and with

the repulse of Breckinridge's command on the left, the fighting for the day was over; and on the field where death had reaped such a heavy harvest, on the last day of 1862, the troops slept on their arms, waiting for what the next day might bring forth. The night was clear and cold. The armies maintained their relative positions, with some picket firing occurring during the night. Rosecrans gave orders that all the spare ammunition should be issued, and it was found that there was enough for another battle, the main question being where the battle was to be fought. During the night Rosecrans, in order to complete the new formation of his lines, withdrew the left from the advanced position it occupied, and placed it in line some two hundred and fifty yards in the rear, on more advantageous ground, the extreme left resting on Stone's River above the lower ford and extending to the railroad. Late in the afternoon the brigades under Colonels Starkweather and Walker, that had been on duty in the rear, arrived at the front and were posted in reserve on the line of battle, the former in rear of McCook's left, and Walker in rear of the left of Sheridan's division near the Murfreesboro pike. On the morning of the 1st they were placed in the front line, relieving Van Cleve, who then returned to his position on the left.

The extent of the disaster on the right was appalling and seemed at one time about to envelop the entire army. As the storm of battle passed down the line it reached Thomas, who cool, calm, and self-sustained, stood the test of one of the fiercest contests of the war. It was to him that Rosecrans first turned in the hour of disaster and in him he trusted most. The commander of the army, too, was sorely tried. He had come to win victory, but in place of it defeat seemed almost inevitable. Reforming his lines and bravely fighting, he had hurled back Bragg's army before it had achieved any decisive success. Rosecrans knew that his losses had been extremely heavy, but those of the enemy had been still more severe. He felt that on a question of endurance his army would come out first, although the dash and onset of the rebels had at the opening been able to sweep all before them. In the face of an earnest effort on the part of some of his general officers to persuade him to fall back to Nashville and then throw up works and wait for reinforcements, Rosecrans determined to await the attack of the enemy in the positions of his lines late Wednesday afternoon. He sent for the provision trains, ordered up fresh supplies of ammunition, and decided that if Bragg should not attack before these arrived, that he himself would then resume offensive operations.

During the morning of January 1, 1863, the rebels made repeated attempts to advance on Thomas's front in the centre, but were driven back before emerging from the woods. Crittenden was ordered to send Van Cleve's division across the river, to occupy the position opposite the ford on his left, his right resting on high ground near the river and his left thrown forward perpendicular to it. The rebel right, under Polk, kept up a brisk skirmish fire on their front. Chalmers's brigade was ordered to occupy the ground in front of the "Round Forest." Bragg, anticipating an attack on his right under Breckinridge on the morning of the 1st, during the night ordered two brigades of that division to recross to the east side of the river. But none was made. About two o'clock in the afternoon the enemy showed signs of movement, by massing large numbers of his troops on our right at the extremity of an open field a mile and a half from the Murfreesboro pike. Here the rebels formed in lines six deep, and massed thus heavily, remained without advancing for over an hour. Gibson's brigade and a battery occupied the woods near Overall's creek, while Negley's was placed as support on McCook's right. The evident design of Bragg during the day was simply to feel the lines of our army to find out if Rosecrans was retreating. Satisfied of this, he felt that while he could maintain his position he was not in condition to attack, after the heavy hammering his army had received the day before.

At daylight the next day Bragg gave orders to his corps commanders to feel our lines and ascertain Rosecrans's position. Fire was opened from four batteries on the centre, and a demonstration in force was made by his infantry, followed by another on McCook; but at all points meeting with a heavy artillery fire, he concluded that our army still occupied the battlefield in force. Bragg ordered Wharton's and Pegram's brigades of cavalry to cross to the right bank of Stone's River immediately in Breckinridge's front. Soon after this a number of his staff officers discovered for the first time that Van Cleve's troops, sent over the day before, had quietly crossed unopposed, and had established themselves on and under cover of an eminence from which Polk's line was commanded and enfiladed. It was an evident necessity either to withdraw Polk's line or to dislodge Van Cleve's. The first alternative was not to be entertained until the failure of an attempt to accomplish the latter. Polk was at once ordered to send over to Breckinridge the remaining brigades belonging to his division still with Polk, and Breckinridge, reporting to Bragg, received his orders. The attack was to be made with the four brigades of Breckinridge's command, the cavalry protecting his right and co-operating with him. The crest of ground near the river, where Van Cleve's division was in position, was the point against which the main attack was to be directed. This taken, Breckinridge was to bring up his artillery and establish it on the high ground, so as to enfilade our lines on the other side of the river. Polk was to open with a heavy fire on our left as Breckinridge commenced his advance. The signal for the attack was to be one gun from the centre, and four o'clock was the hour set for the firing of this gun.

Breckinridge drew up his division in two lines, the first in a narrow skirt of woods, the other some two hundred yards in rear. General Pillow, after the first day's fighting, reporting for duty, was assigned to the command of Palmer's brigade. Pillow's and Hanson's brigades formed the first line, Preston's and Adams's brigades the second. The artillery was placed in rear of the second line, and in addition to that of his brigade, ten Napoleon guns—12-pounders— were sent to aid in the attack.

Van Cleve's division was under the command of Colonel Samuel Beatty, with Price's brigade on the right next to the river, Fyffe's brigade on the left. Grider's brigade formed Beatty's support, while a brigade of Palmer's division was placed in position on the extreme left to protect that flank. Drury's battery was posted in the rear. In front of Breckinridge's line was an open space some six hundred and fifty yards in width, with a gentle ascent which it was necessary for his troops to cross before reaching our lines. Several hundred yards in the rear of the latter was the river, increasing the distance as it flowed beyond our left.

General Rosecrans had ordered Crittenden to send Beatty's division across the river as protection to the troops on the left and centre, as from the high ground near the river the enemy, by an enfilading fire, could sweep these portions of our line. During the morning of the 2d Negley's division was ordered from the right, and placed in position on the west bank of the river, in the rear of Beatty's division, as

reserves, being here on the left of Hazen's and Cruft's brigades of Palmer's division.

As soon as Breckinridge's command entered the open
ground to his front, the artillery massed on the west bank
of the river by order of Crittenden, consisting of all the
guns of the left wing, together with the batteries belonging to Negley's division and Stokes's battery, making 58
guns in position, opened a heavy, accurate, and destructive
fire. Large numbers of the enemy fell before they reached
Beatty's infantry lines. Pressing forward without waiting
to throw out a skirmish line, Breckinridge's command
swept onward, reckless of the artillery fire and that of the
infantry, and struck Price's and Grider's brigades, broke
their lines, drove them from their position on to their support in the rear, which also gave way, when the entire division retreated in broken ranks across the river, taking refuge
behind the line of Negley's division, and there reforming.
Breckinridge reports that he "after a brief but bloody conflict routed both the opposing lines, took 400 prisoners and
several flags, and drove their artillery and the great body of
their infantry across the river." His success, however, was
exceedingly short-lived. Colonel John F. Miller, commanding the right brigade of Negley's division, had, in the absence of Negley in the rear, ordered the troops of his division to lie down under cover of the bluff of the river bank,
and hold their fire until our troops from the other side
crossed over and moved to the rear. As soon as the last of
Beatty's men had passed through Miller's lines, he commanded the division to rise and open fire on Breckinridge's
troops. Miller's fire was so effectively given as to cause the
enemy at once to recoil, Breckinridge's command being also
under the artillery fire on the left, enfilading his ranks. His
division soon wavered, and then began falling back. At

this Miller—Negley still not appearing—ordered the division to charge across the river, and to drive the enemy to their line of intrenchments, which they did. While crossing, Miller received word from Palmer not to cross his command, but as the greater part of his troops were over the river driving the enemy, Miller pressed on in person, and hurried the troops last to cross, up to the support of those in the advance. He was then ordered by Palmer to recross the river, and to support the artillery on the hill on the west bank. The troops under Miller were then advancing through the cornfield, driving the enemy, and as his right flank was fully protected, he had no inclination to turn back, and he ordered the troops forward. One of the enemy's batteries was posted in a wood just beyond the cornfield to the front. It was keeping up a brisk fire on Miller's advance, when he ordered his men to charge this battery, which they did, capturing three guns. At the time of the charge the Twenty-sixth Tennessee was supporting the battery. This regiment was broken by the assault, a large number of them captured, with the colors of the command. Sending the prisoners, guns, and colors to the rear, Miller reformed his line so as to hold the ground until relieved by other troops. These being crossed over the river under Hazen, together with Davis's division, Miller's command returned to the west bank of the river and there reformed the division in line, and took position for the night. Negley himself was not across the river with the command during the engagement.

Bragg was deeply chagrined at the failure of Breckinridge's movement. In his report of the action he says, "The contest was short and severe, the enemy were driven back and the eminence gained, but the movement as a whole was a failure, and the position was again yielded.

Our forces were moved, unfortunately, to the left so far as to throw a portion of them into and over Stone's River, where they encountered heavy masses of the enemy, while those against whom they were intended to operate had a destructive enfilade on our whole line. Our reserve line was so close to the front as to receive the enemy's fire, and returning it took their friends in the rear. The cavalry force was left entirely out of the action." Bragg immediately sent Anderson's brigade across the river, which formed in line on the front of Breckinridge's command, and remained there in position during the night. He also sent Cleburne's division over, and placed Hardee in command of that side of the river. Rosecrans ordered Davis to take and hold the line occupied by Beatty's division. Later, all the troops of Crittenden's corps crossed the river and occupied the crests, intrenching themselves in this position.

During the morning of the 3d Bragg ordered a heavy and constant picket firing to be kept up on his front, to determine whether our army still confronted him. At one point in the wood to the left of the Murfreesboro pike the rebel sharpshooters had all day annoyed Rousseau, who requested permission to dislodge them and their supports, covering a ford at that place. About six o'clock in the evening two regiments from John Beatty's brigade of Rousseau's division, co-operating with two regiments of Spear's brigade of Negley's division, under cover of a brisk artillery fire, advanced on the woods and drove the enemy not only from their cover, but also from their intrenchments a short distance from the rear.

At noon Bragg, on consultation with his generals, decided to retreat, leaving the field in possession of his opponent. At 12.15 of the night of the 2d, after Breckinridge's failure, Cleburne and Withers had sent a communication to Bragg's headquarters, through Polk, stating that there were but "three brigades that are at all reliable, and even some of these are more or less demoralized from having some brigade commanders who do not possess the confidence of their commands." They expressed their fears of great disaster 'which should be avoided by retreat. This was endorsed by Polk at 12.30 A.M., January 3d, "I send you the enclosed papers as requested, and I am compelled to add that after seeing the effect of the operations of to-day, added to that produced upon the troops by the battle of the 31st, I very greatly fear the consequences of another engagement at this place on the ensuing day. We could now perhaps get off with some safety, and with some credit if the affair was well managed; should we fail in the meditated attack, the consequences might be very disastrous."

By 11 P.M. the whole of Bragg's army, except his cavalry, was in retreat in good order to a position behind Duck River. His cavalry held the front at Murfreesboro until Monday morning, when they fell back and covered Bragg's immediate front. Sunday the 4th was spent in burying the dead, and the cavalry was sent to reconnoitre. On the 5th Thomas's entire command, preceded by Stanley's cavalry, marched into Murfreesboro, and encamped on the Manchester and Shelbyville road.

The cavalry under Stanley rendered very efficient service on the advance from Nashville. Dividing these troops into three columns he sent the first brigade under Colonel Minty with Crittenden's corps; the second brigade under Colonel Zahm moved to the right, protecting McCook's right flank; the reserve Stanley commanded in person, and moved with the head of McCook's command on the Nolinsville pike. Colonel John Kennett, in command of the cavalry division, commanded the cavalry on the Murfreesboro pike. There was constant skirmishing between the enemy's cavalry and artillery and each of the columns up to the 31st, as the army advanced, getting into position. At midnight on the 30th, Stanley moved with part of his command to Lavergne, where the enemy's cavalry was interfering with the trains. At 9.30 he was ordered by General Rosecrans to hasten to the right and cover McCook's flank. On reaching there he found McCook's new line formed on the Nashville road, when the enemy's skirmishers advanced and drove Stanley's dismounted cavalry out of the woods to the open field. Here he was reinforced, and charging the rebels routed them, driving them back to their lines. On the 1st Zahm's brigade was sent to Lavergne to protect the wagon trains being sent to Nashville. He had several skirmishes with Wheeler, but finally secured the safety of the train and repulsed every attack of the rebel cavalry.

On the 2d and 3d of January the cavalry was engaged in watching the flanks of our position. On the 4th Stanley discovered that the enemy had fled. Collecting his cavalry he moved to the fords of Stone's River, in readiness to cross, and on the 5th, preceding Thomas, they entered Murfreesboro. Zahm's command went out on the Shelbyville pike six miles, meeting with no opposition. Stanley with the rest of his cavalry marched down the Manchester pike, encountering the enemy's cavalry strongly posted at Lytle's Creek in heavy force. Fighting here until sundown, the rebels were driven from one cedar-brake to another until Spear's brigade came up, when they were driven from their last stand in disorder. The cavalry returned and camped at Lytle's Creek to recuperate, after nine days of active campaigning. During this time the saddles were only taken off the horses to groom them, and were immediately replaced.

Bragg in his retreat left in his hospitals all his wounded in Murfreesboro. By this some 2,500 prisoners fell into our hands to be cared for.

Thus, after seven days' battle, the Army of the Cumberland rested in Murfreesboro. having achieved the object of the winter campaign. The final battle for Kentucky had been fought by Bragg and lost. Nashville, too, was now beyond his hopes, and for the great victory of the 31st, which he claimed, Bragg had but little to show.

In the heavy skirmishing prior to the 31st, success attended every movement of the Federal army. The heavy fighting of the early part of the 31st was all in Bragg's favor up to the time his advance was checked by our centre and the new line on the right. From that time to the occupation of Murfreesboro every movement resulted in favor of the army under Rosecrans, and the retreat of Bragg after the defeat of Breckinridge gave the halo of victory to our army as the result of the campaign. In his retreat Bragg admitted that he had gained nothing but a victory barren of results, at the cost to him of 10,125 killed, wounded, and missing, 9,000 of whom were killed and wounded, over twenty per cent. of his command. Bragg's field return of December 10, 1862, shows an effective total of 51,036, composed of 39,304 infantry, 10,070 cavalry, and 1,662 artillery. By reason of Morgan and Forrest being absent on their raids, Bragg's cavalry was reduced to 5,638. This gave an effective force of 46,604, which was the strength of the army with which Bragg fought the battle.

Rosecrans's force on the battle-field was : Infantry, 37,977 ; artillery, 2,223 ; cavalry, 3,200 ; total, 43,400. His loss was : killed, 1,553 ; wounded, 7,245. The enemy captured about 2,800 men. Making his total loss about twenty-five per cent. of his force in action. Rosecrans lost twenty-eight pieces of artillery and a large portion of his wagon train. Bragg lost three pieces of artillery.

Why did Rosecrans's plan of battle miscarry so fatally and Bragg's come so near absolute success? The fault was not in the plan as conceived by the former. The near success of the latter proved a vindication of that. The originator of the plan was not at fault personally, for at no time during the battle did he falter or prove unequal to his command. When called on to give up his plan of the offensive and assume the defensive to save his army, the wonderful power of Rosecrans as a general over troops was never displayed to a greater advantage. With the blood from a slight wound on his cheek, in a light blue army overcoat, through the mud and rain of the battle-field, he rode along the line inspiring his troops with the confidence he felt as to the final result. To Rosecrans there was but one outcome to the battle at Stone's River, and that was victory. When some of his general officers advised retreat to Nashville, not for an instant did he falter in his determination to " fight or die right here." The demoralization of one of his division commanders was so great, that on Thursday afternoon, when the rebels were massing on Rosecrans's right, this general, commanding a division, announced to his brigade commanders that in the event of the anticipated assault resulting disastrously, he proposed to take his division and cut his way through to Nashville. To his troops—the greater part of whom had never seen Rosecrans under the enemy's fire—when on their return from the cedars, they formed anew in front of the Nashville pike—seeing the Commanding General of the army riding fearlessly on the extreme front, in the heat of battle, cool and collected, giving orders and encouraging his men—his mere presence was an inspiration. His personal bravery was never more fully shown than when he rode down to the "Round Forest" with his staff, under fire, at the time Garesché was killed by a shell that only missed the chief by a few inches. In this ride Rosecrans had three mounted orderlies shot dead while following him. When the entire extent of McCook's disaster in its crushing force was revealed to him, he felt the full burden of his responsibility, and rising to the demands of the hour he was superb. Dashing from one point to another, quick to discern danger and ready to meet it, shrinking from no personal exposure, dispatching his staff on the gallop, hurrying troops into position, massing the artillery and forming his new lines on grounds of his own choosing, confident of ultimate success, and showing his troops that he had all confidence in them, it was worth months of an ordinary life-time to have been with Rosecrans when by his own unconquered spirit he plucked victory from defeat and glory from disaster.

But if the plan was not at fault, what was? Rosecrans started from Nashville for an offensive campaign, and before his plan of battle had met the test, he was compelled to abandon it, and assume the defensive. Where was the fault and who was to blame? The fault was McCook's defective line, and in part Rosecrans was responsible for it. He ought never to have trusted the formation of a line of battle so important to the safety of his whole army to McCook alone, and he certainly knew this. Rosecrans gave his personal attention to the left, but he should at least have ordered the change his quick eye detected as necessary in McCook's line, and not trusted to chance and McCook's ability to withstand the attack with his faulty line. No one who saw him at Stone's River the 31st of December will say aught against the personal bravery and courage of McCook under fire. All that he could do to aid in repairing the great disaster of that day he did to the best of his ability. He stayed with

6*

Davis's division under fire as long as it held together, and then gave personal directions to Sheridan's troops, in the gallant fight they made against overwhelming odds. As Rosecrans himself says in his official report of McCook, " a tried, faithful, and loyal soldier, who bravely breasted the battle at Shiloh and Perryville, and as bravely on the bloody field of Stone's River." But there is something more than mere physical bravery required in a general officer in command of as large a body of troops as a *corps d'armee*. As an instructor at West Point, McCook maintained a high rank. As a brigade and division commander under Buell, there was none his superior in the care and attention he gave his troops on the march, in camp, or on the drill-ground. His division at Shiloh as it marched to the front on the second day did him full credit, and in his handling of it on that field he did credit to it and to himself. What McCook lacked was the ability to handle large bodies of troops independently of a superior officer to give him commands. This was his experience at Perryville, and it was repeated at Stone's River. With the known results of Perryville, McCook ought never to have been placed in command of the " right wing." Rosecrans at Stone's River, of necessity was on the left, and being there he should have had a general in command of the right with greater military capacity than McCook. Rosecrans's confidence was so slight in his commander of the left that he felt his own presence was needed there in the movement of the troops in that part of the plan of battle.

Rosecrans in his report repeatedly speaks of "the faulty line of McCook's formation on the right." But he knew of this on the 30th, and told McCook that it was improperly placed. McCook did not think so. Rosecrans told him that it faced too much to the east and not enough to the south, that it was too weak and long, and was liable to be flanked. Knowing all this and knowing McCook's pride of opinion, for McCook told him he " did not see how he could make a better line," or a "better disposition of my troops," it was the plain duty of Rosecrans to reform the line, to conform to what it should be in his judgment. The order to McCook to build camp fires for a mile beyond his right was another factor that brought about the combination that broke the line on the right. Rosecrans was correct in the conception of this, in order to mislead Bragg and cause him to strengthen his left at the expense of his right. Had Bragg awaited Rosecrans's attack, this building of fires was correct—if it took troops away from the right to reinforce the left; but this it did not do. Bragg moved McCown and Cleburne's divisions from his right to his left on Tuesday, but after this Bragg brought none of his forces across the river until Wednesday afternoon. The building of the fires caused Bragg to prolong his lines, lengthening them to the extent that before Hardee struck Kirk's and Willich's brigades, he thought our line extended a division front to their right. Finding this not to be the case, he whirled his left with all the force of double numbers on to the right of McCook. The rebels then swinging around threw themselves in the rear of Johnson's division before they struck any troops on their front. Of course it is mere guess-work to say just what the outcome might have been of any other formation of the line, but it is safe to say that had the left instead of the centre of Hardee struck the right of McCook, there would have been a better chance for the troops on the extreme right of his line to have shown the spirit that was in them, before they were overpowered by mere superiority of numbers.

Then there were some minor mistakes that aided in a great degree the bringing about of that mishap which imperilled the safety of the entire army. Even granting that

Johnson was not in any way responsible for the position occupied by his troops on the front line of battle, still it is
hard to find any excuse or even explanation for a general
officer in command of a division who, knowing the enemy
was in force on his front, and intending to attack his command at daylight the next morning, would place his headquarters a mile and a half in the rear.   This too, when he
knew that the post of honor and responsibility for the safety
of the entire army had been committed to his keeping.
What then shall be said for him when it appears by the
report of the commanding officer of his reserve brigade
that when it returned from the support of a cavalry reconnoissance, the general commanding the division ordered
this brigade, on the eve of battle, to take position in the
woods, "near the headquarters of the division," instead of in
supporting distance of the front line ?   He could not have
thought that the division headquarters needed the support
of the reserve more than the line of battle.   It is safe to say
that had the line of Johnson's division been properly formed,
so as to give the most strength to the command—short and
well centred, with a good brigade like that of Baldwin's in
reserve, with all officers in their places—these troops would
have given a very different account of themselves when the
blow struck the right.   There was no commanding officer in
the front with Johnson's division, of greater command than
a regiment—save General Kirk.   The troops of Willich's
brigade on the right flank refused to come to his assistance,
because there was no one to give them orders.   Johnson
says in his official report that " In consultation with Major-
General McCook, late in the afternoon of December 30th, he
informed me that he had reliable information to the effect
that the centre of the rebel line of battle was opposite to
our extreme right, and that we would probably be attacked

by the entire rebel army early on the following morning."
Johnson then coolly adds: "His prediction proved true."
Yet with these facts staring them in the face, McCook and
Johnson made no other efforts to strengthen the right of the
line, and Johnson, on the arrival of his reserve brigade later,
posted it in the woods a mile and a half from his front "near
his headquarters." General Kirk was mortally wounded in
the attack on his command, but lived long enough after the
battle to make a report of the part taken in the engagement
by his brigade. He states in his report, that he suggested
to Johnson to send his reserve brigade to support the main
lines, and that Johnson declined to do so.

The location of Johnson's headquarters, and Johnson being there, makes him responsible for the capture of Willich, and the breaking up of that fine brigade. Willich had
been on the line for an hour before daylight with his brigade under arms, and from what he heard of the movements
of the enemy in his front, he was satisfied that a change
should be made in the position of the division, and started
to Johnson's headquarters to communicate with him. Before he could return to his troops, the enemy was upon
them, and drove them from the position they held, without
their making a stand. Being without either division or
brigade commander, they drifted to the rear. Willich had
a horse shot under him, and was captured without giving an
order, before he reached his command.

When the artillery was posted in line of battle on the
30th, roads were cut through the cedars to allow the batteries to reach the front line. The heavy loss of guns, reported by Rosecrans, was occasioned by these batteries being
unable to reach the roads through the cedar thickets in the
retreat, and in many instances guns were abandoned in the
woods, through which it was impossible to haul them.

Bragg alleges in his official report that our troops were surprised, and cites the fact that his men passed through the camps where breakfast was being prepared. He was right as to his fact, but wrong in his deduction. Willich's brigade was the only one that was not through the morning meal, and this was by reason of his troops being under arms for nearly two hours prior to this time, after which Willich gave them orders to prepare their meal. Kirk's brigade had been under arms since five o'clock in the morning, ready for action an hour before the battle commenced, and in Post's brigade the men were in order of battle for an hour before the first dawn of light. The front of all these brigades was covered with heavy picket lines well thrown out. General Sill reported to General Sheridan at two o'clock in the morning, " great activity on the part of the enemy immediately in his front, with movements of troops to their left," and from four o'clock in the morning until seven, Sheridan's troops were standing under arms, and the cannoneers were at their places.

It is difficult to determine which to admire the more, the heavy, quick, decided onset of the rebels, as with ranks well closed up, without music, and almost noiselessly, they moved in the gray light of the early December morning, out of the cedars, across the open fields, hurling the full weight of their advancing columns upon our right, with all the dash of Southern troops, sweeping on with rapid stride, and wild yells of triumph, to what appeared to them an easy final victory ; or, later in the afternoon, when our troops that had been driven from the field early in the morning, were re-formed under the eye of the commanding general, met and threw back from the point of the bayonet, and from the cannon mouth, the charge after charge of the same victorious troops of the earlier portion of the day. One was like the resistless sweep of a whirlwind in its onward course of destruction, the other the grand sturdy resistance of the rocky coast, which the waves only rush upon to be dashed to pieces. In each of these, the two armies displayed their distinctive feature to the best. Under Thomas, the Centre of the army evinced, in a marked degree, the staying qualities of that commander, which afterward were shown so conspicuously at Chickamauga.

CHAPTER IX.

IN MURFREESBORO.

DURING the first six months of 1863, the military operations of the Army of the Cumberland were of a minor character. The exhaustion attending the severe fighting of the last week of the previous year, kept that army in camp for some time to restore the losses of arms and material, to reclothe the army, to recruit the strength of the troops, to forward the needed supplies, and to build the necessary works to fortify Murfreesboro as a new base. The rebuilding of the Muldraughs Hills trestleworks, and the heavy repairs elsewhere needed on the railroad north of Nashville, together with having the road from Nashville to Murfreesboro placed in proper order, all required time and were necessary to be done, to supply the wants of the army in the immediate present. But the future was what demanded the greatest thought and most careful planning. The problem that gave Buell the greatest trouble to solve—the protection of his lines of communication and supplies—was now forced upon Rosecrans. The enemy with more than one-half his cavalry force absent during the battle of Stone's River, under Morgan in Kentucky and Forrest in West Tennessee, outnumbered that arm of the service in the Army of the Cumberland during the battle almost two to one. These troopers were nearly all old veterans, accustomed to the severest hardships of service, and it was wonder-

ful the rapidity with which they got over ground and the
amount of fatigue they could undergo. To afford perfect
protection to his line supplying the army from its base at
Louisville, as against these raiding bands, if infantry was to
be employed, Rosecrans's entire force was needed, posted
by brigades at the vulnerable points. To make an advance
and thus lengthen his lines, simply increased the present
difficulties. Without making the necessary preparation to
protect his line of supplies, Rosecrans would hamper his
forward movement and retard and cripple his advance when
commenced. The only proper force to meet the enemy's
troopers was cavalry. In the early days of the Army of the
Ohio, under Buell, a number of unsuccessful attempts were
made to chase and fight cavalry with infantry, and in every
instance the effort was crowned with failure, the only result
being the discomfort and complete exhaustion of the marching troops.

The repair of the most complete wrecking the Louisville
road ever suffered, demanded Rosecrans's attention the first
thing after the Battle of Stone's River. When the army
left Nashville, on the advance to meet Bragg, the supplies
in that city were very limited. With the disabling of the
road it was impossible at that time to forward sufficient
supplies to meet the wants of the command, and for the
first few weeks while the army remained at Murfreesboro
the troops were on half rations, and many of the articles
constituting the "ration" entirely dispensed with, leaving
but three or four on the list. The surrounding country for
miles was scoured for forage and provisions. Everything of
that kind was gathered in by raiding parties, not leaving sufficient for the actual necessities of the inhabitants. To
such an extent did this go, that to the officers with means to
purchase such provisions as were to be had, potatoes and

onions became luxuries. The whole army was threatened
with scurvy.

The number and extent of these raids, and the damage
sustained by the Louisville and Nashville Railroad during
the year from July 1, 1862, is concisely set forth in the report of the superintendent of that road. His report shows
that during this time "the road has been operated for its
entire length only seven months and twelve days;" "all the
bridges and trestleworks on the main stem and branches,
with the exception of the bridge over Barren River and
four small bridges, were destroyed and rebuilt during the
year. Some of the structures were destroyed twice and some
three times. In addition to this, most of the water stations,
several depôts, and a large number of cars were burnt, a
number of engines badly damaged, and a tunnel in Tennessee nearly filled up for a distance of eight hundred feet."

By reason of this condition of things, Rosecrans determined
to increase the cavalry arm of his army, so that he could
meet the ten or twelve thousand cavalry of the enemy in
their detached raids on more of an equal footing. From the
commencement of operations in Tennessee under Buell, the
enemy's cavalry had been steadily increasing in numbers
and in efficiency, until at this time it was a greater problem
how to meet this arm of the enemy's force than his infantry.
Rosecrans made repeated urgent applications to the Department at Washington for additional cavalry; for horses
and improved arms for those already under his command.
He detailed infantry to be mounted and armed as cavalry,
organizing a brigade of "mounted infantry" under Colonel
John T. Wilder.

On Bragg's retreating from Murfreesboro, he took position
with a portion of his army and established his headquarters
at Shelbyville. He then ordered part of his command to

move to Tullahoma, and there intrench, throwing up extensive earthworks and fortifications. Later, he placed his troops in winter quarters. In addition to the cavalry that had formerly been under Bragg, Van Dorn in February reported to him with his command of three brigades of cavalry, about five thousand effective troops. Bragg placed Van Dorn and Wheeler to protect the front and flanks of his army, assigning the former to the left, with his headquarters at Columbia, and directing the latter to take position on the right, constituted each command a corps. In Wheeler's command he assigned Morgan's, Wharton's, and Martin's divisions. Forrest's command was assigned to Van Dorn. Some important events took place during the first six months of 1863, that had a bearing on the fortunes of the Army of the Cumberland.

On January 9th, in recognition of the services of that army, by General Order No. 9 of War Department, that command was reorganized, and the Centre, Right, and Left were constituted *corps d'armee*, with the designation of Fourteenth, Twentieth, and Twenty-first Corps, under the same commanders, who were thus advanced to this higher command. During this month, Steedman, in command of Fry's old division, was ordered from Gallatin to the front, and posted at Triune and La Vergne. Reynolds's division was ordered from Gallatin to Murfreesboro. A slight change was also made in the boundaries of the Department. On the 25th, by order of the War Department, the commands of Fort Henry and Fort Donelson were transferred from the department under Grant, to that under Rosecrans, and later Fort Heiman. To Rosecrans was then committed the care and control of the Cumberland River, his second and secondary line of communication and supplies connecting his two principal depots.

On January 26th, Bragg ordered Wheeler on an expedition to capture Fort Donelson. Wheeler directed Forrest to move his brigade with four guns on the river road, via the Cumberland Iron Works, to the vicinity of Dover, which was the real position occupied and fortified by the Federal forces, and not the old site of Fort Donelson, while Wheeler with Wharton's command of some twenty-five hundred men moved on a road to the left. Rosecrans, hearing from his scouts that this movement was contemplated, ordered Davis in command of his division and two brigades of cavalry under Minty, to march by the Versailles road, and take Wheeler in the rear. Steedman was directed to watch Wheeler's movements by way of Triune. Davis despatched Minty to move with his cavalry around by way of Unionville and Rover, while he moved with the infantry direct to Eaglesville. At Rover, Minty captured a regiment of some three hundred and fifty men. Davis and Steedman's forces united at Franklin, the latter marching by way of Nolinsville. Wheeler, advancing rapidly, passed between the troops in pursuit, and, on February 3d, his entire force attacked the post at Dover, occupied by Colonel Harding with the Eighty-third Illinois, some six hundred men in the command. The rebels opened fire at once, and made a vigorous assault in force upon Harding's position. His little command repulsed the enemy with heavy loss. Again they advanced, making a more determined assault than before, but again they were driven back with still greater loss. In this last repulse Harding ordered his men to charge beyond his works, which they did with great gallantry, capturing forty-two of the rebels. Wheeler then withdrew with a total loss of one hundred and fifty killed, four hundred wounded, and one hundred and fifty captured. Colonel Harding lost sixteen killed, sixty wounded, and fifty captured. Efforts were made to cut off the retreat of Wheeler's force by Davis's command, reinforced by five hundred cavalry, which went as far west as Kinderhook and Bon Aqua Springs, but Wheeler took the road through Centreville, where he crossed Duck River.

In the latter part of the engagement at Dover, Harding was aided by the fire from six gunboats which were acting as convoys for a fleet of transports conveying reinforcements to Rosecrans's command, consisting of eighteen regiments of infantry, with four batteries of artillery that had been serving in Kentucky under the command of General Gordon Granger. The troops forming this column were under the immediate command of Crook, Baird, and Gilbert. After the danger at Dover had passed, the fleet steamed up to Nashville, and there the troops disembarked. During February Crook was sent with his command to take post at Carthage, on the Cumberland River, and watch the movements of the enemy from there to Rome, and Gilbert was ordered to proceed with his brigade to Franklin.

On March 4th, Gilbert at Franklin ordered Colonel Coburn, with five regiments of infantry, four detachments of cavalry under Colonel Jordan, and Aleshire's battery, the whole command nearly three thousand strong, to proceed south from Franklin with a wagon-train of one hundred wagons, ostensibly on a foraging expedition, but also to reconnoitre the enemy's front toward Columbia. Coburn's command, some twelve miles south of Franklin, was to meet a force moving from Murfreesboro toward Columbia, and these commands were to co-operate and determine the position of the enemy. Unknown to Gilbert, Van Dorn, on assuming command at Columbia, in February, determined to establish outposts and picket-lines within sight of Franklin and Triune, and to move his headquarters north of Duck River to Spring

Hill. Jordan's cavalry struck the enemy only three miles from town, formed in line of battle. Opening with artillery, Jordan advanced, and, after a sharp conflict, the enemy retreated to Spring Hill. That night Coburn notified Gilbert that he was confronted by a largely superior force, and suggested that he fall back. Gilbert, however, ordered him to advance. Proceeding next morning, the column met the enemy drawn up in line of battle a short distance from Thompson's Station. Forrest's command occupied the extreme right, with a battery of artillery on the left of this, and some paces retired was Armstrong's brigade. On the left of his command and in line with it was the Texan brigade under Whitfield, with two guns on each side of the Columbia turnpike, making a force of 10,000 men under Van Dorn. It was about half-past nine o'clock in the morning when Coburn struck these troops in line. He immediately deployed his infantry across the pike and to the right, and ordered his command to advance. The enemy's battery posted at the pike opening fire, Coburn's troops charged on it handsomely, his entire command moving in line of battle down the pike. When within one hundred and fifty yards, Armstrong's and Whitfield's brigades sprang forward and opened a destructive fire. Coburn's troops held their lines for over half an hour under heavy fire, replying with the same, when he ordered his command to fall back. Finding this large force in his front, he directed Jordan with his cavalry to cover his retreat. Van Dorn now advanced his line, pressed forward his right and left to surround Coburn and capture the entire force. Jordan formed two detachments, dismounted behind a stone fence to check the advance of Forrest and enable the artillery to escape. Forrest made two sustained attempts to dislodge these detachments from their position, but he was repulsed each time; on a third attempt they were surrounded and captured. The regiment in charge of the train with the artillery and cavalry now moved off rapidly on the pike to Franklin, and Coburn, being surrounded by the rebels in overwhelming numbers, and finding his ammunition exhausted, surrendered. His loss was 40 killed, and 150 wounded, and 2,200 prisoners, including his wounded. The enemy's loss was 35 killed and 140 wounded. The rebels lost heavily in officers, several of the most valued of Forrest's falling in the repulses of his command.

The surrender of Coburn weakened the forces at Franklin, and revealed the enemy in such strong force on the immediate front, that Gordon Granger at once ordered Baird to proceed by rail to Franklin, and moving his own headquarters there, assumed the command in person.

On the 7th, Sheridan's division was ordered to the front to reconnoitre the enemy's position. He reached Franklin, and the force at that place was further increased by the arrival of a brigade from Nashville. On the 9th, Minty's brigade of cavalry also reported, and on the day following, Granger with his troops advanced from there upon Van Dorn's encampment at Spring Hill. In support of Granger's movement on Van Dorn, Rosecrans ordered Davis to move with his division from Salem to Eaglesville, with R. S. Granger's brigade in supporting distance, posted at Versailles. Gordon Granger drove Van Dorn from Spring Hill, and the next day compelled his entire command to retire south of Rutherford's Creek. On account of the high water the pursuit was not continued farther.

During March the rebel cavalry under Morgan met with one of the most decisive repulses yet experienced by that command. On the 18th of March Colonel Hall with his command, the second brigade of Reynolds's division, was sent from Murfreesboro after Morgan. Starting northeast from that place he advanced beyond Statesville, when hearing that Morgan was advancing on him he retired toward Milton, posted his command on some high ground near that place and awaited the attack. Morgan endeavored first to turn the right and then the left of Hall's command, but in each of these attempts he was driven off with heavy loss. He then dismounted the main portion of his command and ordered an attack to be made on the front. A vigorous assault was at once made with a heavy force, but this was also repulsed, Morgan losing a large number of men. After an engagement lasting some four hours, in which Hall's brigade fought with the utmost determination, Morgan's command, being repulsed at all points and in every assault, withdrew from the field with a loss of some ninety-five killed, three hundred and fifty wounded, and twenty prisoners.

Early in April, Morgan's troopers were defeated with great loss. On the 2d of April Stanley advanced with his cavalry to Liberty, where Morgan met them with his entire command. The two forces encamped within two miles of each other. On the morning of the 3d, Stanley advanced, intending to engage Morgan's command at once, but found that he had retreated to what he regarded as a very strong position at Snow Hill. Morgan, however, had left a strong force at Liberty to watch Stanley's movements. As Stanley advanced, he struck this force and quickly drove them back on to their main body, and then dashed upon it with part of his command, sending a portion around to the right, which turned the enemy's left flank. Pressing Morgan's command from both positions, it soon gave way at all points, and was in full retreat. Morgan's officers tried to rally their men, but the latter were thoroughly demoralized and had no fight in them. The teamsters became panic-stricken and added to the general rout. It was two weeks before Morgan succeeded in getting his men together again.

Early in April, Rosecrans ordered Colonel Streight to the command of a brigade he had organized for the purpose of making a raid on the lines of communication of the rebels, and to move through the country south and southeast, destroying as he went all property of use to them. Streight's command started from Nashville, partially mounted, going by way of Clarksville to Fort Henry, at which place he took steamer for Eastport, Miss. *En route* to Fort Henry his command secured as many animals as they could, but only four-fifths of the men were mounted, and they poorly. The animals were nearly all mules, and very few of them were fit for the service required. It was expected that the command would capture enough good animals to carry the expedition successfully through, but this was not realized. Leaving Eastport on the 21st, he passed through Tuscumbia three days later, and reached Moulton on the 26th. From here on the 28th he pressed forward through Day's Gap on Sand Mountain, in the direction of Blountsville. In the gap their rear guard was overtaken and attacked on the 30th by the enemy's cavalry under Forrest, who had pressed forward, riding night and day. Selecting the best mounted of his men, he pushed at once to Streight's camp. Here coming upon the rear of Streight's force as it was leaving camp, Forrest opened with artillery firing. Dismounting his men, Streight formed his command on the crest of a hill on each side of the road and awaited the enemy's attack. As Forrest advanced, Streight ordered a charge to be made which drove the enemy at all points, capturing their two pieces of artillery. Forrest lost in killed and wounded seventy-five men, a large percentage of whom were killed. Streight's loss was twenty-one killed and wounded. A good many of

VII.—7

horses were captured from the enemy, on which Streight mounted a number of his men. On the same afternoon the enemy attacked again, but was driven back with considerable loss, after a severe engagement lasting from three o'clock until dark. On May 1st, the Federal forces reached Blountsville at noon. Here all the wagons save one were burned, and the ammunition placed on pack mules, after distributing to the men all that they could carry. At three o'clock Streight started again, and skirmishing commenced at once on their rear. Pressing on, the command marched until twelve o'clock that night. Resuming their march in the morning, the rear skirmished all the forenoon of the 2d with the rebels. Arriving at Gadsden, Streight remained long enough to destroy a large quantity of provisions in store there for the enemy. It was expected at this place that a small steamer would be found, upon which a detachment of men could be sent to capture Rome. In this Streight was disappointed. From this point Streight's animals became much exhausted, and the men were falling to the rear and getting captured. To prevent this the command had to go much slower. Forrest coming up about one o'clock on the 2d, attacked the command while the horses were being fed at Blount's farm. Here Colonel Hathaway fell, shot through the breast. Again the rebels were repulsed, but they constantly pressed upon the rear of Streight's command, keeping up a brisk skirmish fire. The enemy were kept in check at Blount's farm until after dark. In the meantime the main command had crossed the Coosa. Here the river was so high that the ammunition was damaged by being wet. From this place Streight sent a detachment to burn the Round Mountain iron works, one of the principal manufactories of munition of war in the South. It was burned to the ground and all the machinery destroyed. On arriving at the other branch of the Coosa a bridge was found, and, as soon as the command had crossed, it was destroyed. On the morning of the 3d, as the men were preparing their breakfast, the enemy again attacked. Shortly afterward Forrest sent in a flag of truce, demanding the surrender of the entire command. This was at first refused, but on consultation with his officers, and considering the damaged condition of his ammunition and the complete exhaustion of his command, Streight, after making a personal inspection of Forrest's artillery, finally yielded, and the entire force of 1,466 officers and men was surrendered.

On April 20th, Thomas sent J. J. Reynolds with three brigades of infantry and Minty's brigades of cavalry, together with Wilder's brigade of mounted infantry, to proceed to McMinnville, capture what force was there, destroy the railroad from Manchester to McMinnville, and co-operate with a force to move from Carthage against Morgan. Reynolds made a successful raid on the railroad and nearly destroyed it ; burned all the bridges, trestle-work, cars, and locomotives on the road, also the depôt in McMinnville, and several cotton mills. A large amount of supplies was captured, some one hundred and eighty prisoners taken, and over six hundred animals picked up. The command from Carthage failed to aid in the expedition, and Morgan's command in the main effected their escape.

Colonel Lewis D. Watkins on the 27th made a gallant charge on the Texas Legion, encamped close to Van Dorn's main command near Spring Hill. Dashing in on the enemy early in the morning, he was among them before they could rally for defence, capturing one hundred and twenty-eight prisoners, over three hundred animals, and their camp equipage without the loss of a man.

It was during the six months waiting at Murfreesboro

that the unfortunate controversy arose between Rosecrans and the authorities at Washington, represented by General Halleck, as Commander-in-Chief, and Mr. Secretary Stanton of the War Department. The Army of the Cumberland, during the period of the active movements of that command, congratulated itself that the field of operations was so far removed from Washington City, that it did not come under the influence of the authority that seemed to paralyze every effort of the commands immediately around the seat of war at the East. But in this they were mistaken. The future student of the history of the war, in the light of the full official records, will wonder most at the fact that, under the orders from Washington, the commanders in the field were at all able finally to crush the rebellion. It was only when the armies at the East were placed under a general who was practically untrammelled in the exercise of his power, and who conducted his campaigns upon military principles, and not as the result of orders from Washington that the beginning of the end of the rebellion in the East began to dawn. In Tennessee we have seen how Halleck gave Buell orders, and then attached such conditions to them as to render their proper execution absolutely impossible. There was nothing to prevent Buell from occupying Chattanooga in June, 1862, as he was directed, while Bragg with his command was in Northern Mississippi, except the utterly useless condition attached to his orders, that he should repair the Memphis and Charleston Railroad as he moved east. Buell urged, in forcible terms, the foolishness and even impropriety of this delay, but Halleck, who knew much of the theory of war as learned from books, and in a general way wished to apply these principles to the practical movements of troops, overruled Buell. The latter knew that the enemy in his front always resolutely refused to be bound in his operations by such rules in conducting campaigns. The result of Halleck's wisdom soon became manifest when Bragg started for Kentucky, after the waste of Buell's time in repairing this railroad, which, when completed, was at once turned over to the enemy in good condition for immediate use against our own forces. On Buell fell the force of the blow that some one had to bear for this failure to take advantage of patent opportunity. Buell's obedience to Halleck's orders rendered Bragg's advance into Kentucky possible, while Buell's failure to bring Bragg to a decisive action in Kentucky, and his refusal to follow Bragg into the mountains of Eastern Kentucky and Tennessee, was deemed sufficient cause by Halleck to issue the order removing him from his command. If Halleck's order to Buell to repair this railroad had never been issued, Bragg's campaign in Kentucky would never have been made. Halleck's removal of Buell was the direct result of the latter's obedience to orders received from the former. On Rosecrans assuming command, almost the first order he received from Halleck was one directing him to advance into East Tennessee after Bragg. With a full knowledge of the military situation obtained from Buell, Rosecrans proceeded at once to protect the line established by Buell, and await the advance of Bragg in the vicinity of Nashville. The battle of Stone's River was for the time sufficient to prove, even to Halleck, that Buell and Rosecrans were correct, and Rosecrans was allowed for the time to attend to his command without being interfered with. During the encampment at Murfreesboro, the first object of Rosecrans was to properly mount and equip his cavalry. In this he received at first faint encouragement, which soon ceased altogether.

On March 1st Halleck, as Commander-in-Chief of the Armies of the United States, wrote a letter, sending a copy

to Rosecrans and Grant, offering the position of the then
vacant major-generalship in the regular army, to the general
in the field who should first achieve an important and decisive
victory. Grant very quietly folded up the letter, put it by
for future reference, and proceeded with the plans of his
campaign, saying nothing. To Rosecrans's open, impulsive,
and honorable nature, engaged with all his powers in fur-
thering the interests of the Government and the general wel-
fare of his command, this letter was an insult, and he treated
it accordingly. On March 6th he prepared his reply, and
forwarded it to Washington. In this letter he informs the
General-in-Chief that, "as an officer and as a citizen," he
felt "degraded at such an auctioneering of honors," and
then adds: "Have we a general who would fight for his
own personal benefit when he would not for honor and for
his country? He would come by his commission basely in
that case, and deserve to be despised by men of honor. But
are all the brave and honorable generals on an equality as to
chances? If not, it is unjust to those who probably deserve
most."

The effect of this letter was to widen the breach between
the authorities at Washington and Rosecrans. Halleck's
letter and Rosecrans's reply were both characteristic of the
men. Halleck, fresh from the results of a large law practice
in California—principally devoted to the establishment of
the validity of land grants in favor of his clients, in the
success of which large contingent fees were gained—saw
nothing improper in such an offer to an officer of sufficient
ability and standing to be in command of one of the armies
of the United States. With Rosecrans, all the honest, gen-
erous impulses of a high-principled, honorable gentleman,
who had imperilled his life on many a battlefield, fighting
solely from a sense of duty to his country, led to the ex-

pression of his contempt for the author of such an offer.
The mistake that Halleck made was in thinking that
what would prove a tempting offer to a man like himself, would be so to Rosecrans. No one will attempt to
maintain the wisdom of Rosecrans's course as a matter of
policy, however much they may sympathize with and admire the spirit of his letter. It was an impolitic letter,
and one that aided in drawing the ill-will and resentment
of Halleck and Stanton upon him in full force later.

From this time forward, all the requests of Rosecrans for
the improvement of the efficiency of his army were treated
with great coolness, and in many instances it was only after
the greatest importunity that he was able to secure the
least attention to his recommendations for the increased
usefulness of his command. His repeated applications for
more cavalry, and that they be armed with revolving rifles,
were treated with little attention. In the meantime nearly
every communication from Washington intimated that he
was unnecessarily delaying his advance upon Bragg in his
works at Shelbyville and Tullahoma. Grant, on his Vicksburg campaign, became very anxious for the advance of
the Army of the Cumberland, to engage Bragg and prevent reinforcements being sent from him to Pemberton
or Johnston, operating on his front and rear; and urged
Rosecrans to move, and wrote to Halleck, requesting him
to direct an advance of the Army of the Cumberland on
Bragg's position. Rosecrans regarded it for the best interests of the country for his army to remain constantly
threatening Bragg, in order to hold the entire army of the
latter in his immediate front, and also in the event of the
defeat of Grant, and a concentration of the enemy on Rosecrans's position, that he should be close to his base, his
army being then the reserve. If an advance succeeded in

driving Bragg from Tullahoma, a greater danger than his
remaining inactive on our front might ensue. To Bragg,
the occupancy of Middle Tennessee was of sufficient importance to justify him in remaining inactive with his entire command, waiting for the advance of Rosecrans some
six months.   If driven from Tennessee, his troops were
ready to unite with the command in Mississippi and defeat
Grant's movements. If Bragg could be held in Tennessee
until after Grant's success was assured, then, by waiting at
Murfreesboro with his army quiet, Rosecrans could render
better service than by moving on the enemy. This was
a matter of military judgment, on one side espoused by
Rosecrans and all his corps and division commanders, who
were on the ground, and on the other by Halleck, Stanton,
and Grant ; and this question served to increase the feeling
against Rosecrans in those quarters. Bragg also considered
that his presence on the front of the Federal army would prevent any troops from it being sent to aid Grant. And thus
the year wore away until early summer. Still another consideration with Rosecrans, was the character of the soil in
Tennessee from a short distance south of Murfreesboro to
the foot of the Cumberland Mountains. This was a light
sandy loam, that in winter and spring, during the rains of
those seasons, became like quicksand, allowing the artillery
and wagon to sink almost to the hub, and rendering the
rapid movement of a large army absolutely impossible.

During the early part of June, Rosecrans commenced
placing his troops in position, preparatory to a general advance. He ordered the brigade that had been encamped at
Gallatin, under General Ward, to Lavergne, and despatched
Gordon Granger to take post at Triune, moving his command from Franklin up to that place. Crook was ordered
from Carthage to report to Murfreesboro, and on his ar-

rival, was placed in Reynolds's division. Rosecrans organized a reserve corps, consisting of three divisions designated as First, Second, and Third, under Baird, J. D. Morgan, and R. S. Granger, respectively, and he assigned Gordon Granger to the command of this corps.

Early in June, Garfield, then Chief-of-Staff of the General commanding, urged Rosecrans to make an advance movement, both as a military and political measure with reference to the sentiment of the North. General Rosecrans had matured his plans for an advance, but decided to refer the question to his general officers in command of corps and divisions. The matter being submitted to them, the universal sentiment of these officers was that the movement should be further delayed. However, on the 23d of June, Rosecrans having made all necessary arrangements for his command, according to his plans, and learning of the favorable prospects at Vicksburg, and of the movement of the force under Burnside into East Tennessee to take and hold Knoxville, issued the necessary orders for the advance of his army on that of the enemy.

7*

CHAPTER X.

THE ADVANCE ON TULLAHOMA.

At the time of the advance of the Army of the Cumberland, Polk's corps of Bragg's army occupied the main position at Shelbyville, strongly intrenched behind heavy works thrown up during the six months of waiting. These added to the natural strength of the position, and extended from Horse Mountain on the east, to Duck River on the west, and were covered by a line of abattis. The town was noted for the strong Union sentiment of its inhabitants, of which fact the rebels took full advantage to the loss and distress of the people. It is situated about twenty-five miles south of Murfreesboro, and some twenty miles north of Tullahoma, on a branch railroad from the main Nashville line, starting west from Wartrace. Bragg's right was posted at Wartrace, with Hardee's corps occupying the passes at Liberty, Hoover, and Bellbuckle Gaps. These gaps were all held by strong forces of the enemy, supported by the main command. Polk had an advance in Guy's Gap with his entire command in supporting distance. Bragg's extreme right was protected by cavalry with headquarters at McMinnville, while his cavalry on the left, under Forrest, had headquarters at Columbia, threatening Franklin.

At this time the main base of supplies of the enemy was at Chattanooga, to which the entire country south of Duck River had been made tributary. From Duck River, south,

the country is rough, with rocky ranges of hills, which divide
the "barrens" from the fertile parts of Middle Tennessee.
These "barrens" constitute a high rolling plateau of ground
between the ranges of hills at Duck River and the Cumberland Mountains. It is here that the soil during a rainy season offers the greatest obstacle to active campaigning. Situated on the "barrens," at the junction of the McMinnville
branch with the Nashville and Chattanooga Railroad, was
Tullahoma, a small straggling village, where Bragg had established his main depot and made a large intrenched
camp. The defiles of Duck River, a deep, narrow stream
with but few fords or bridges, covered its front, with a rough
rocky range of hills immediately south of the river. The
principal roads as they passed through these hills bore
southwardly toward the line of the enemy's communications and Tullahoma. The Manchester pike passed through
Hoover's Gap and reached the "barrens" by ascending
a long, difficult cañon called Matt's Hollow. The Wartrace road passed through Liberty Gap, and from there it
ran into the road along the railroad through Bellbuckle
Gap. The direct road to Shelbyville goes through Guy's
Gap.

Rosecrans was satisfied from the information he had received that Bragg intended to fight in his intrenchments at
Shelbyville, in the event of the army advancing in that direction. The "effective total present," as reported by Bragg
as the strength of his army on June 20, 1863, at Shelbyville,
was 43,089, of all arms. If he were attacked at Shelbyville
and beaten, he would then be in good position to retreat to
his strong intrenchments at Tullahoma, and on his retreat
could so retard Rosecrans's advance through the narrow
winding roads leading up to the "barrens," as to fully
protect his own line of retreat and inflict severe loss on the

advancing force without exposing his own troops. Rose-crans's plan of campaign was to render useless Bragg's in-trenchments by turning his right, and then if possible secure his line of retreat by moving on the railroad bridge at Elk River. Bragg by this means would either be forced to accept battle on ground chosen by Rosecrans, or be com-pelled to beat a retreat on a disadvantageous line, neither as direct nor by as good roads as he would have from Shel-byville and Tullahoma due south. To carry out this plan it was necessary to impress Bragg with the idea that our ad-vance would be in force on Shelbyville, and, if possible, to keep up this impression until the main body of our army reached Manchester. The success of this would keep Bragg's attention on the movement on his front at Shelby-ville, and enable our army to pass through the dangerous defile of Hoover's Gap, a narrow passage-way three miles long, between high hills, and so on through Matt's Hollow, an equally dangerous defile, being a gorge two miles long with hardly room anywhere for wagons to pass each other. These passes were only eight miles from Hardee's head-quarters and sixteen from Shelbyville.

The plan then of Rosecrans in the advance on Tullahoma, was to make a feint with Granger's corps and the main por-tion of the cavalry, on Polk's command in his strong position at Shelbyville, and to mass the three main corps on Bragg's right at Wartrace. The army being all ready for the open-ing campaign, on the 23d of June General R. B. Mitchell with his command—the First Cavalry Division—commenced the advance from Triune on the Eaglesville and Shelbyville pike, in the feint on Polk's command, made a furious attack on Bragg's cavalry and drove in his infantry guards on their main force, pressing the whole line on that front. Granger, with the three divisions of his corps and Brannan's division of Thomas's corps, on that day moved with three days' rations from Triune to Salem.

On the same day, Palmer's division and a brigade of cavalry marched to the vicinity of Bradyville, for the purpose of seizing with his advance the head of the defile leading over an obscure road by Lumley's Station to Manchester, and so up to the "barrens." All the other troops were supplied with twelve days' rations of bread, coffee, sugar, and salt, with six days' pork and bacon, and six days' meat on hoof, and were held in readiness to move southward. These movements being made, the next day the entire army pressed forward on the advance.

In the evening of the 23d, the corps commanders met at army headquarters. The plan of the campaign was fully explained to them, and each one received in writing his orders as to his part in the movement.

"Major-General McCooks' corps to advance on the Shelbyville road, turn to the left, move two divisions by Millersburg, and advancing on the Wartrace road seize and hold Liberty Gap. The Third Division to advance on Fosterville and cover the crossing of General Granger's command from the Middleton róad, and then move by Christiana to join the rest of the corps.

"General Granger to advance on the Middleton road, threatening that place, and cover the passing of General Brannan's division of the Fourteenth Corps, which was to pass by Christiana and bivouac with the rear division of the Twentieth Corps.

"The Fourteenth Corps, Major-General Thomas, to advance on the Manchester pike, seize and hold with its advance, if practicable, Hoover's Gap, and bivouac so as to command and cover that and the Millersburg road, so that McCook and himself could be within supporting distance of each other.

"Major-General Crittenden to leave Van Cleve's division of the Twenty-first Army Corps at Murfreesboro, concentrate at Bradyville with the other two, and await orders."

One brigade of cavalry under Turchin was sent with Crittenden to establish a lookout toward McMinnville. All the remaining cavalry under Stanley was to meet Mitchell as he came in from Versailles and at once attack the rebel cavalry at Middleton.

These movements were all promptly executed in the midst of heavy drenching rains, as it only could rain in the mountains and hills of Tennessee, whenever the Army of the Cumberland made a forward movement. The ground was so softened on all the dirt roads as to render them next to impassable.

The Twentieth Corps, consisting of Johnson's, Davis's, and Sheridan's divisions, started on the Shelbyville pike, and by different cross roads moved to the left to Millersburg, where Davis's and Sheridan's divisions encamped for the night. Johnson's division was advanced up to Liberty Gap, with the Thirty-ninth Indiana, under Colonel Harrison, thrown forward to skirmish. Harrison developed the enemy in front of the Gap. Willich's brigade was moved forward, and drove the skirmishers in the rebel front back upon their main line, placed on the crest of the hills, on each side of the entrance to the gap. Here the enemy was too strongly posted to attack his front. Another brigade under Colonel John F. Miller, who had been transferred from Negley's division to Johnson's, was then brought forward. These two brigades were at once deployed in line, making a front of such length as to envelop both flanks of the enemy's line, and advancing, these brigades gallantly drove the rebels through the defile, a distance of two miles. After clearing the gap, the troops returned to the north end of it and there bivouacked. On the following day, late in the afternoon, an attack was made on Willich's and Miller's brigades, to drive them out of the north end of the gap. Johnson's failure to hold the southern entrance enabled the enemy again to enter it, and to secure it entirely they made this attack. The engagement opened with a heavy fire on the centre of the command, the enemy attacking in force. They were handsomely repulsed. Renewing the attack, Hardee then endeavored to secure positions on the hills to the right and left, so as to command Johnson's flanks with his fire, but each movement was met by Johnson's troops, supported by Carlin's brigade of Davis's division, and every attack was repulsed. Beaten at every point, late in the evening the enemy withdrew entirely, taking position at Bellbuckle. The fighting at Liberty Gap was the most severe of the campaign, and in this attack Johnson's command, including Carlin's brigade, lost two hundred and thirty-one killed and wounded. The enemy's loss was still greater. It was in repelling one of the attacks on the left that Colonel Miller fell severely wounded with a minie ball through his left eye while leading his brigade.

On the 24th, General Thomas moved direct on the Manchester pike from Murfreesboro, Reynolds's division in advance, starting at 4 o'clock in the morning, under orders, if possible, to seize and hold Hoover's Gap. At 7 A.M., Rousseau's division followed in support of Reynolds's division, which encountered the mounted videttes of the enemy a few miles beyond our picket station, forced them upon their reserve, and then resolutely pressing on drove the entire force on the run, through Hoover's Gap and beyond McBride's Creek. Wilder, finding the enemy about to attack him with two brigades from the direction of Fairfield, occupied a strong position on the hills at the southern entrance of the gap. Reynolds at once moved his two infantry brigades forward and occupied the gap in the rear of Wilder's command, prepared to resist the enemy on the front. Wilder's brigade was immediately attacked by the enemy's force. Reynolds supported him at once with his other brigades, which were posted on the ridge of woods on the extreme right to prevent the enemy turning our right flank, then heavily engaged by a superior force. With these reinforcements the enemy was driven back out of the woods, and three regiments were posted on the right, making that position secure. Major Coolidge, commanding the brigade of regulars of Rousseau's division, was ordered to reinforce Reynolds, and every preparation was made for an attack on the following morning. The other brigades of Rousseau's command, with Negley's division, occupied the gap in the rear of Reynolds during the night. Early on the morning of the 25th, Scribner was ordered with his brigade to the front, in support of the batteries and to form picket line on the extreme left.

On the 24th, Crittenden, with Wood's and Palmer's divisions, marched to Bradyville, leaving Van Cleve's division to garrison Murfreesboro. Granger, with his three divisions and Brannan's, advanced from Salem to Christiana. Turchin's division of cavalry under Stanley moved on the Woodbury pike to Cripple Creek, and thence through Salem. During the day Mitchell advanced from Rover through Versailles to Middleton, where he had a sharp engagement with the enemy's cavalry.

The plans of the enemy not being yet fully developed, and in view of the uncertainty that existed whether he would fall on McCook's front, or mass on Thomas near Fairfield, Rosecrans issued the following orders for the 25th:

" Major-General Crittenden to advance to Lannon's Stand, six miles east of Beech Grove, and open communications with General Thomas.

" General Thomas to attack the rebels on the flank of his advance position at the forks of the road, and drive the rebels toward Fairfield.

"General McCook to feign and advance, as if in force, on the War-trace road by the Liberty Gap passes.

"General Stanley, with his cavalry, to occupy their attention at Forsterville, and General Granger to support him with his infantry at Christiana."

In the event that Thomas succeeded in his attack and drove the enemy toward Wartrace, he was then to cover that road with a division, and taking the remainder of his troops was to move rapidly on Manchester. McCook was then to move in and take Thomas's place at Beech Grove, holding Liberty Gap with a division, and was finally to withdraw that and follow Thomas with his entire command to Manchester.

The same day that Crittenden's command marched to Holly Springs, Brannan's division reached the main command of Thomas, and went into camp with Rousseau at Hoover's Mills. Reynolds had a slight skirmish with the enemy on his front. On the night of the 25th, Rousseau was ordered up with his division to take position immediately in the rear of Reynolds, preparatory to an attack on the enemy's position at Beech Grove the next morning. Minty's brigade of cavalry pressed forward at all points and drove the enemy to Guy's Gap. Long took position at Lumley's Station. The remainder of Turchin's division moved in the advance with General Crittenden.

The incessant rains that had fallen since the opening of the campaign delayed the advance, by preventing Brannan joining the Fourteenth Corps as soon as was expected. During the night of the 25th it rained so continuously that it was almost impossible for the troops to move, but by extraordinary exertions the divisions were all in position by 10.30 A.M. At 4 o'clock in the morning Brannan's division moved up to take part in the attack. At 8 A.M. Negley's division took

position to support the attack of the other divisions. If the
enemy's position at Beech Grove was carried, then Rousseau
and Brannan were to push on to Manchester that night if
possible. At 10.30 A.M. the advance was ordered. Moving
forward on the rebels in force on the heights north of Garrison Creek, our army drove them steadily and rapidly
toward Fairfield, Rousseau and Brannan operating on their
left flank from the hills north of the Fairfield road, while
Reynolds advanced against their front and right. The enemy
had prepared for an obstinate resistance, and attempted to
enfilade Thomas's troops from the high ground on his right.
This was effectually prevented by a gallant charge of Walker's brigade and the regulars under Major Coolidge, who
drove the enemy from this position. Thomas pushed forward his troops, driving the rebels in the direction of Fairfield, who covered their retreat with two batteries of artillery, occupying positions behind strong lines of skirmishers
flanked by heavy cavalry force. The rebels thus retired to
Fairfield, near to which place our pickets were advanced.
Reynolds's division and the baggage moved forward during
the night toward Manchester. Late in the afternoon Wilder's brigade seized Matt's Hollow, and thus secured that
passage. Thomas placed his divisions in line of battle extending from the Fairfield road to within five miles of Manchester. McCook remained in camp at Liberty Gap during
the day, while Granger rested at Christiana. Crittenden's
command pressed forward as rapidly as possible on toward
Manchester, struggling over almost impassable roads.

Rosecrans's headquarters, on the 27th, reached Manchester. The advanced position secured by Thomas's command
rendered the concentration of the whole army on the enemy's left, through Hoover's Gap, at this time an easy matter. With this done, Bragg would either be forced to fight,

in resisting the further advance of the army under Rosecrans, or abandon Middle Tennessee altogether. Early on the morning of the 27th, Reynolds's advance brigade—Wilder's mounted infantry—took possession of Manchester, capturing forty prisoners, a guard at the railroad depot, and taking the town completely by surprise. Reynolds's entire division reached Manchester during the morning. General Thomas then moved Rousseau's and Brannan's divisions in pursuit of the enemy, driving him as far as Fairfield, and ascertained at that place that the rebels had retreated entirely. These two divisions then turned into the Fairfield and Manchester road, Brannan's reaching the latter place at 10 P.M. and Rousseau's at midnight. Negley's division had, during the day, been moving in support of these two divisions toward the Fairfield road, by way of Noale Fork, and arrived at Manchester at 8 P.M. Thomas's corps being now together, it was manifest that the enemy must leave his intrenchment at Shelbyville, and that our army must be prepared to meet him at Tullahoma, only twelve miles distant. Rosecrans gave the necessary orders at once to the other corps commanders to close up their columns on Manchester, and be prepared for the contest.

On the extreme right our cavalry, on the 27th, did brilliant work. Supported by the reserve corps under Granger, Stanley advanced from Christiana to Guy's Gap, where the advance of the rebel army under Wheeler, with Martin's and a portion of Wharton's divisions, was encountered. Charging down on them with Minty's brigade, closely followed by Mitchell's division, Stanley routed and drove them out of the gap into their intrenchments just north of Shelbyville. Here they again made a stand. Dashing ahead, Minty encountered them in their works, and drove them in disorder from their intrenchments into Shelbyville.

While Minty was pushing them on the front, Mitchell came up, turned their right, cutting off their direct line of retreat, and both forces united in driving them beyond the town, completely defeated.   Wheeler lost all his artillery and some five hundred prisoners.   A large number of the rebels were driven into Duck River and drowned while attempting to cross.   The flight was so hurried that Wheeler himself only escaped by swimming the river.   This successful movement established the fact that Bragg had abandoned his strong line of defence at Shelbyville, and the question now to be answered was whether he would accept battle at Tullahoma, or retire with his entire command across the Cumberland Mountains and the Tennessee River, fighting as he fell back.

While the concentration of his command at Manchester was being effected, Rosecrans determined to break the line of railroad in the rear of Bragg's army, if possible.   On the morning of the 28th Wilder, with his brigade of mounted infantry, started at reveillé by way of Hillsboro, to burn Elk River bridge, and to destroy the railroad between Dechard and Cowan.   John Beatty, with his brigade of infantry marched to Hillsboro for the purpose of covering and supporting Wilder's movement.   The latter reached Elk River and crossed his command, floating his mountain howitzers on a raft made of an old saw-mill.   He then moved on to Dechard, where, after a slight skirmish with a detachment of the enemy, he destroyed the depot full of commissary goods, the water tanks, the railroad bridge over the Winchester road, and tore up some three hundred yards of the railroad.   Earlier in the day Wilder sent part of his command, under Colonel Munroe, to destroy the railroad bridge over Elk River.   Withers's division of Bragg's army reached this point only a few moments ahead of Munroe, and prevented the burning of the bridge. Finding that the enemy was in pursuit of him at all points, Wilder next moved to Tantalon and Anderson with detachments of his command, but was compelled to retire, as these points were strongly guarded by heavy forces of the enemy's infantry. Crossing the mountains that night on his return over the Tracy City road, and so on to Pelham, the troops slept at the foot of the mountains, and started the next morning just in time to escape Forrest, who was in pursuit with ten regiments of cavalry. Wilder reached Manchester at 1 P.M. of the 30th.

Sheridan's division of McCook's corps reached Manchester on the 29th. The command—troops and animals—suffered severely on their march over the heavy roads. Crittenden's command, which had been on the road since the 26th, reached Manchester also on the 29th, after marching with all speed, badly worn, by reason of the terrible rains and fearful roads. The condition of the latter may be inferred from the fact that it required four days of incessant labor for Crittenden to advance the distance of twenty-one miles. The concentration of the entire army being effected, orders were given for the final movement on the 30th, as follows:

"The Fourteenth Corps to occupy the centre at Concord Church and Bobo Cross Roads, with a division in reserve.

"The Twentieth Corps to take the right on Crumpton's Creek, two divisions in echelon retired, one in reserve.

"The Twenty-first Corps to come up on the left near Hall's Chapel, one division in front and one in reserve."

The rain had rendered the roads over which this movement was to be made as soft and spongy as a swamp, into which the wagons cut to the hubs, and even horses could only pass over with the greatest exertion. The troops on the

30th were compelled to drag along the artillery through the mud into position. While the orders for the movements of the troops were being executed on the 30th, Thomas sent Steedman's brigade of Brannan's division, and two regiments of Negley's division on separate roads to reconnoitre the enemy's position, and Sheridan sent Bradley's brigade of his own division on another road, for the same purpose. These reconnoissances all returned, and reported having found the enemy in force within a mile or two of Tullahoma, on all roads except the one leading to Estill Springs. Scouts coming in confirmed this, adding that it was the general belief that Bragg would not leave his intrenchments at Tullahoma without a fight.

On the same day Rosecrans ordered his topographical engineers to ascertain the nature of the ground, in order to determine the practicability of moving by columns in mass in line of battle from the position in front, to gain the rear of the rebel position. Their report being favorable, all arrangements were completed, and the second division of Crittenden's corps was moved into position.

On July 1st, Thomas, hearing from a citizen that the enemy were evacuating Tullahoma, ordered Steedman with his brigade, supported by two regiments of Reynolds's division on the left, to advance cautiously and ascertain if the report was true. Pushing forward his advance, Steedman, meeting with no opposition, entered the place at noon, capturing a few prisoners. Rosecrans being at once notified of this, immediately ordered Rousseau's and Negley's divisions in pursuit. Pressing forward with all possible haste by Spring Creek, these divisions overtook the rear guard of the enemy late in the afternoon at Bethpage Bridge, two miles above the railroad crossing, where, after a sharp skirmish, in which a good many of our men were wounded, the rebels were driven steadily back, until darkness prevented further pursuit. The enemy, occupying the heights south of the river, commanded the bridge with their artillery, which they had placed behind epaulements.

On the 2d, the ammunition was brought forward, and McCook, with Sheridan's and Davis's divisions, was ordered in pursuit on the roads west of the railroad. Sheridan, on arriving at Rock Creek Ford, found Elk River so swollen with the heavy rains of the past week as to be barely fordable for cavalry. On the south bank of the river the enemy had posted a force of cavalry to resist the crossing. Sheridan opened fire at once on them, drove them away, and occupied the ford. During the night the enemy burned the bridge on the line of advance of Thomas, who found equal difficulty in crossing. Here the river was very deep, and he ordered Rousseau's, Brannan's, and Reynolds's divisions up the river to Jones's Ford. Hambright's brigade was thrown across the river, and the other troops went into camp on the north bank. Hambright captured several rebel prisoners, who told him that Bragg's army was in full retreat by way of Pelham and Cowan, across the Cumberland Mountains. Turchin, with a small brigade of cavalry, moved forward from Hillsboro on the Dechard road. On reaching the fords of Elk River at Morris Ferry he found the rebel cavalry strongly posted. He attacked them at once, reinforced by Mitchell's command, and forced a passage of the river after a sharp fight. Night closed the pursuit.

On the 3d, Sheridan succeeded in crossing Elk River, supported by Davis's division, and pursued the enemy to Cowan, where he learned that Bragg had crossed the mountains with part of his artillery and infantry by the University and Sweden's Cove, sending Hardee's corps into Sequatchie

Valley, and covering his retreat with his cavalry. Thomas crossed Rousseau's and Brannan's divisions at Jones's Ford and ordered them to take position on the Winchester and Hillsboro road. He directed Negley and Reynolds to cross their divisions at the ford on the Winchester and Manchester pike. On the 4th, Rousseau was ordered to march to the Dechard and Pelham roads, and to take up position at Brackenfield's Point toward the University. Reynolds encamped at Penningtown, and Brannan's division at Taite's. The cavalry sent from Sheridan's position, and by Stanley from the main column, developed the fact that the enemy was entirely across the mountains, and the troops were now ordered into camp to await supplies from the depot at Murfreesboro.

Bragg's army reached Chattanooga the first week in July. Here he established his headquarters with Polk's corps retained in and around town for the purposes of observation, with the exception of Anderson's brigade of Withers's division, which was ordered to Bridgeport, at the crossing of the Nashville and Chattanooga Railroad over the Tennessee River. Hardee's corps was distributed along the line of the Knoxville Railroad, with Tyner's Station as the centre. At Chattanooga Bragg at once commenced fortifying his position, which work he steadily prosecuted for some weeks, awaiting the development of Rosecrans's plans. He also threw up defensive works at each of the crossings of the Tennessee as far north as Blyth's Ferry. Forrest was sent to Kingston, on the north bank of the Tennessee River, with orders to picket the approaches to the river from Sequatchie Valley, as well as the various crossings of the river, and to maintain a watchful observation of Burnside's movements in East Tennessee.

The Tullahoma campaign, with the exception of the one

immediately following, which placed the army of the Cumberland across the Tennessee and terminated in the battle of Chickamauga, was the most brilliant of the great strategic campaigns carried to a successful issue by General Rosecrans. The movements of the army occupied nine days, during which time the enemy was driven from two strongly fortified positions, with a loss in prisoners captured of 1,634, eleven pieces of artillery, and a large amount of stores and supplies. The result of this campaign gave to Rosecrans possession of Middle Tennessee, and placed the armies back in the relative positions occupied by them prior to Bragg's advance into Kentucky, a little less than one year previous. The campaign was conducted throughout, in one of the most extraordinary series of rain-storms ever known in Tennessee at that season of the year. This, with the resistance interposed by Bragg to our advance at Hoover's Gap, retarded operations thirty-six hours, and in front of Manchester a detention of sixty hours occurred. These delays and the storms prevented us getting possession of Bragg's communication and forcing him to a very disastrous battle. General Rosecrans in his official report of this campaign says: "These results were far more successful than were anticipated, and could only have been obtained by a surprise as to the direction and force of our movements."

Bragg made no official report of the Tullahoma campaign, but in a statement to General J. E. Johnston of his operations at that time, he says that he offered battle behind his works at Shelbyville to Rosecrans, which was refused; that the latter passed to his, Bragg's, right on two occasions, threatening his rear. He being not able to cope with the Federal army retreated to the Tennessee. Bragg adds: "The Tennessee will be taken as our line."

During these nine days of active campaigning the Army

VII.—8

of the Cumberland, numbering less than sixty thousand effective men, with a loss of 560 killed, wounded, and missing, compelled the army under Bragg, numbering something less than forty-five thousand effective men, to retreat a greater distance and out of far stronger positions than the united armies under Sherman were able to compel the same army with but slight additional strength under General Joe Johnston, to fall back, in four months of active field campaigning, with a very much larger relative loss. The proportion of the forces of the opposing armies during the Tullahoma campaign was far nearer equal than that on to Atlanta, while the natural and military obstacles to be overcome were largely the greater in the Tullahoma campaign. To Bragg the forward movement of the Federal army in full strength was a surprise, but to find that army so far in his rear and so near to cutting his line of communications was a much greater surprise. These might not have been guarded against, but nothing displayed the marked superiority of Rosecrans over his opponent, as a great strategist, so much as the grand success of the final movement of the campaign, from Manchester south. The general who—as even the rebels, in their worship of their leader General Lee, admitted —was able in Western Virginia to completely outgeneral Lee, on the Tullahoma campaign again demonstrated his ability as the greatest strategic general of the war.

Brilliant campaigns, however, without battles, do not accomplish the destruction of an army. A campaign like that of Tullahoma always means a battle at some other point. This was true after the Atlanta campaign, where Sherman got the glory and Thomas did the fighting. This was equally true as to the Tullahoma, and the fact that these two armies were yet somewhere to meet and engage in deadly strife, was apparent to the commanders of both armies. Where and when that meeting was to be was the problem that engaged the minds of both these commanders. In the Tullahoma campaign the elements were on the side of Bragg's army, both in preventing the rapid movements of the Federal army, and in furnishing a perfect barrier to a successful pursuit when the retreat was under way, by the high water in the swollen streams, the bridges over which Bragg destroyed as he fell back.

The concluding line of Bragg's letter to Johnston, that "The Tennessee will be taken as our line," demonstrated that, to his mind at least, his Kentucky movement of the year before did not meet with the success he anticipated. Here now he was waiting his opportunity to contest his last foothold on the State of Tennessee at the far corner in Chattanooga. With Rosecrans, his army required after these days of hard campaigning a rest to repair the wear and tear of the heavy marching, and the resupplying of his entire command. The railroads in his rear required his attention first. These were placed in order up to his army, and the repairs on the road to the front were then to be pushed to the Tennessee River. In three weeks time these were completed, and on the 25th, the first supply train was pushed through to the Tennessee River. Then Rosecrans established his new depot of supplies at Stevenson, Alabama, and hastened, as rapidly as he could, the accumulation of supplies at that point.

Chickamauga Campaign.

CHAPTER XI.

THE MOVEMENT TO CHICKAMAUGA.

THE withdrawal of the army under Bragg to Chattanooga again made that point the objective of a campaign. But several things had to be taken into consideration before this was entered into. Burnside had been ordered from Cincinnati to East Tennessee through Kentucky, and it was necessary to know the force and position of his command. If Knoxville and Cumberland Gap were under his control, then it would be reasonably safe to follow out a plan of operations looking to flank Bragg's left by a movement across the Tennessee over the ranges of mountains of Northern Georgia. But to do this, part of the force under Grant, now inactive after Vicksburg, should be ordered up at least as far east as the Tennessee, to protect the line of supplies and prevent any movement of the enemy to the rear on that flank of Rosecrans's army. Another weighty consideration was that of forage for the animals of the command. By the middle of August, corn in the valleys of Southern Tennessee and Northern Alabama would be ripe, and subject to the wants of the army. It was General Rosecrans's plan to wait until these movements could be accomplished and until the corn had ripened, and knowing the difficulties in the way at the best, of his successfully accomplishing his plans for the campaign, he wished at least to have that best in his favor.

In making his final preparations for his operations against

Chattanooga, General Rosecrans considered two plans. One was to appear on the front of Chattanooga and attempt a direct attack on the town and reduce it by a lengthy siege. The other was to flank Bragg out of Chattanooga, as he had been compelled by the movement on the Tullahoma campaign to abandon his strongholds one by one.

The first plan could hardly be entertained, as Bragg was at his base, with but short lines to all important points under control of the rebel government, and at a place where in a very short time heavy reinforcements could be sent him, while Rosecrans in front of Chattanooga would be in a rough, sterile country, far away from his base of supplies, with a long wagon-haul over rocky mountain ranges from his nearest depôt. To attempt the movement on the left, or through Sequatchie Valley, would concentrate Bragg's entire army at the contemplated point of crossing the Tennessee. This plan Bragg was prepared for, and was resting, quietly awaiting the movements of our army carrying it into effect. But it was not the purpose of Rosecrans to meet this expectation of his opponent. The genius of Rosecrans contemplated one of the most brilliant military movements of the war to obtain possession of this great stronghold of Nature, the gateway to East Tennessee and Northern Georgia, Chattanooga. At that time this place was of the utmost importance to each of the contending forces, and the highest prize in a military point of view that the Army of the Cumberland ever contended for.

To properly understand the magnitude and importance of the campaign that Rosecrans was now entering on, it is necessary that the topography of the country should be considered. The position of our army after the Tullahoma campaign was on the northwestern base of the Cumberland range, in camp occupying McMinnville, Tullahoma, Dechard, and Winchester, with Chattanooga south of east. Immediately in front was the first great barrier in the advance movement—the Cumberland Mountains—a lofty range of rocks dividing the waters flowing into the Cumberland and Tennessee Rivers. The range rises far to the north and extends to the southwest into Alabama. North of Chattanooga the mountains are much bolder, more difficult to cross, with almost sheer declivities on each of the sides.

Beyond the main range, in the direct road to Chattanooga, running south, flows the Sequatchie River through the valley of that name, formed by another range jutting off slightly to the east from the main range, and between it and the Tennessee River. This spur is known by the name of Walling's Ridge, after an early settler and Indian hunter. It abuts close on the Tennessee in precipitous rocky bluffs.

South of the Tennessee, and separated from the mountain ranges north by this river, are the two ranges known as Sand and Lookout Mountains. The northern extremity of the former is called Raccoon Mountain. Here the river cuts its channel as a great chasm through these mountain ranges, so sharply defined that the masses abut directly upon the water in heavy palisades of rock.

The tops of all these mountain ranges are of poor soil but generally with considerable timber; rough, with but few roads, and these almost impassable for wagons and nearly destitute of water. The western slope of Sand Mountain reaches nearly to the Tennessee River. Between this latter range and Lookout Mountain is Lookout Valley with the creek of that name flowing through it into the Tennessee a short distance below Chattanooga. This valley is also known as Wills Valley, and at that time was traversed by a railroad branching from the Nashville road at Wauhatchie, terminating at Trenton.

Beyond this was Lookout range, 2,400 feet above the sea, with almost perpendicular sides, heavily wooded and with little water, abutting abruptly on the Tennessee, some two miles south of the town, with only three practical wagon roads over it—one close to the river, one at Johnson's Crook, and the third at Winston's Gap, twenty-six and forty-two miles respectively south of Chattanooga.

To the east of Lookout Mountain is Chattanooga Valley with the town at the head of it and the creek of that name flowing through, with Dry Creek as a branch emptying its waters into the Tennessee just south of the town. Beyond this to the east is Missionary Ridge, and parallel to it and just beyond is Chickamauga Valley, with the creek of that name running through it emptying into the river above Chattanooga, formed by East, Middle, and West Chickamauga Creeks, uniting with Pea Vine Creek between the latter two as a tributary. Chattanooga and West Chickamauga Creeks have a common source in McLemore's Cove, which is formed by Pigeon Mountain on the east, jutting to the north as a spur of Lookout Mountain, with the latter on the west, Missionary Ridge running out as it enters this cove. The wagon road from Chattanooga to Rome, known as the La Fayette road, crosses Missionary Ridge into Chickamauga Valley at Rossville and proceeds thence nearly due south, crossing Chickamauga Creek at Lee and Gordon mills, thence to the east of Pigeon Mountain, passing through La Fayette some twenty-two miles south of Chattanooga; it then continues on to Sumnerville, within twenty-five miles of Rome, and so on to the latter place.

Beyond these ranges is Taylor's ridge, with a number of lesser ranges between it and the Atlanta Railroad, running through Dalton. Both Pigeon Mountain and Taylor's Ridge are very rough mountain ranges, with but few roads, and these only through gaps. At Dalton is the junction of the East Tennessee with the Atlanta Railroad, in the valley of the head waters of the Coosa River, which valley is here some ten miles wide and is the great natural passage-way into East Tennessee from the south.

To follow Bragg to Chattanooga and to cross the Tennessee above that place involved moving the army either to the north of the Sequatchie Valley by Dunlap or by Therman and Walling's Ridge, some sixty-five to seventy miles through a country poorly supplied with water, with no forage, and by narrow and difficult wagon roads. This route would take Rosecrans further away from his base of supplies and line of communication than that south of the river. It was over this northern route that Bragg anticipated the onward movement of the Army of the Cumberland. This would enable him to make a protracted defence of the town and retard the advance for weeks, if not months. But Rosecrans's plan of the campaign contemplated a much more hazardous movement and a far speedier one for the possession of Chattanooga. To accomplish this, however, it was necessary to cross the Cumberland Mountains with subsistence, ammunition, a limited supply of forage, and a bridge train ; then to cross his army over the Tennessee River, after that over Sand or Raccoon Mountain into Lookout Valley, and from there to cross Lookout Mountain, and finally the lesser ranges—Missionary Ridge—if he went directly to Chattanooga, or to cross Missionary Ridge, Pigeon Mountain, and Taylor's Ridge, if he struck the railroad at Dalton or south of it. This involved the carrying by his army of ammunition for two great battles and twenty-five days' subsistence.

As soon as the repairs were made on the main line to Stevenson, Rosecrans ordered Sheridan's division to make an advance movement with two brigades to Bridgeport and

8*

one to Stevenson. Van Cleve had been ordered up with his division from Murfreesboro and was posted at McMinnville. On August 8th, stores being accumulated at the front, orders were issued to corps commanders to supply their troops, as soon as possible, with rations and forage sufficient for the general advance.

The movement over the Cumberland Mountains began on August 16th, and the troops were ordered to move as follows:

"Crittenden's corps in three columns to move through the Sequatchie Valley. Minty's cavalry to move on the left by Sparta, and after covering the left flank of Van Cleve to proceed to Pikeville.

"Thomas to move Reynolds and Brannan from University by way of Battle Creek, where they were to take post, concealed near its mouth. Negley and Baird to go by way of Tantallon and halt on Crow Creek between Anderson and Stevenson.

"McCook to move Johnson by Salem and Larkin's Ford to Bellefont. Davis by Mount Top and Crow Creek to near Stevenson. The three brigades of cavalry by Fayetteville and Athens to cover the line of the Tennessee from Whitesburg up."

These orders were all complied with, and the movements completed by the evening of August 20th. Crittenden sent Hazen's brigade on a reconnoissance to Harrison's Landing, where he found the enemy throwing up works. On the next day Hazen took post at Poe's cross-roads. Wilder was sent to reconnoitre from Harrison's Landing to Chattanooga. On reaching Chattanooga, he was supported by Wagner's brigade, and both commands opened fire on the next day, shelling the town from across the river. This bombardment of the place caused it to be evacuated by the rebel troops, to points beyond range outside, and the withdrawal by Bragg of his stores to points of convenience on the railroad to the rear. Bragg then ordered Anderson's brigade to withdraw from Bridgeport.

The feint under Crittenden was so well timed that Bragg concentrated his immediate command at and above Chattanooga, leaving the crossing of the river by the main portion of our army later, unobstructed. Rosecrans had posted his army so that demonstrations were made simultaneously from Whitesburg to Blythe's Ferry, a distance of one hundred and fifty miles, and Bragg did not know just where to look for his real advance, but definitely concluded that it would *not* be made anywhere in the vicinity of Bridgeport. On the 26th, five days after the surprise at Chattanooga, Burnside's advance into East Tennessee was announced by the presence of his cavalry in the vicinity of Knoxville. Bragg then ordered Buckner to evacuate Knoxville, and occupy Loudon. The demonstration at Blythe's Ferry on the Tennessee, opposite the mouth of the Hiawasse, caused Bragg to order him to retire to Charleston, and soon thereafter to Chattanooga. On the 30th, information was given General Thomas that Johnston, with 15,000 men from Mississippi, had reinforced Bragg.

Under cover of the apparent activity of the left of our army in front of and above Chattanooga, Rosecrans effected safely the crossing of the first great barrier to the objective point, and reached the banks of the Tennessee opposite the enemy, concealing as far as he could the movements of his troops, and the position of his pontoons and trains. He then had the river reconnoitred, that the best points might be selected and the means at once provided for the crossing. As soon as the crossings had been determined on, the proper dispositions were made to begin the movement.

The Tennessee River, at the various points where our army was to cross, is very wide; and, swollen by recent rains, was quite high for that season of the year. The troops crossed the river at four points. As there were not enough pontoons for two bridges, Sheridan had commenced trestlework for part of one at Bridgeport. Reynolds advanced to Shellmound, seizing the place. Here he captured a number of boats, and with these and other material picked up, he was enabled to cross at that point, while Brannan crossed his division from the mouth of Battle Creek on rafts. The main crossing of McCook's corps was at Caperton's Ferry, about forty miles below Chattanooga, where the pontoon bridge was laid by Davis's division, after driving a detachment of rebel cavalry from the opposite side.

The movement across the river was commenced on August 29th, and completed on September 4th. Baird, in command of a division of Thomas's corps, crossed the river at Bridgeport after the repairs were completed to the bridge. Negley's division crossed at Caperton's Ferry. The four divisions of Thomas's corps with great difficulty crossed Sand Mountain, and concentrated near Trenton in Will's Valley, east of Sand Mountain. On September 6th Negley's division, being in the advance, reached Johnson Crook, where Beatty's brigade was sent at once up the mountain to seize Stevens's Gap. Before proceeding far he met the enemy's pickets, and, night coming on, he went into camp just west of the gap. The Eighteenth Ohio went a short distance on the road to the top of Lookout Mountain, met the enemy's pickets and withdrew. The next day, Baird's division supporting Negley, the latter with two brigades, moved forward, and with his advance gained possession of the top of the mountain, and secured the forks of the road. The entire of Negley's division reached this point on the 9th, at the head of Johnson's Crook, and with one brigade held the pass while another was sent a short distance north on the mountain to seize Cooper's Gap, with a regiment in the advance to occupy and hold the entrance on the east. Another regiment was sent forward to hold Stevens's Gap, which was found heavily obstructed with fallen timber. Negley still being in the advance, moved the day following across Missionary Ridge, and took up a position in McLemore's Cove on the road through Dug Gap. Here he found the enemy's cavalry drawn up in line, and learned from citizens that the rebels were in strong force concentrated in his front in Dug Gap, with infantry, artillery, and cavalry. Baird's division was in supporting distance of. Negley.

Early in the morning of the 9th Reynolds sent the Ninety-second Illinois (mounted infantry) to make a reconnoissance along the top of Lookout Mountain, to discover the enemy's movements and to determine the rumors in regard to the evacuation of Chattanooga. At 11 A.M. the regiment entered the town as the rear of the enemy's column was leaving the place. The next day the four divisions of the Fourteenth Corps were in supporting distance of each other, with Negley still in front of Dug Gap, the enemy holding the east entrance with a heavy force, and the Gap full of obstructions. Negley discovered early on the following day that the rebels were advancing on him in such superior force that his situation was critical, and that he was in danger of losing his train. He determined to fall back to a strong position in front of Stevens's Gap, which movement he proceeded to execute, and succeeded in the face of the enemy by his energy and skill, with the prompt co-operation of Baird, in securing his position in front of the gap without the loss of a single wagon. The next day the location of Bragg's army at La Fayette with Johnston's reinforcements was fully determined, and Thomas's corps now awaited the movements of the other troops with reference to the concentration of the army.

In the meantime Davis's and Johnson's divisions of Mc-Cook's corps, crossing the river at Caperton's Ferry, moved over Sand Mountain into Will's Valley, and thence—Davis being in the advance—moved into and seized Winston's Gap, some twenty-five miles from Caperton's Ferry, and about forty-two from Chattanooga. Sheridan's division crossed the river at the railroad bridge, moved through Trenton, and on the 6th encamped twelve miles from Winston's Gap. McCook sent several detachments on the 8th and 9th to different points, reconnoitring the enemy. One went to Alpine and two into Broomtown Valley, but nothing was discovered of Bragg's whereabouts. On the evening of the 9th Rosecrans sent orders to McCook, stating that the enemy had evacuated Chattanooga and were retreating southward, and directing him to move rapidly upon Alpine and Summerville in pursuit, to intercept his line of retreat, and to attack on his flank. The day following McCook reached Alpine, where he discovered the situation. The enemy had not retreated very far from Chattanooga, the exact location as yet unknown. McCook learned that he could not communicate with Thomas, as his couriers could not pass through the valley, occupied as it was by the enemy in force, and that his corps was entirely isolated at Alpine. That, had he gone to Summerville, he would have been exposed to an attack from the entire rebel army, which his reconnoissance later determined was concentrated in force near La Fayette. On the following day McCook remained in camp waiting for Thomas to move up on him. He, however, sent his wagon-train back to the summit of Lookout Mountain. On the 12th McCook waited in camp for reports from the cavalry as to the position and movements of the enemy.

Crittenden's corps had during the time moved down the Sequatchie Valley, in readiness for an active campaign. He then crossed the river at Bridgeport, Shell Mound, and Battle Creek, and on September 4th his entire corps was across the river. He was ordered to move up the valley of Running Water Creek and Whiteside, leaving one division on the line of the Nashville and Chattanooga Railroad, and to push forward as near as possible to Chattanooga, threatening the enemy in that direction. At 6 A.M. on the 9th Crittenden was informed by a despatch from Rosecrans that Chattanooga had been abandoned by the enemy, and that he was to push forward at once with five days' rations and make a vigorous pursuit. During the morning Crittenden with Wood's division occupied the town, and Wood was placed in command. Palmer's and Van Cleve's were turned off south after they passed the spur of Lookout Mountain, and encamped at Rossville, five miles south of Chattanooga. In the afternoon of the same day Crittenden was ordered to leave a brigade at Chattanooga, and with the balance of his command to pursue the enemy with the utmost vigor, the line of march to be through Ringgold and on to Dalton. The next day Crittenden left Wagner—who had crossed the river from the front of the town during the night—in command, and ordered forward Palmer's, Van Cleve's, and the two brigades of Wood's division in pursuit, marching on the Rossville and Ringgold road. During the afternoon Palmer reported the enemy's cavalry strong on his front, that he had only been able to march six miles, had encamped at Chickamauga Creek, and that his advance had been checked by a charge of the rebel cavalry. That night Crittenden received several reports from his front that the enemy was in force near La Fayette, and threatening to retake Chattanooga.

During the 11th, Wood, with his two brigades, was on a reconnoissance at Gordon's Mills, and Crittenden was ordered to occupy Ringgold and report. These movements deter-

mined to Rosecrans's satisfaction the position of the enemy
in force in the vicinity of La Fayette. He immediately
ordered Crittenden to close his entire command upon Wood,
crossing as quickly as possible to the Rossville and La Fayette road, to some point near Lee and Gordon's Mills. Early
on the morning of the 12th, Wilder was ordered back to
Ringgold and directed to follow on the line of march of the
infantry, covering the left flank. Crittenden succeeded during the day in effecting a concentration of his command at
Lee and Gordon's Mills, which point Wilder's brigade reached
after a severe skirmish during the day near Leet's tanyard,
where he lost thirty men killed and wounded. With the
knowledge that Bragg was concentrating his forces awaiting
reinforcements behind Pigeon Mountain, in the vicinity of
La Fayette, and that his own army was scattered a distance
of thirty miles from flank to flank—from Lee and Gordon's
Mills to Alpine—Rosecrans felt that it was a matter of life
and death to effect the concentration of his army in the short-
est possible space of time.

During these movements of the army under Rosecrans,
what was Bragg doing? On August 20th, the movement of
our army over the Cumberland Mountains was reported to
Bragg, and he then knew that he might look for an immediate advance. The movement of our army across the Tennessee was also reported to Bragg by his scouts, but was regarded by him as incredible. These reports were soon after
confirmed by the news that our cavalry had occupied Trenton
and had advanced up the Will's Valley Railroad as far as Wauhatchie, within seven miles of Chattanooga, as a covering force
under which Rosecrans's columns of infantry were advancing. Our army was now as near the line of communication
of the rebel army, as the latter was to the line to Nashville,
and with less risk in its advance movements should Bragg

commence operations to the north. Bringing his cavalry forward at once, Bragg soon ascertained that the general movement of our army was toward his left and rear in the direction of Dalton and Rome, keeping Lookout Mountain between the armies. He then determined to meet our army as its columns debouched from the defiles of the mountains. To hold Chattanooga would require at least two strong divisions, and he felt that his force would not permit this and make a successful attack also. Bragg put his army in motion on September 7th and 8th, and took up position from Lee and Gordon's Mills to La Fayette, on the road running south from Chattanooga, with front to the east side of Lookout Mountain, and on the east bank of Chickamauga Creek, establishing his headquarters at the former place.

The positions of our detached corps was fully known to Bragg on the 8th. Learning of Negley's movement of the 9th into McLemore's cove, Bragg rightly interpreted it to mean that a hurried pursuit was being made after his force, under the idea that he was in full retreat. With his own force concentrated in front of the centre, Bragg at once saw how Rosecrans had exposed the corps of his army to be attacked and defeated in detail, and that evening he gave orders to Hindman to prepare his division to move against Negley, and ordered Hill to send or take Cleburne's division, join Hindman, and immediately move upon Negley. On receipt of these orders, Hill replied that his part of the movement was impracticable, as Cleburne was sick, and that both gaps—Dug and Catlett's—had been closed by felling timber, which would require twenty-four hours to remove. Hindman having marched during the night of the 9th some ten miles, was now in position, some three miles from Negley in the cove. Bragg not wishing to lose so favorable an opportunity of striking his opponent's force, ordered Buckner with

his command to move from Anderson and join Hindman in
the cove, which he did during the afternoon of the 10th.
After these commands had united, the commanders held a
consultation and determined that a change in the plan of
operations should be made. Bragg having removed his headquarters to La Fayette, "so as to secure more prompt and
decided action in the movements ordered against the enemy's
centre," now directed Polk to send his remaining division to
support Hindman during the operations in the cove. De-
spatching an officer to Bragg with a report as to this change
of plans, Hindman and Cleburne waited his return. Bragg
refused to make any change, and sent a verbal order to Hindman to proceed at once to carry out his previous instruction.
Bragg at the same time sent written orders by courier to
Hindman, notifying him of the movements of our forces,
that Polk had been directed to cover his rear, and ordered
him to attack and force his way through Negley to La Fayette at the earliest hour in the morning, and adds " Cleburne
will attack in front the moment your guns are heard."
Walker's reserve corps was also ordered to move promptly,
join Cleburne's division at Dug Gap and unite in the attack.
All obstructions were removed from Dug and Catlett's Gaps,
and Breckenridge's division of Hill's corps was kept in position south of La Fayette to check any movement of our
troops from that direction, thus putting 30,000 troops in
position to crush Negley and Baird. Bragg shortly after
daylight joined Cleburne, where they waited nearly all day
for Hindman's guns to open—when Cleburne was to attack—
on the flank and rear of Negley and Baird's divisions. After
waiting long past noon in great anxiety for Hindman's attack,
about the middle of the afternoon his first gun was heard.
Cleburne at once pressed forward and discovered that Negley
had fallen back to Stevens's Gap.

Bragg, finding his attempt against Thomas's corps a failure, then determined to hurl his columns upon Crittenden's divided corps, approaching from Chattanooga, by withdrawing the troops engaged in the movement on Thomas's command to La Fayette, and directing Polk's and Walker's corps to move immediately in the direction of Lee and Gordon's Mills. Bragg knew Crittenden's corps was divided, but supposed only one division had been sent to Ringgold. At six o'clock on the evening of the 12th, Bragg wrote again to Polk, notifying him of Crittenden's position of the 11th, and stated: "This presents you a fine opportunity of striking Crittenden in detail, and I hope you will avail yourself of it at daylight to-morrow. This division crushed, and the others are yours. We can then turn on the force in the cove. Wheeler's cavalry will move on Wilder so as to cover your right. I shall be delighted to hear of your success." Later in the evening two additional orders were issued to Polk, urging him to attack promptly at "day-dawn," on the 13th; that our army was concentrating, and that it was "highly important that your attack in the morning should be quick and decided." At eleven o'clock that night Polk sent a dispatch stating that he had taken a strong position for defense and asked that he be heavily reinforced. Bragg sent him an immediate order not to defer his attack, as his command was numerically superior to the opposing force, and told him that to secure success, prompt and rapid movements on his part were necessary. Early on the morning of the 13th, Bragg, at the head of Buckner's command, went to the front, and found no advance had been made by Polk as ordered, and that Crittenden had united his forces and recrossed the Chickamauga.

Again the attempt to strike our army in detail had failed, and now Bragg gave orders to his commanders to concentrate along the east bank of Chickamauga in position for battle, and as soon as his reinforcements under Longstreet from Virginia were up to attack with the entire command. Wheeler, with two divisions of cavalry on the extreme left, was ordered to engage the attention of Thomas in McLemore's Cove, covering the main movement of the rebel army; Forrest with his own and Pegram's divisions of cavalry covered the right and front. Bragg ordered B. R. Johnson's brigade from Ringgold, where he had been stationed protecting the railroad, to take position near Reed's bridge on the extreme right of his line. Walker's corps was then formed on Johnson's left, opposite Alexander's Bridge. Buckner's corps was formed on the left of Walker, near Ledford's Ford. Polk's corps was placed in line opposite Lee and Gordon's Mills on Buckner's left, with Hill on the extreme left. Two brigades that had just arrived from Mississippi were placed under Johnson on the right, making his command a division of three brigades strong. To this division in the earlier movements three brigades of Longstreet's corps from Virginia were temporarily attached. On the 18th, Hood reporting, was placed in command of this column on the right.

The rebel army on the 17th were in position, and that evening Bragg issued his orders for his forces to cross the Chickamauga, commencing the movement at six o'clock on the morning of the 18th. Bragg's plan of battle for the 18th was for the column under Johnson—later under Hood— to cross in force at Reed's Bridge, rapidly turn to the left by the most practicable route, and sweep up the Chickamauga toward Lee and Gordon's Mills. Walker's corps next on the left, crossing at Alexandria Bridge, was to unite in the movement, pressing our army vigorously on flank and rear, in the same direction. Buckner, crossing at Ledford's Ford, was to join in the movement to the left, pressing our army back up the stream from Polk's front.   The latter to push forward to the front at Lee and Gordon's Mills, and if not able to cross there, to bear to the right and cross at Dalton's Ford or Alexander's Bridge, and unite in the attack wherever he could find an opposing force.   Hill, to cover the left flank of the rebel army from an advance by our forces in the cove, to ascertain by pressing his cavalry to the front if we were reinforcing our corps at Lee and Gordon's Mills, and if so to attack on the flank.   This plan contemplated the destruction of the left of our army, the seizing of the La Fayette road, and, if possible, occupying and holding the roads in Chattanooga Valley, cutting off all access from Chattanooga.   These movements were not executed as rapidly as was contemplated by Bragg, owing to the resistance made by our cavalry and Wilder's mounted infantry, and the difficulties arising from bad and narrow roads.   Johnson was repeatedly urged to commence the movement on the right, but he delayed his advance until late in the afternoon, when Hood arrived and effected the crossing.   Walker moved up to Alexander's Bridge, at which point Wilder hotly contested his crossing, and finally broke up the bridge.   Walker moved down the creek to Byron's Ford, where he crossed and joined Hood on the right during the night.   On Walker's crossing, Wilder was compelled to fall back.

The concentration of our army continued on the 13th, Thomas held his position of the 12th, with Negley's, Baird's, and Brannan's divisions remaining in camp, waiting the arrival of McCook, who had been ordered to close up to the left.   Reynolds's division was concentrated on the road from Cooper's or Frick's Gap to Catlett's Gap, and the next day moved forward and took position at Pond Spring, with his two infantry brigades, and was joined here by Wilder.   Reynolds sent Turchin to make a reconnoissance with the Ninety-second Illinois mounted infantry, to the mouth of Catlett's Gap, driving the rebel cavalry pickets from Chickamauga Creek to the gap, where he found the enemy posted with strong reserves.   Brannan on the same day reconnoitred the position of the enemy toward Dug Gap, sending a brigade to Chickamauga Creek, east of Lee's Mills, one mile to the right and south of Reynolds, at Pond Spring.   Turchin made another reconnoissance on the 16th toward Catlett's Gap, and found the enemy strongly posted there with infantry and artillery.   The next day Thomas moved his entire corps and closed up on Crittenden's right along Chickamauga Creek, and was joined at night by McCook on his right.   The four divisions of Thomas's command on the afternoon of the 18th moved to the left to Crawfish Springs.   Here Rosecrans, anticipating the movement of Bragg to secure the road to Chattanooga, and recognizing the importance of holding it, ordered Thomas with his corps to march on the cross-road leading by the Widow Glenn's to the Chattanooga and La Fayette road, and take position on that road near Kelly's farm, connecting with Crittenden's corps on his right at Gordon's Mills.   During the entire night of the 18th the troops of Thomas's corps were moving to the left, and at daylight on the 19th the head of the column reached Kelly's farm; Baird's division in the advance, taking position at the forks of the road, facing toward Reed's and Alexander's Bridges over the Chickamauga.   Wilder had been driven across the State road to the heights east of Widow Glenn's house the evening before, by the advance in force of the enemy over these bridges, and Baird's right rested close to Wilder's brigade.   Baird's division was closely followed by Brannan, who was placed in position on the left of Baird, on the two roads leading to the bridges.

Orders were received by McCook at midnight on the 13th,

directing two divisions of his corps to move to Thomas's support, and that he send his train back under guard of his remaining division. McCook moved his command, by way of Valley Head, up the mountain at Alpine on the night of the 13th, and down on the 14th into Lookout Valley, except one brigade from each division forming his train guard under command of Lytle, encamped at Little River in the mountains. Sheridan's marched down Lookout Valley to Johnson's Crook, while Johnson's and Davis's divisions were sent from Valley Head on the direct road to Stevens's Gap. General Lytle was ordered to make a reconnoissance with two brigades toward Dougherty's Gap at the head of McLemore's Cove. McCook's corps was concentrated on the 17th at Mc-Lemore's Cove, and on the night of the 18th General Lytle joining the corps with two of his brigades, McCook's command was closed up on the Fourteenth Corps, except Post's brigade of Davis's division, ordered by General Rosecrans to hold Stevens's Gap at all hazards.

Crittenden on the 13th, under orders from headquarters, posted Wood's division in a strong position at Lee and Gordon's Mills, under orders to resist any advance of the enemy to the last, and in case of extremity, if Granger was not in position to support, then to fall back to some point where he could guard the road to Chattanooga and the one around the point of Lookout Mountain, and hold both roads, as long as he had a man under him. The next day Crittenden moved the two remaining divisions of his corps to a position on the southern spur of Missionary Ridge, his right communicating with Thomas, where he was to remain, covering the road in Chattanooga Valley. Finding no movement of the enemy on his front, on the 15th Crittenden was ordered to return with his command and take position near Crawfish Spring, with Van Cleve on the left and Palmer on the right. During the day Minty with the cavalry made an extended reconnoissance on the front, finding the enemy in force at all points. Wood, holding position on Chickamauga Creek, at Lee and Gordon's Mills, on the morning of the 18th reported the enemy advancing with strong line of skirmishers on his left and asked for supports. Van Cleve was placed on Wood's left and Palmer then took Van Cleve's position on Wood's right. Wilder in the afternoon reported Minty's cavalry driven back after being reinforced with two of his regiments; that the enemy was flanking him and that he would fall back on Wood. Palmer later in the day was placed on the left of Van Cleve's new position on the line of Chickamauga Creek, his last brigade reaching its position at four o'clock on the morning of the 19th; Wood holding his position on the creek at Lee and Gordon's Mills, which at this point runs between steep rocky bluffs in an eastwardly course, with the road to Chattanooga *via* Rossville crossing it at right angles; Van Cleve on his left and Palmer on the left of Van Cleve; the general course of the line being northeasterly along the Chickamauga and Rossville road.

CHAPTER XII.

THE BATTLE OF CHICKAMAUGA.

COLONEL DAN. McCOOK, of Granger's reserve corps, who had been posted on the road leading to Reed's Bridge, on the evening of the 18th, made a reconnoissance to Chickamauga Creek as far as Reed's Bridge, which he burned. On the 19th, meeting Thomas, he reported that an isolated brigade of the enemy was on the west side of the creek, and as the bridge was destroyed a prompt movement in that direction might succeed in capturing the entire force. Thomas ordered Brannan to post a brigade on the road to Alexander's Bridge as support to Baird, and with his other brigades to reconnoitre the road to Reed's Bridge in search of this brigade of the enemy. Brannan moved at nine o'clock A.M., and Baird, under orders from Thomas, threw forward his right wing so as to get into line with Brannan. Baird was also ordered to keep a sharp outlook on his right flank and watch the movements of the enemy in that quarter. Shortly after these movements a part of Palmer's division reported to Thomas and was placed in position on the right of Baird. Rosecrans, when he sent Thomas to the left—the critical point—told him that he was to hold the road to Rossville, and if hard pressed, that he should be reinforced with the entire army.

Under Bragg's orders, Walker's corps on the 18th crossed to the west side of Chickamauga a little below Alexander's Bridge and then moved up the stream opposite this point.

Battle of Chickamauga.

Bushrod Johnson's command the same day crossed at Reed's bridge, and then marched up the stream some three miles and took position on the morning of the 19th. Walker resumed his movement to his left up the stream, under the impression that our centre was still at Lee and Gordon's Mills, Bragg's plan being to mass Walker's and Johnson's commands and attack our left flank. The advance movement of Brannan's division, Croxton's brigade in front, about ten o'clock encountered the enemy, being the cavalry under Forrest with Wilson's and Ector's brigades of infantry, and drove them nearly half a mile, when it met with obstinate resistance. This reconnoissance of Brannan in pursuit of the brigade reported by Dan. McCook developed the relative position of the opposing contending forces, which up to this time was unknown to the respective commanders of each. It gave to Bragg the knowledge that his right was greatly overlapped by Thomas on our left, and that his flank was in danger of being turned. It compelled him at once to halt Walker's command on its march, and to direct it to retrace its steps and reinforce Forrest, now engaged with Croxton, whose movement brought on the battle of Chickamauga before Bragg had his troops in the position ordered.

Thomas then ordered Baird's division forward to Croxton's support. Moving at once with two brigades on the front, with Starkweather's in reserve, Baird and Croxton drove the enemy steadily for some distance with great loss, capturing many prisoners. Croxton's brigade having exhausted its ammunition in the severe fighting of over an hour, was then moved to the rear, and Brannan's and Baird's divisions with united forces drove the enemy from their immediate front. Here the line was halted and readjusted. Baird learning from his prisoners that the rebel army was in heavy force on his immediate front, gathering for an attack in mass, drew back his right wing and waited the assault of Bragg's right on his line, which was made in heavy force by Walker, who had reached his new position. Before Baird had completed the reforming of his line, Walker's corps, in overwhelming numbers was upon him, assaulting Scribner's and King's brigades, and driving them back in disorder.

McCook, early on the morning of the 19th, had taken position with his corps at Crawfish Spring, and was now beyond the extreme left of the rebel army, massing his troops at this point and waiting for orders. At a little after ten o'clock in the morning he was directed to take command of the right and the cavalry on that flank. This included Negley's division of the Fourteenth Corps, which was watching the fords of Chickamauga near Crawfish Spring, one brigade of his command being then engaged with the enemy. The same order directed McCook to send Johnson's divisions to the left to report to Thomas, and following this came another one from Rosecrans, directing McCook to send Davis's division also to Thomas. On Baird being driven back, General Thomas ordered Johnson's and Reynolds's division of his own corps—both of whom had opportunely arrived by this time—immediately to advance and drive the enemy back. Johnson arriving first was ordered at once to advance his left, connecting with Baird's right, Palmer was immediately placed on Johnson's right and Reynolds still to the right of Palmer, with one brigade of his division in reserve. As soon as the line was thus formed the troops advanced, attacking Walker's corps on the flank with great vigor, driving it in confusion back to its first position, while Brannan's division, fighting them on the front, drove back the head of the column and retook the artillery which had been captured from Baird when he was driven back. Bragg then ordered up Cheatham's division, which had been in reserve, reinforcing Walker. With these two commands united, the rebels pressed forward with loud yells, determined on the destruction of our left. As these two commands advanced, a gap was made in their lines, into which Bragg threw Stewart's division. As they encountered our line, these troops moved forward. Striking Johnson first, they drove him from his position in disorder, then Palmer was compelled to retire, when Van Cleve coming to his support was also beaten back. Reynolds then in turn was overpowered and the rebels seemed to be sweeping every thing before them as at Stone's River. By this time Davis had reported with his division, and moving at once to the front checked the rebel advance, when Wood coming up to his assistance, our lines were reformed, and Cheatham's, Stewart's, and Walker's troops were driven in rapid retreat back to their original line. Sheridan, under orders, had left Lytle's brigade to hold Lee and Gordon's Mills on our extreme right, and moved to our left in support of the new line near Wood's and Davis's divisions. He reached the position opportunely and aided in driving back the rebels, Bradley's brigade recapturing the Eighth Indiana battery previously taken by the enemy. A large number of prisoners were captured belonging to Longstreet's corps.

Bragg, finding that his plan of battle was discovered by his opponent, and that the latter intended to dispute to the end for the possession of the Rossville and Chattanooga road, ordered Polk to cross the creek with his remaining division at the nearest ford and to assume command in person on their right. Hill with his corps was also ordered to move across the Chickamauga below Lee and Gordon's Mills and to join the line on the right.

The rebels made another desperate assault at about half past two o'clock on our right. Hood's corps, with Bushrod Johnson's division from the enemy's centre, moved forward in

heavy masses, assaulting furiously Reynolds's and Van Cleve's
divisions. Here they met with 'fearful loss from the heavy
infantry and artillery fire, portions of six batteries opening with canister on their advancing columns, but still on
they came. Soon the roar of battle was heard approaching near to the Widow Glenn's house, where Rosecrans's
headquarters were. Our right centre now was pierced and
the enemy was on the La Fayette road. Negley, from the
right under McCook, was immediately ordered up with his
division, Brannan from Thomas's left joining him. These
two divisions were at once sent in to the fight. Moving
rapidly forward to the attack, with cheer on cheer, they
hurled back Hood and Johnson, steadily driving them until
darkness ended the combat, our troops re-occupying their
old positions.

Thomas, wishing to reform his lines—which had become
greatly extended in driving the rebels—and concentrate
them on more commanding ground in the rear preparatory
to the engagement to be renewed on the morrow, selected a
new position for Baird's and Johnson's divisions, the former
on the extreme left. These positions were designated to
them and were occupied at once. Palmer and Reynolds
were ordered into position in line on the right of Johnson, with Brannan to the rear and right of Reynolds as reserve. While these movements were being made, Cleburne
with his fresh division of Hill's corps, who had been ordered
to the extreme right by Bragg, under orders to attack immediately, advancing in full force, supported by Cheatham,
assaulted Johnson first and then Baird with tremendous
force. The onset was so determined that some confusion in
the line resulted, but in a few minutes our troops rallied
and the enemy was repulsed in fine style. This conflict
lasted for some time after dark with heavy losses on both

sides, the heavy firing lighting up the struggle. At this point our artillery was again used with good effect. Wilder's brigade had occupied a position during the day on the La Fayette road about a mile north of Lee and Gordon's Mills, with Minty close by. The latter was now ordered to report to Granger at Rossville, to hold in check the enemy's cavalry operating on their right. Granger, with his reserves, protected the roads to the rear toward Rossville and covered our left flank.

With night the fighting ceased, and the troops, worn out after the marching of the night before—moving from the right to the extreme left—and the heavy fighting of the day, slept on their arms, awaiting the heavier conflict of the morrow. Though weary, the troops were in most excellent spirits, and confident of final victory. It was known throughout the army that we had been fighting during the day largely superior forces. That Bragg had been heavily reinforced from Mississippi and East Tennessee, and by Longstreet's command from Virginia, and that the enemy was fighting most desperately. Bragg's great aim had been to conceal his main attack on our left by the feint on the centre, and supposed that our centre on the morning of the 19th was still at Lee and Gordon's Mills. Presuming this to be the case, Bragg had massed heavily on our left, intending to repeat his movement made on our right at Murfreesboro. His plan contemplated the breaking our left, sweeping it before him in broken masses, crushing our centre, and destroying our right, and then occupying the road to Chattanooga in force he would have the Federal army completely in his power. The movement made by Croxton compelled Bragg to open the battle in heavy force on the left, before his troops had secured the positions assigned them, and then, to his surprise, he found that during the night our left had been greatly prolonged, and that Rosecrans was in force, occupying a position far to the north of what he had been led to expect. During the night Bragg ordered up by forced marches all reinforcements arriving by railroad. Three brigades of fresh troops reached the enemy during the night, and were placed in line early in the morning of the 20th. These, with the troops ordered late the day before from the east bank of the Chickamauga, gave Bragg a large number of fresh troops, which he placed in line of battle on the 20th. During the night Bragg summoned his generals to meet him at his camp fire, and there gave them orders for the following day. He divided his entire force into two commands, to which he assigned his senior Lieutenant-Generals Longstreet and Polk. The former—who had reported during the night—to the left, composed of six divisions where his own troops were stationed, and the latter continuing in his command of five divisions on the right. Bragg's plan of battle for the 20th was for Polk to assault in force, with Breckinridge's division on his extreme right at day-dawn, when the attack was to be taken up rapidly in succession by the divisions to his left. The left wing was to await the movement on the right, and when the attack was made there to take it up promptly. When the entire line became engaged it was to move forward vigorously and persistently throughout its entire length, the whole army wheeling on Longstreet's left as a pivot, but constantly pressing our left to get possession of the road to Chattanooga.

The battle of the 19th was a series of brilliant charges and counter-charges, in favor of first one side and then the other. During the day our troops, at times broken and driven by the enemy, always promptly rallied and drove the rebels in disorder to·their lines by brilliant and effective dashes, moving to the attack with vigor and determination. In the main the results of the day were in our favor. Bragg had been forced to fight before he was in position, and had been foiled in his attempt to secure the roads, which on the evening of the 19th remained even more securely in our possession than before, fully protected on both flanks by our cavalry. As this was the object of the severe conflict of the 19th, that day's fighting was a success for our arms, both the Rossville and the Dry Valley roads being firmly held by our troops that night.

But the battle was not yet over. During the night Rosecrans assembled his corps commanders at his headquarters at the Widow Glenn's house, and after a consultation with them on the state and condition of their commands, gave orders for the disposition and movements of the troops for the next day. Tho divisions of Thomas's corps, with those which had reinforced him, to hold the road to Rossville, in the same position as then occupied by them in line of battle, with Brannan in reserve. McCook, with Sheridan's and Davis's divisions was to maintain his picket line until it was attacked and driven back. His left division—Davis's—was to close on Thomas, and to have his right refused covering the position at Widow Glenn's house. Crittenden was to hold two divisions, Wood's and Van Cleve's in reserve near where the line of McCook and Thomas joined to reinforce the front line as needed.

During the night Thomas received word from Baird on the extreme left, that the left of his division did not reach the road to Reed's Bridge, as had been anticipated. Thomas immediately requested that Negley's division be ordered to report to him to take position on Baird's left and rear, securing this flank from assault. At daylight Rosecrans, rid-

9*

ing the line, ordered Negley to join Thomas at once, and directed McCook to relieve Negley, who was on the front line. He also ordered McCook to adjust his right, as it was too far out on the crest, and to move Davis's division to the left, and close it up compactly. Crittenden was also directed to move his two divisions to the left and Palmer, on Thomas's line, was instructed to close up his front. On reaching the left Rosecrans was convinced that the first attack would be made on that flank, and returned at once to the right to hurry Negley over to Thomas. Arriving there he found that this division had not moved, and that McCook's troops were not ready to relieve him. Negley was then ordered to send his reserve brigade under John Beatty, and to follow with the other two when relieved from the front. Impatient at McCook's delay in relieving Negley, and anticipating momentarily the attack of the enemy on our left, Rosecrans ordered Crittenden to move Wood's division to the front, to fill the position occupied by Negley of which McCook was notified by Rosecrans in person. Rosecrans, when first at McCook's line, was greatly dissatisfied with McCook's position. He now called McCook's attention to the defects in his line, that it was too light, and that it was weakened by being too much strung out, and charged him to keep well closed up on the left at all hazards. Leaving McCook, Rosecrans then returned to Negley, and found to his surprise that the brigades in front had not yet been relieved and started to Thomas after his repeated orders, as Wood's division had only reached the position of Negley's reserve. Greatly irritated at this, Rosecrans gave peremptory orders and Wood's division was at once placed in front, closed up on the right of Brannan.

A heavy fog hung over the battlefield during the early

morning. Bragg, before daylight with his staff, took position immediately in the rear of the centre of his line, and
waited for Polk to begin the attack, waiting until after sunrise with increasing anxiety and disappointment. Bragg
then sent a staff officer to Polk to ascertain and report as to
the cause of the delay, with orders urging him to a prompt
and speedy attack. Polk was not found with his troops, and
the staff officer learning that he had spent the night on the
east side of Chickamauga Creek, rode over there and deliv-
ered his message. Bragg, impatient at the delay, proceeded
in person to his right wing and there found the troops wholly
unprepared for the movement. Messengers were sent for
Polk in hot haste, and on his reporting he was urged to a
prompt execution of his orders and to make a vigorous attack
at once.

During the night our troops threw up temporary breastworks of logs and rails. Behind these Thomas's command
awaited the attack. After Bragg had sent for Polk, he ordered a reconnoissance in his front on the extreme left of
our line, and crossing the main road to Chattanooga developed the fact that this position so greatly desired by him
was thus feebly held. At half past eight o'clock the rebel
attack opened on our left with skirmish firing. Pushing
forward with a heavy line of skirmishers to develop Baird's
position, with Breckinridge's division on the right and
Cleburne to his left, the rebels made, about an hour later,
a tremendous assault. Beatty's brigade of Negley's division
being now in line on Baird's left, received the full force of
the blow from the brigades of Adams and Stowall on the
right of Breckinridge's division, and was driven back in
disorder. Helm's brigade and Cleburne's division, advancing on the front of Baird, encountered the troops behind
their breastworks but were here met with a terrific fire of

canister and musketry, and their advance checked so thoroughly that it was not regarded as safe to send the two brigades now overlapping Baird to attack his rear. These brigades, however, had reached and crossed the La Fayette road. Beatty in falling back was relieved by several regiments of Johnson's division, which were placed in position by Baird. These regiments were joined by Vanderveer's brigade of Brannan's division and a portion of Stanley's brigade of Negley's division, which had been hurried to the left and thrown into action. These forces advancing checked the assault of the enemy and then drove him entirely from Baird's left and rear. Immediately following the attack on Baird, the enemy's assault, being taken up by the divisions on Breckinridge's left, pressed on and struck Johnson, then Palmer and Reynolds successively with equal fierceness, maintaining the attack for two hours, the enemy in repeated assaults bringing fresh troops constantly to the front was each time met and hurled back by the splendid fighting of our troops. Here Bragg exhausted his utmost energies to drive in the centre and to dislodge Thomas's right, and failing in this after repeated attacks fell back and occupied his old position.

McCook, early in the morning, on going to the front found that Wood's division, not having the battle-front of Negley's, did not occupy the entire of the rude barricade thrown up by Negley's troops, and that a portion of it on Wood's right was not occupied by any of our forces. Wood, on meeting McCook, explained to him that his left was well protected, resting on Brannan's right, and that his orders were to keep well closed up on Brannan. On the right of this gap to the right of Wood, McCook had posted Wilder with his brigade, who had been ordered to report to McCook and receive orders from him. McCook then directed Sheridan to bring

forward one of his brigades and occupy with it the space
between Wood's right and Wilder. As McCook started to
leave this portion of the line, he met Davis's division marching toward this vacant space. Davis was directed at once to
post one of his brigades in this part of the line, holding the
other in reserve. When the brigade Sheridan sent arrived,
McCook placed it in column as support to Davis on his
right and rear. At this time Thomas again reporting that
he needed reinforcements and the right as yet not being
actively engaged, Rosecrans concluded that Bragg's efforts
were still looking to the possession of the roads on our left,
and that he was massing his troops on his right, thus pro-
longing his line on that flank.   He then, at 10.10 A.M.,
ordered McCook to withdraw as far as possible the force
on the right and reinforce Thomas, stating that "the left
must be held at all hazards, even if the right is withdrawn
wholly back to the present left." Five minutes after the
receipt of this order McCook received one dated 10.30 A.M.,
directing him to send two brigades of Sheridan's division
at once with all possible dispatch to support Thomas and
to send the third brigade as soon as it could safely be
withdrawn.   McCook immediately sent Lytle's and Walworth's brigades of Sheridan's division on the double quick
to the support of Thomas.

The battle increasing in fury and volume was gradually
approaching the centre from the left, but Thomas still sus-
taining the brunt of the fight was compelled to send again
and again for reinforcements.   Beatty's and Stanley's brigades of Negley's division had been sent from the right.
Vanderveer with his brigade of Brannan's division also reported.   Barnes's brigade of Van Cleve's division had also
been ordered to Thomas, and now the two of Sheridan's division were under orders to proceed to the left.   About this

time Lieutenant-Colonel Von Schrader of Thomas's staff, who had been riding the lines, reported to Thomas that there were no troops on Reynolds's right, and a long gap existed between Reynolds and Wood; not aware that Brannan's division although not in front line was still in position, retired in the woods a short distance back, but not out of line. This information was at once sent by Thomas to Rosecrans, who immediately directed Wood to close up the line on Reynolds and support him, and sent word to Thomas that he would be supported if it required all of McCook's and Crittenden's corps to do so.

On receipt of this order—impossible for him to execute literally—Wood undertook to carry it out by withdrawing his entire command from the front, leaving a gap of two brigades in the line of battle, moving to the rear past Brannan's division, to where Reynolds was posted in line. Into the gap thus made by Wood, Davis attempted to throw sufficient force to hold that portion of the line thus vacated, by posting his reserve brigade.

Just at this time the order of battle on the enemy's line had reached Longstreet's command, who, seeing this gap, ordered his troops, formed in heavy columns, to advance. Into this gap there poured Stewart's, Hood's, Kershaw's, Johnson's, and Hindman's divisions, dashing impetuously forward, with Preston's large division as supports. Our right, disabled as it was, was speedily turned, the line of battle on the enemy's front extending nearly from Brannan's centre to a point far to the right of the Widow Glenn's house, and from the front of that portion of the line Sheridan's brigades had just been taken. McCook, to resist this fierce assault, had only Carlin's and Hey's brigades of Davis's division and Laibold's brigade of Sheridan's division. On finding the rebel troops pressing through the space vacated by Wood, McCook ordered Lytle and Walworth to change front and return to assist in repelling the enemy. Wilder and Harrison closed in on Sheridan with their commands as speedily as possible, and aided in resisting the enemy's attack. Davis, being overpowered by the immense numbers of the rebels, was compelled to retire to save his command. Laibold was in turn driven back in confusion, and the tide of battle then struck Lytle and Walworth, who contended nobly against the overpowering columns, and for a time checked the advance of the enemy on their immediate front. The rebel troops swarming in, turned the left of these brigades, and they were compelled to withdraw to escape being surrounded. At this point the gallant Lytle was killed. Here our army lost several thousand prisoners, forty guns, and a large number of wagon-trains.

Once more the right of the army was broken all to pieces, and five brigades of that wing cut off entirely from the rest of the command. In the meantime Bragg, determined to turn Thomas's left, and cut him off from Chattanooga, was making his preparations for a second assault on his right in heavier force. Bragg directed this movement in person. Extending his right by moving Breckinridge's division beyond its former position, he ordered Walker's corps in line on Breckinridge's left, and connected Cleburne's right on the left of Walker. Bragg's plan was for Breckinridge to advance, wheeling to the left, and thus envelop Thomas's exposed left flank, striking it in the rear. Breckinridge, advancing, was soon in position on the Chattanooga road, partly in rear of Thomas. But he was now detached from the main body of the rebel troops engaged in the movement, and, making a bold assault on the rear, he was here met by the three reserve brigades under Vandeveer, Willich, and Grose, and hurled in rout back on his original line. On

reaching it he there found the other troops that had taken
part in this charge, and that they had been repulsed at every
point by Baird's, Johnson's, and Palmer's divisions.

Beatty, just prior to the repulse of the enemy on the left
by Thomas, applied in person to the latter for at least a brigade to support him in the attack of the rebels he was then
expecting. Thomas sent an aid to hurry Sheridan up. This
officer returned soon afterward, and reported that he had
encountered a heavy force of the enemy in the rear of Reynolds's position, which was advancing slowly, with a strong
line of skirmishers thrown out; that he had met Harker,
who, with his brigade posted on a ridge a short distance to
Reynolds's rear, was watching this force approaching, and
was of the opinion that these troops were Sheridan's coming
to Thomas's assistance. Thomas then rode forward to determine the character of the advancing troops, which he
soon did, and ordered Harker to open fire upon them, resisting their farther advance. Thomas then selected the crest
of a commanding ridge, known as "Horseshoe Ridge," on
which to place Brannan's division in line, which—on Longstreet's sweeping McCook's lines from the right—had been
struck in the flank on the line of battle. On the spurs to
the rear he posted his artillery. On Thomas leaving Harker, the latter opening fire with his skirmishers, then posted
his right to connect with Brannan's division and portions of
Beatty's and Stanley's brigades of Negley's division, which
had been ordered over to this point from the extreme left.
Thomas then went to the crest of the hill on the front,
where he met Wood with his division, who confirmed him in
the opinion that the troops advancing were those of the
enemy. Thomas was not aware at that time of the extent
of the disaster to the right. He ordered Wood to place
his division in line with Brannan's, and to resist as long as

possible the advance of the enemy.   On receipt of his order
Wood immediately threw his troops on the left of Brannan,
and had barely time to form his lines when the enemy was
upon then in a heavy, fierce assault like those early in the
day.   This, however, was handsomely repulsed, the enemy
charging again and again with fresh troops, but their efforts
were successfully resisted.   These were Bushrod Johnson's
men, with Patton Anderson's brigade on his right, which
had been formed on the brow of the secondary spur of the
ridge, and at about two o'clock moved forward, making a
most determined assault on our forces.   Part of his line
reached the crest held by Wood, but was hurled back to its
original position under as determined a counter-charge.

Away off at Rossville Gordon Granger with three brigades
of the reserve corps was stationed.   He had heard during
the morning heavy firing from the front, in the direction of
Thomas, and as the firing increased in volume and intensity
on the right, he judged that the enemy were pressing him
hard.   He then determined, although contrary to his orders,
to gather what troops he could and go to Thomas's assistance.   Ordering Whittaker's and Mitchell's brigades under
the immediate command of Steedman to move to his front,
he placed Dan McCook's brigade at the Mc Afee church, to
cover the Ringgold road.   Thomas was at this time heavily
engaged on "Horseshoe Ridge," between the La Fayette
and the Dry Valley roads, about three miles and a half from
Granger's headquarters.   Pushing forward his troops rapidly,
Granger moved past a detachment of the enemy some two
miles out, and ordered Dan McCook forward to watch the
movements of the rebels, to keep open the La Fayette road,
and to cover the open fields on the right of the road intervening between this point and Thomas's position.   McCook
brought up his brigade as rapidly as possible, took and held

his position until late that night. Granger moving to the front arrived with his command about three o'clock, and reported at once to Thomas, who was then with this part of his command on "Horseshoe Ridge," where the enemy was pressing him hard on front and endeavoring to turn both of his flanks. To the right of this position was a ridge running east and west nearly at right angles with it. On this Bushrod Johnson had reformed his command, so severely repulsed by Wood. Longstreet now strengthened it with Hindman's division and that of Kershaw, all under the command of Hindman, who formed it in heavy columns for an attack on the right flank and rear of Thomas's troops. Kershaw's division had possession of a gorge in this ridge through which his division was moving in heavy masses, with the design of making an attack in the rear. This was the most critical hour of this eventful day. Granger promptly ordered Whittaker and Mitchell to hurl themselves against this threatening force. Steedman gallantly seizing the colors of a regiment, led his command to the charge. Rushing upon the enemy with loud cheers, after a terrific conflict, only of some twenty minutes' duration, with a hot infantry and artillery fire, Steedman drove them from their position and occupied both the ridge and gorge. Here the slaughter was frightful. The victory was won at a fearful cost, but the army was saved. After Hindman was driven back, Longstreet about four o'clock, determined to re-take the ridge. Asking Bragg for reinforcements from the right, he was informed by him "that they had been beaten back so badly that they could be of no service to me." Longstreet then ordered up his reserve division of fresh troops under Preston, four brigades strong, supported by Stewart's corps, and directed him to attack the troops on the ridge. Advancing with wild yells, confident of success, Preston dashed boldly up the hill, supported by Kershaw's troops, with Johnson's—part of Hindman's—and later on by those of Stewart's. But once more the enemy was driven back with frightful slaughter, and thus with charge and counter-charge at this part of the field, lasting for nearly two hours, the day wore away until darkness settled down, night find-ing Thomas's command—the troops under Brannan, Wood, and Granger—still holding the ridge. Some unauthorized person had ordered Thomas's ammunition train back to Chattanooga, and the supply with the troops on the field was running very low. The ammunition that Granger brought up with him was divided with the troops on that part of the field where his command fought—Brannan's and Wood's di-visions—but this supply was soon exhausted. The troops then gathered what could be found in the cartridge-boxes of the slain, friend and foe being alike examined. With the fresh charges of the enemy, the troops were ordered to use their bayonets and give the rebels cold steel, and in the final charges the enemy was met and repulsed in this way.

In the breaking up of our right, two brigades of Davis's division, one of Van Cleve's, and the entire of Sheridan's di-vision was caught in the whirl and sent adrift from the main command, the enemy in heavy columns completely controlling all access to Thomas and the remaining divisions with him, except by way of the Dry Valley road across the ridge and on to Rossville, thence back on the La Fayette road to Thomas's left. The troops of Sheridan's and Davis's divisions were rallied a short distance in the rear of the line, and taking the Dry Valley road, endeavored to unite with Thomas's command. They were placed in position on the Rossville road leading to the battlefield.

Rosecrans was watching on the rear of Davis's right for McCook to close up his line to the left when Longstreet's men poured through the gap left by Wood's withdrawal. Seeing that some disaster had occurred, Rosecrans hurried in person to the extreme right, to direct Sheridan's movements on the flank of the advancing rebels. But it was simply impossible to stem the tide and our men were driven back as the enemy advanced. Leaving orders for the troops to be rallied behind the ridges west of the Dry Valley road, Rosecrans endeavored with Garfield, his chief of staff, and a few others of his staff, to rejoin Thomas by passing to the rear of the broken portions of the right. Riding down in this direction, some two or three hundred yards under a heavy fire, he found the troops that had been driven from the right far over toward the left, and from all indications it appeared doubtful if the left had been able to maintain its position. He then concluded to go to Rossville and there determine whether to join Thomas on the battlefield or whether his duty called him to Chattanooga, to prepare for his broken army if his worst fears should be realized. On reaching Rossvillé it was determined that Garfield should go to the front to Thomas and report, and that Rosecrans should go to Chattanooga and make the necessary dispositions for the troops as they came back in rout.

Rosecrans on arriving at Chattanooga at once sent out orders to Thomas to assume command of all the troops at the front, and with Crittenden and McCook to take a strong position and assume a threatening attitude at Rossville, where ammunition and rations would be sent to meet him. Thomas determined to hold his position until nightfall, if possible, before withdrawing. He then distributed ammunition to the commands and ordered the division commanders to hold themselves in readiness to fall back as soon as ordered. Reynolds at half-past five was notified to commence the movement. Leaving the position he had held near Wood, Thomas started to meet Reynolds and show him the position he wanted him to occupy, forming the line covering the retirement of the troops on the La Fayette road on the left. Just before meeting Reynolds, Thomas was informed of a large rebel force in the woods ahead of him, drawn up in line and advancing toward him. This was Liddell's division on the extreme rebel right, under orders from Bragg, moving to a third attack on Thomas's left. Reynolds arriving at this time, Thomas ordered him to at once change the head of the column to the left, form line perpendicular to the road and to charge the enemy then in his immediate front, while the artillery opened a converging fire from the right and left. Turchin charged with his brigade upon the rebel force and drove them in complete rout far beyond Baird's left. Robinson's command—King's brigade—closely supporting Turchin, was posted on the road leading through the ridge to hold the ground, while the troops on our right and left retired.

Shortly after this Willich with his brigade was placed in position on commanding ground to the right of the ridge road, and assisted in covering the withdrawal of our troops. Turchin's brigade, having cleared the front, returned and took position on this road with Robinson and Willich.

Thomas having made this disposition of the troops, ordered Wood, Brannan, and Granger, to fall back from their positions. These troops were not molested, but Baird and Johnson as they were retiring were attacked. By the exercise of care and foresight they retired without confusion and with but slight loss. This attack was led by L. E. Polk's brigade, but the rebel lines had become so changed that they formed an acute angle and their troops were firing into each other in the dark. So quietly was the army withdrawn that it was not until after sunrise on the 21st that Bragg discovered that Thomas had retired. Having effected the withdrawal of his troops, General Thomas, accompanied by Granger and Garfield, proceeded to Rossville and placed the command in position at that place, ordering one brigade of Negley's division to hold the gap on the Ringgold road with the other two brigades posted on the top of the ridge to the right, joining on the brigades in the road, with Dan McCook's brigade in reserve. On the right of Negley Reynolds's division took position, reaching to the Dry Valley road, with Brannan's division as a reserve in rear of Reynolds's right. On the right of the Dry Valley road, extending to the west, McCook's corps was placed, his right extending to Chattanooga Creek. Upon the high ground to the left of the Ringgold road the entire of Crittenden's corps was placed. As a reserve Steedman's division of Granger's corps was posted on his left, while Baird's division was also in reserve and in support of the brigade of Negley's division holding the gap. Thrown out on the Ringgold road, a mile and a half in advance of the gap, Minty's brigade of cavalry held the road at that point during the night. Here the weary troops rested undisturbed the night after the heavy fighting and nothing was seen of the enemy until about nine o'clock of the 21st, when their advance appeared in heavy force of infantry and cavalry on Minty's front. Thomas, withdrawing Minty through the gap, posted his command on our left flank and directed him to throw out strong reconnoitring parties across the ridge, watching the enemy's movements on our left and front. There was no object in attempting to hold the position at Rossville Gap, beyond the gaining of a day to select the final position for the troops at Chattanooga on their retirement to that place,

the location of the lines, and the preparation for throwing up earthworks. This was all accomplished on the 21st
and preparations made to fall back. All wagons, ambulances, and surplus artillery-carriages were sent to the
rear before night and the troops were held in readiness
to move at a moment's notice. The orders to withdraw
reached Thomas about six o'clock P.M., and the movement
commenced about nine P.M.

Brannan's division was posted at six P.M. on the road
about half way from Rossville to Chattanooga, covering the
movement. Orders were sent by Thomas for each division
commander to throw out a strong skirmish line, to be withdrawn at daylight, concealing the movement to the rear.
This line was to be supported by Baird's division and
Minty's brigade of cavalry, which was to retire after the
skirmishers were withdrawn. During the night the movement was completed without the loss of a single man, and
at seven o'clock on the morning of the 22d, the Army of the
Cumberland, again united, was in position, holding the cov-
eted prize, still strong enough to prevent the enemy from attempting further to dispute our possession of the town.
The temporary works were strengthened from day to day
until all apprehension of an attack from the enemy on the
front was at an end.

Taking all the surroundings into consideration, the campaign from the western slopes of the Cumberland Mountains,
ending in the battle of Chickamauga, was the most brilliant
one of the war, made as it was, in the face of the strong
column of the enemy, whose business it was to watch every
movement, and as far as possible to retard and cripple the
advance. Rosecrans, with his masterly manœuvring, in every
instance deceived his opponent down to the withdrawal of
Bragg from Chattanooga. While recognizing the genius of

the military leader who could plan the campaign that was
made from the time of the crossing of the Cumberland
Mountains, Bragg regarded the obstacles to be overcome on
such a campaign so stupendous that he was incredulous that
any movement south of the Tennessee was contemplated by
the Federal leader.   Every preparation was made by Bragg
to meet the crossing of our army over the Tennessee north
of Chattanooga, watching all the fords with strong detachments of infantry and artillery, holding the main portion of
his command ready to move to the north at any moment, he
watched the movement of our troops through the Sequatchie
Valley and so on to the Tennessee.   Withdrawing his only
brigade that was south and west of Chattanooga on the advance of Crittenden, he threw open the gateway for Rosecrans's advance.   When the full scope of the movement
dawned upon him, Bragg abandoned Chattanooga and
gathered his troops wherever he could reach them from all
quarters to concentrate for the destruction of our army.
Bragg never intended his withdrawal from Chattanooga to
be permanent; all the indications he left behind him pointed
that way.   None of the bridges were destroyed as he retired.
All storehouses, hospitals, and other buildings used by his
army were left standing, and Rosecrans's mistake was in con-
struing Bragg's withdrawal to be a demoralized retreat and
in ordering his army to pursue before this was definitely
determined.   However, all advices that Rosecrans had were
to the effect that the rebels were in hasty flight and would
not stop anywhere north of Dalton, and that their probable
destination was Rome.   This information was sent to him
from Washington, and Bragg aided in confirming this belief
by sending numbers of his soldiers as " deserters " into the
Federal lines with the same report.

As late as the 11th, Halleck telegraphed Rosecrans that

after he occupied "the mountain passes to the west of Dalton" it would be determined what his future movements would be; and on the 13th, Halleck telegraphed Rosecrans that if Bragg should go to Alabama he must not be allowed to re-enter Middle Tennessee. On the 13th, Foster, at Fortress Monroe, telegraphed Halleck that trains of cars had been running day and night southward for the past thirty-six hours. On the following day Foster sent Halleck another despatch, that Longstreet's corps was reported going south, which Meade on the same day confirmed. Then Halleck sent urgent messages to Hurlbut and Burnside to move to Rosecrans's support. But it was too late. These commands were many days' marches away, and at that moment the Army of the Cumberland was engaged in the earlier movements of the life and death struggle it was peremptorily ordered by Halleck to encounter alone with its old enemy, under Bragg, heavily re-enforced, while large numbers of Federal troops which might have been within helping distance, had orders been given in due season, as asked for by Rosecrans, remained inactive.

It was not until McCook had received and partly executed his orders to occupy Alpine that the actual facts as to Bragg's movements were developed, and that he was concentrated at La Fayette, there waiting for reinforcements, but strong enough without them to crush the Army of the Cumberland in detail. Rosecrans, when aware of Bragg's movements, grasped the situation at once. Bending every energy to the concentration of his army before Bragg should strike, on the 12th he issued orders for McCook's immediate return, and despatched the same in all haste by courier. Hearing nothing definite from McCook, on the next day Rosecrans repeated his orders and duplicated them in the afternoon of that day. Still learning nothing positive as to

VII.—10

McCook's movements, on the 14th repeated orders were sent to him urging him to consummate his rearward movement with all possible haste. After a sleepless night, Rosecrans on the 15th left Chattanooga for the front, to hasten, if possible, McCook's movements. After another sleepless night, information was had from McCook as to the position of his command, and on the 17th the concentration of the army was effected in McLemore's Cove, five days after McCook's first orders were dated.

The delay attending McCook's movements was almost fatal to the Army of the Cumberland. Had Bragg received his promised reinforcements at the date he expected them, our army would in all probability have been completely annihilated in detail. McCook claims that his delay was only incident to the route he was compelled to take to join Thomas. This took him back over Lookout Mountain, to Valley Head, then down that valley, crossing the mountain again at Cooper's Gap, and then up and down Missionary Ridge into McLemore's Cove, a long, difficult road, nearly all of it over rough mountains. This route, McCook from the information received, regarded as the better one to take, as between it and the one on which he was ordered to move, which was a road on the mountain into the head of McLemore's Cove, through Dougherty's Gap.

The battle for Chattanooga would never have been fought at Chickamauga had not the safety of McCook's corps demanded it. Could the Army of the Cumberland have been withdrawn in safety to Chattanooga and there concentrated behind earthworks, as it was later, while Bragg doubtless would have made his attack there, yet the surroundings would have been far more favorable for our army, especially as the troops afterward sent might have reached Rosecrans in time to have defeated Bragg, as he was later at the battle of Missionary Ridge. But the reinforcements that were hurried from all points *after* the disaster, by the officials at Washington were not to benefit Rosecrans.

While the battle of the 19th was severe at times, and some slight advantages were gained by the enemy, still nothing had been accomplished to mark that day's fighting as a great, distinctive battle. The delay on the part of Negley in reporting as ordered, to Thomas on the left, placed that position in extreme peril, had Polk made his attack as ordered at daydawn on the 20th. Fortunately, Polk slept outside of his lines that night—not as he was accustomed to—and was not awakened as early as he would have been had he remained in camp. For this reason the attack, was not made until after Beatty's brigade had reached Baird's left. While this was too weak to successfully resist the attack, still with this command rallied after it was driven back and aided by the troops sent to its support, Thomas was able to repulse Breckinridge's first charge of the morning. The delay from six o'clock until after nine was of great service to the Army of the Cumberland. Negley's delay in reporting at an early hour with his entire division was owing to Wood's failure to relieve him. Sheridan had at an earlier hour been ordered to Negley's position on his front, but Thomas representing the urgency of the movement, Crittenden was ordered to send Wood, who was only a short distance from Negley. Wood, on receiving his orders to relieve Negley, simply moved forward and occupied the position that had been vacated by Negley's reserve brigade, already started for Thomas's left. On Rosecrans's return from the extreme right, he found that Negley had not yet reported to Thomas, although more than an hour had elasped since he was so ordered, and then discovered that Wood had failed to relieve him on the front. Repeating his orders in such plain

English that there could be no further misapprehension of them, Rosecrans moved Wood's division into position, relieved Negley at once, and started him in all haste to Thomas. Negley did not reach the left until after ten o'clock. Rosecrans, impatient at the delay that occurred in the execution of this order, expressed himself very forcibly to Wood, much to the dissatisfaction of the latter. After seeing Negley at last *en route* to Thomas, Rosecrans then went to the right and was watching the movements of the troops when the word reached him of the supposed gap to the right of Reynolds, on the left of Wood. Rosecrans's plan of battle being to keep his line well closed up on the left, he directed an aid to send Wood an order to close up on Reynolds, which he did as follows.

HEADQUARTERS OF THE ARMY OF THE CUMBERLAND.
Brigadier-General Wood, Commanding Division:
  The General Commanding directs that you close up on Reynolds as fast as possible, and support him,
                              Respectfully, etc.,
                                    FRANK S. BOND,
                                      Major and Aid-de-Camp.

This order was written by an officer who had no military experience prior to the war, and, as the order shows on its face, embraced much more than the General Commanding intended it should. The orderly who carried this order to Wood reported on his return that "General Wood on receipt of the order remarked that he 'was glad the order was in writing, as it was a good thing to have for future reference.' That he carefully took out his note-book, safely deposited the order in it, and then proceeded to execute it." Wood's official report contains the order written out in full. He says that it was eleven o'clock when it reached him.

"General McCook was with me when I received it. I informed him that I would immediately carry it into execution, and suggested to him that he should close up his command rapidly on my right, to prevent the occurrence of a gap in the line. He said he would do so, and immediately rode away."

McCook says, in reference to the movement of Sheridan to the aid of Thomas, which he had just ordered, "Simultaneously with this movement, and much to my surprise, Wood's division left the position it had in line of battle on Davis's left, marching by the left flank, leaving a wide gap in the line." Wood also says in his official report that when he started to execute the order he met Thomas, and told him of his order. He says, "I exhibited my order to him, and asked him whether he would take the responsibility of changing it. He replied he would, and I then informed him that I would move my command to the support of General Baird." The first mention Thomas makes in his official report of seeing Wood, is when in riding "toward the crest of the hill," coming from the left, he met Wood on the way, and directed him to take position on Brannan's right. Later, he says, "About the time that Wood took up his position, General Gordon Granger appeared," etc. This was over three hours after what General Wood styles "the disastrous event of the right" occurred. It seems strange, if Wood was properly executing an order from the Commanding General, that he should try so hard to shield his action by the authority of these two corps commanders, especially when he was under the direct command of neither of them.

General Wood was a graduate of West Point, had been in the army all his life, and knew the full meaning of all technical terms used to describe military movements. The order bore on its face a direction to him to make a movement with his front in line of battle, and at the same time to occupy a position in the rear of the division, on which he was ordered to join his left in line on the immediate battle-front. He knew he could not execute the order literally as given, and from the wording of it must have known that there was some mistake about it. Instead of sending a short distance to the rear, or going himself to Rosecrans and finding out just what was meant by the order, he chose to give it a meaning that it was never intended to convey, and moved to the rear from the front of battle, when he knew, as he says in his report, " although I had not been seriously engaged at any time during the morning, I was well satisfied the enemy was in considerable force in my immediate front." Wood says in his official report, " Reynolds's division was posted on the left of Brannan's division, which in turn was on the left of the position I was just quitting ; I had consequently to pass my command in the rear of Brannan's division to close up on and go into the support of Reynolds." If " Reynolds's, division was posted on the left of Brannan's division," then there was no gap, and no place for Wood to place his division as ordered, and he knew it. He could support Reynolds, but to do this he was compelled to disobey the first part of his order, which *in its spirit and intent was to keep him on the line of battle*, simply moving his division to the left. This space by his own official report he shows was occupied by Brannan's division, and with this knowledge he undertook to execute an order that directed him to make an impossible movement sooner than ask an explanation of it from his commanding officer. No wonder he wanted to keep his order safe where he could produce it if occasion required. Wood, irritated at the reprimand of Rosecrans earlier in the day, intent on maintaining his dignity, chose rather to undertake to carry out an order in the execution of which he felt safe, so long as he had it in writing and where he could produce it if occasion demanded it, than to suspend its execution long enough to ride a short distance to the rear, and find out just what the order meant ; *and to this extent he is responsible* for the great disaster which swept the right wing of the Army of the Cumberland from the field of battle on the 20th.   That Wood must have known that there was a mistake in regard to the order is plain, from the fact that he himself says that his troops had not been seriously engaged that morning.   It was hardly possible that Reynolds's division, which was only a division front from his, could be so hardly pressed as to need supports, and that his division should "not be seriously engaged."   In fact, when Wood undertook to carry out this order, he says he met Thomas and was told by him that Reynolds did not need supports, and that he, Wood, "had better move to the support of General Baird, posted on the extreme left, who needed assistance," showing that the conflict had as yet not reached down the line to Reynolds.   The spirit in which General Wood fought the battle of Chickamauga is shown by the following extract from his official report, where, in speaking of Garfield's arrival on the battlefield later in the afternoon of the 20th, he says, "After the disastrous event of the right, General Garfield made his way back to the battlefield, showing thereby that the road was open to all who might choose to follow it where duty called." After Wood reported to Thomas there was no more splendid fighting done on that field of terrific conflict on the 20th than was done by Thomas J. Wood and his division.   To the last he aided Thomas in holding Horseshoe Ridge, and was one of the last divisions to retire.

In the tide that swept down the Dry Valley road, Rose-crans was caught with the members of his staff. He breasted this for a while, and endeavored to join his left and cen-tre under Thomas by a direct route. After riding along a short distance, under the heavy fire of the rebels with both artillery and musketry, he discovered that that road was effectually closed by the enemy in strong force. He then started over the ridge to the Dry Valley road, and made his way as rapidly as possible through the swarming masses of broken troops from the right of the battlefield to Rossville, with the intention of joining Thomas from that place down the La Fayette road if the left and centre were not also in rout, and on the road to Chattanooga. On reaching Rossville, Rosecrans and Garfield halted in the midst of the driving masses of teamsters, stragglers, and fugitives from Thomas's command, all striving in hot haste to be among the first to reach Chattanooga. Making in-quiry of these men as to the condition of affairs at the front, they were informed "that the entire army was de-feated, and in retreat to Chattanooga." "That Rosecrans and Thomas were both killed, and that McCook and Crit-tenden were prisoners." Asking a small detachment of troops the command they belonged to, Rosecrans was in-formed Negley's division. He then asked as to the where-abouts of Negley. He was informed that he was a short distance from Rossville, though some distance from the battlefield, "rallying stragglers," and that the entire divi-sion "was knocked all to pieces." Knowing that one of the last orders he had given on the battlefield was for Negley's division to report to Thomas to take position on his extreme left, Rosecrans was satisfied that if these soldiers reported truly the left and centre were routed and that the whole army as a broken mass would be back in

Chattanooga very shortly. At this time there was a lull in the firing at the front. Dismounting from their horses, Rosecrans and Garfield placing their ears to the ground, endeavored to determine from the sound as it reached them the truth of the reported rout. Hearing no artillery firing, and detecting only what appeared to be a scattering fire of musketry, the conclusion was forced on Rosecrans that his army was entirely broken. His information prior to the battle led him to believe that the rebels outnumbered him two to one, and if this proved true, the disaster in part could be accounted for. Conferring with Garfield as to what was the best thing to be done under the circumstances, Garfield told him that if these reports were true that then his, Rosecrans's, place was in Chattanooga, where he could receive and reorganize, if possible, his army on its reaching that place. That he, of all persons, had more influence with the army, and if it was broken that his duty was to go to that place and make such disposition of the troops as might possibly save the army from complete destruction. That he, Garfield, would ride to the front, try and find Thomas, if alive, and would report immediately to Rosecrans at Chattanooga as to the condition of affairs at the front. Unfortunately, this plan was carried out. The reverse of this should have been done. Rosecrans should at once have gone to the front, and by his presence there aided, as he did at Stone's River, more than any other thing to retrieve the fortunes of the day, and pluck victory from disaster. Had Rosecrans gone to the front, and discovered from a personal observation the true condition of affairs, and the spirit and *morale* of the troops there, the chances are that he never would have ordered their retirement to Rossville the night of the 20th. That was the turning-point, and his hour had arrived.

10*

On reaching Chattanooga, General Rosecrans rode up to Department Headquarters there, and was helped from his horse into the house. He had the appearance of one broken in spirit, and as if he were bearing up as best he could under terrible blow, the full force and effect of which he himself did not at that time clearly perceive and only partly felt. This was about four o'clock in the afternoon. He had been in the saddle all day from before daylight, with nothing to eat since then. Rarely has mortal man been called on to undergo the terrible mental strain that had been on him during the week just past, of which for two nights in succession his anxiety for McCook was so great as to prevent his sleeping. During the past week the peril of his army had weighed on him to the extent that his nervous system was stretched to its utmost tension. When he saw the rout of his right, supposing that it extended to his entire army, the blow was so strong that it staggered him. A short time after Rosecrans arrived, McCook and Crittenden, also caught in the drift from the right, reached headquarters. While seated in the adjutant-general's office comparing notes with each other as to the events of the day, Rosecrans received a despatch from Garfield, who had reached the front. Hastily reading it over he exclaimed, "Thank God!" and read the despatch aloud. In it Garfield announced his safe arrival at the front, that he was then with Thomas, who had seven divisions intact with a number of detachments, that Thomas had just repulsed a heavy assault of the rebels, and felt confident that he could successfully resist all attacks against his position. Waving this over his head Rosecrans said, "This is good enough, the day isn't lost yet." Turning to McCook and Crittenden he said, "Gentlemen, this is no place for you. Go at once to your commands at the front." He then directed Wagner, in command of the post, to take his entire brigade, stop the stragglers and all others from the front on the edge of the town, and ordered rations and ammunition for his troops to be at once sent out to meet them at Rossville.

During the heavy fighting of the 20th, Thomas was the only general officer on the field of rank above a division commander. Learning some time later in the day of the disaster on our right, he gathered his troops together from all parts of the field to the position selected by himself after the break on the right. Here in a more marked degree even than at Stone's River, he displayed his great staying qualities. Posting his troops on the lines he designated, he, so to speak, placed himself with his back against a rock and refused to be driven from the field. Here he stayed, despite the fierce and prolonged assaults of the enemy, repulsing every attack. And when the sun went down he was still there. Well was he called the "Rock of Chickamauga,'' and trebly well for the army of the Cumberland that George H. Thomas was in command of the left at that battle. On the 20th, when the hour of supreme trial came and he was left on the field with less than one half of the strength of the army that the day before had been barely able to hold its own against the rebel assaults, he formed his 25,000 troops on "Horseshoe Ridge," and successfully resisted for nearly six long hours the repeated attacks of that same rebel army, largely reinforced until it numbered twice his command, when it was flushed with victory and determined on his utter destruction. There is nothing finer in history than Thomas at Chickamauga.

All things considered, the battle of Chickamauga for the forces engaged was the hardest fought and the bloodiest battle of the Rebellion. Hindman, who fought our right at Horseshoe Ridge, says in his official report that he had "never known Federal troops to fight so well," and that he "never saw Confederate soldiers fight better." The largest number of troops Rosecrans had of all arms on the field during the two days' fighting was 55,000 effective men. While the return of the Army of the Cumberland for September 20, 1863, shows 67,548 "present for duty equipped," still, taking out the troops guarding important points within the Department, the actual force was reduced to the figures just given. Of Gordon Granger's nine brigades, only two were on the battlefield. Wagner, of Wood's division, was in Chattanooga, and Dan McCook was holding Rossville. Post's brigade was guarding the wagon trains and was not in the action. Rosecrans losses aggregated killed, 1,687; wounded, 9,394; missing, 5,255. Total loss, 16,336. Bragg, during the battle, when his entire five corps were engaged, had about 70,000 effective troops in line. Among Bragg's troops were large numbers of prisoners of war captured at Vicksburg and Port Hudson, who had been falsely declared by the rebel authorities as exchanged and released from their parole, and in violation of the cartel were again placed in battle. His losses, in part estimated, were 2,673 killed, 16,274 wounded, and 2,003 missing, a total of 20,950. A full report of the rebel losses was never made.

To the enemy the results of the engagement proved a victory barren of any lasting benefits, and produced no adequate results to the immense drain on the resources of his army. In a number of places Bragg's official report shows that his army was so crippled that he was not able to strengthen one portion of his line, when needed, with troops from another part of the field, and after the conflict was over his army was so cut up that it was impossible for him to follow up his apparent success and secure possession of the objective point of the campaign—Chattanooga. This great gateway of the mountains remaining in possession of the Army of the Cumberland, after Bragg had paid the heavy price he did at Chickamauga, proves that his battle was a victory only in name, and a careful examination of the results and their cost will show how exceedingly small it was to the enemy.

CHAPTER XIII.

THE SIEGE OF CHATTANOOGA.

On taking position at Chattanooga, after the battle, the Army of the Cumberland, between the rebel troops in front and the forces of Nature in the rear, was practically in a state of siege. The lines around the town were held by our troops behind extensive rifle-pits, strengthened with heavy earthworks covering all approaches on the front. Bragg's army moved up immediately, and invested our lines, throwing up rifle-pits within a short distance of those of our army. To the rear of these Bragg threw up two other lines of intrenchments and on the right of his command erected a more permanent line of earthworks on the crest of Missionary Ridge, massing however, the bulk of his troops in Chattanooga Valley on our immediate front. As our army retired within its works at Chattanooga, the troops holding the road over Lookout Mountain were withdrawn, and this point was immediately occupied by the enemy and strengthened by extensive works, Bragg sending Longstreet's corps into Lookout Valley to occupy the extreme left of the besieging line, and to cut off all communication with Bridgeport, on the south bank of the Tennessee River. The lines were now fully occupied from the river on the north to the bank south of the town, and the rebel army in force on our front. To the rear the only road that was open was over Walling's Ridge, through Sequatchie Valley, down to Bridgeport, a distance of sixty miles ; the short road on the north side down to Bridgeport being closed by the rebel batteries and sharpshooters, while their troops holding the road to the south of the river compelled all supplies of every kind to be hauled over these sixty miles of road. To thus supply the army during good weather was a very great undertaking, even with the teams of the various commands in good condition, but with the rainy season that soon set in, and the incessant hauling wearing out the mules, the daily rations for the army were constantly growing less and less. On October 1st, Wheeler crossing the Tennessee with Martin's and Wharton's divisions of cavalry moved up the Sequatchie Valley upon our line of supplies at Anderson cross-roads. Here he captured a large number of trains loaded with rations for the front, burned over three hundred wagons, and killed a large number of animals. Colonel E. M. McCook with his cavalry division, moving rapidly from Bridgeport, overtook Wheeler on the 2d, and drove him with great loss in a sabre charge from the trains, recapturing some eight hundred mules. After this Wheeler was driven from Shelbyville on the 6th by Mitchell's cavalry, and on the 8th from Farmington by Crook, and from here he re-crossed the Tennessee with a small portion of his command, the rest having been killed or captured. This loss in wagons, with the roads becoming almost impassable by reason of the heavy rains and the growing weakness of the animals, lessened daily the amount of supplies brought into the town, so that our troops were suffering for food and were in danger of being starved out of Chattanooga. This was what Bragg was quietly waiting for. To supply an army some forty thousand strong, by wagon transportation over rough mountain roads a distance of sixty miles, Bragg knew was an impossibility, and that unless other lines were opened up, the evacuation of the place was only a question of time, and he could then walk in and take undisturbed possession. As the forage became reduced, the artillery horses, for which there was no immediate need, had their rations cut off, and they died in large numbers, starved to death. The supplies grew so small that parts of crackers and corn dropped in handling the packages were eagerly seized and eaten to stay the demands of hunger, and still the pressure was growing daily, and no one knew how it would ultimately end. However, not for an instant was the idea entertained of abandoning the town, to say nothing of the extreme hazard of attempting that, in the face of the strong force of the enemy on our front. The Army of the Cumberland had won Chattanooga and there they proposed remaining.

Immediately after the battle of Chickamauga, the authorities at Washington sent hurried orders to Burnside, Hurlbut and Sherman to move forward without delay to Rosecrans's assistance, and on September 24th the latter was informed that " Hooker, with some fifteen thousand men," was *en route* from the East as fast as rails could take him, and that he would be in Nashville in about seven days. While reinforcements were the thing needed before the battle, now the pressing demand of the hour was the opening of the line of communication to the rear, over which adequate supplies could be forwarded to the troops at the front. To add to the number of men there simply increased the difficulties of the situation.

On the arrival of Hooker with the Eleventh and Twelfth Army Corps at Nashville, Rosecrans directed him to take position on the line of the Chattanooga Railroad, securing that road from the attacks of the rebel cavalry while supplies were being accumulated at Stevenson awaiting the opening of communication with the army at Chattanooga.

Without driving back the entire of Bragg's army in Lookout and Chattanooga Valleys, it was impossible to use the railroad from Bridgeport east in bringing up supplies. The wagon-trains could no longer be depended on, and, under the spur of necessity, Rosecrans was preparing a plan to utilize the river with boats. A new one had been built at Bridgeport and another captured at Chattanooga had been repaired. By thus using the river he could secure his supplies over a wagon-road of only eight miles from Kelley's Ferry, *via* Brown's Ferry. The course of the Tennessee River at Chattanooga is due west; after passing the town it flows south to the foot of Lookout Mountain, from which point it then sweeps, after a short curve to the northwest, due north, forming here what is known as "Moccasin Point." Crossing the river at the town, a road leads southwest across this point on to the other side, where the river, as it sweeps north, is reached at Brown's Ferry. Shortly after passing Brown's Ferry, the river again makes a sharp bend to the south, forming another point of land running northwardly. Across this point on the east bank, as the river passes south, is Kelley's Ferry. At the extreme angle of this bend the river rushes through the mountains, which here crowd down closely, forming a narrow channel through which the waters rush headlong. This chasm is known as the "Suck." The velocity of the water is so great that steamers in high water cannot stem the current at this point, which necessitated the landing of supplies at Kelley's Ferry, and then hauling them over land across the bridge at Brown's Ferry to Chattanooga.

Immediately after the battle, under orders from the War Department, the Twentieth and Twenty-first Army Corps were consolidated and designated the Fourth Army Corps and Gordon Granger was placed in command. McCook and

Crittenden were relieved from the command of these corps, and ordered North to await a "Court of Inquiry," "upon their conduct on September 19th and 20th."

By War Department order of October 16th, the Departments of the Ohio, the Cumberland, and the Tennessee were constituted "The Military Division of the Mississippi," under the command of Grant. By the same order Rosecrans was relieved of the command of the Department and Army of the Cumberland, and Thomas was assigned to that command. Halleck, in his report of operations for the year 1863, says this change was made on the recommendation of General Grant. These orders were promulgated on the 19th.

On Rosecrans's return from a visit to Brown's Ferry and Williams's Island on the 19th, where he had been with William F. Smith, his chief engineer, making his plans for bringing supplies to that point, he found the order awaiting him relieving him of his command. Quietly .making his preparations for his departure that night over the mountains to Stevenson, he wrote out his farewell order, to be printed and issued the next day, and, without even bidding his staff good-bye, placed Thomas in command and started for his home in Cincinnati. Rosecrans, in the summer of 1862, was under Grant at Iuka and Corinth. Here some hasty criticism made by him brought him into collision with Grant, which now bore fruit.

When it was known that Rosecrans had been relieved, and that he had left the army for the north, there was universal regret that the troops that had loved and trusted him should no longer follow his skilful leadership. Every soldier in his army felt that he had a personal friend in "Old Rosy." His troops never for a moment faltered in their devotion to him or confidence in him. They felt that he had been made the victim of a foolish interpretation of an order that brought ruin and disaster upon his army, for which he was not responsible, but for which he was made to suffer.

General Rosecrans, to his subordinates, was one of the most genial of men. Kind and good-natured, he at times failed to act as decisively as occasion required, deterred by the fact that, should he do so, some of his subordinates would suffer. His restless activity led him to give attention to details that he should have been entirely relieved of by his subordinates. But no amount of work daunted him. He lived almost without rest and sleep, and would wear out two sets of staff officers nightly, and then, if occasion required it, be up and out before daylight. To his superiors he unfortunately allowed his high spirit to get the better of his judgment, and many times when he was in the right he ruined his position by his hasty temper. His fame, despite his enemies—and no general in the field had stronger nor more unscrupulous ones—as the greatest strategist of the war, is permanently fixed in history. What it might have been had he not been hampered, annoyed, and insulted as no other commanding general was at any time by both the Secretary of War and the General-in-Chief, is merely problematical. Personally, he regarded all this as mere "incidents of the service," and strove to the best of his ability to do his whole duty to his country. His combination with Thomas—Rosecrans to plan brilliant campaigns, with Thomas's great abilities to aid him in carrying them out—made the Army of the Cumberland the great aggressive force moving on the centre, gaining territory after each campaign. But it was as well for Rosecrans and the service that he was relieved when he was, with the combination of the armies under Grant. He had faithfully performed his duty up to this time, but now the surroundings were so changed that both for his sake and the good of the service the change was a fitting one to be made. Rosecrans could never again serve as a subordinate, and as the change was determined on, when Grant arrived it was as well for Rosecrans to retire.

When Anderson in 1861 applied for George H. Thomas to be one of the brigadier-generals to accompany him to Kentucky, to help him in the task he was set to accomplish there, Mr. Lincoln told him he was afraid to give the order for Thomas, as he was a Southerner, and from Virginia. Anderson and Sherman, who were present, both responded in the strongest terms, vouching for Thomas's earnest patriotism and deep devotion to the Union, and the order was given. And now it bore full fruit. The quiet, patient soldier, who from his first day's service in Kentucky had never swerved a line from the strict performance of his duty to his Government, according to his oath, without reference to self, had now met his reward. His fame had steadily grown and rounded from the time he gained the first Federal victory in the West, at Mill Springs, up to the battle of Chickamauga, where he saved the Army of the Cumberland to the nation. He had always been the main stay of that army, holding the command of the centre—either nominally or actually the second in command. Upon his judgment and military skill every commander of that army depended, and no movement was made without his approbation. Yet so modest was he that his face would color with blushes when his troops cheered him, which they did at every opportunity; and so diffident, that, prior to the battle of Chickamauga, he doubted his ability to handle large bodies of troops upon the battlefield, and for this reason refused to accept the command of that army, just prior to Perryville, when tendered him. His kind consideration for the feelings of others was one of his marked characteristics. With a pure mind and large heart, his noble soul made him one of the greatest of Nature's noblemen—a true gentleman. The experience of Chickamauga ripened his powers and developed him to his full height. As the General who won the first victory in the West, who saved an army by his skill and valor, and who was the only General of the war on either side able to crush an army on the battlefield, George H. Thomas, "the true soldier, the prudent and undaunted commander, the modest and incorruptible patriot," stands as the model American soldier, the grandest figure of the War of the Rebellion.

One of Grant's first acts on taking command was to telegraph Thomas to hold Chattanooga at all hazards. The commander who had seen his troops on less than half rations for nearly a month, with steadily approaching signs of starvation, hardly needed an intimation that what had been gained by the sacrifice on Chickamauga's field was not to be yielded up without a struggle. Thomas replied "We will hold the town till we starve." On the 24th, Grant, in company with Thomas and W. F. Smith, made a personal inspection across the river of the situation, with reference to carrying out the plan of Rosecrans for the opening of the road by Brown's Ferry, and, approving of it, Thomas was directed to proceed to execute it. This plan required the greatest secrecy of movement, otherwise Longstreet's entire command would resist the landing, and contemplated the co-operation of Hooker's moving up from Bridgeport, holding the road to Kelley's Ferry. The latter was to meet a force sent from the town down the river in pontoons under cover of night, which was to seize the landing on the left bank of the river, driving back the rebel pickets and fortifying their position, and then swinging the bridge across the river. Thomas says in his official report of the battle of Wauhatchie, that "preliminary steps had already been taken to execute this vitally important movement before the command of the Department devolved on me." Thomas on the 23d ordered Hooker to concentrate the Eleventh Corps, and Geary's division of the Twelfth Corps at Bridgeport and sent him instructions as to his movements, and directed him to advance as soon as possible, co-operating with the force from Chattanooga. Hooker was also ordered to move into Lookout Valley, and to protect the bridge when laid from any attack by Longstreet in that direction. Thomas also sent two brigades under Palmer to co-operate with Hooker. Palmer moved across the river to Brown's Ferry, and then took the road through Whitesides to Rankin's Ferry, establishing himself securely at these points, protecting the river communication from attack from the south. Thomas placed W. F. Smith in charge of the expedition, and detached Turchin's and Hazen's brigades, with three batteries under Major John Mendenhall. Smith was directed to organize a picked force, armed from these brigades, to be divided into fifty squads of twenty-four men each, under the command of an officer, who were to float down the river in pontoons that night—a distance by the bends of the river of some nine miles. The boats were placed under the charge of Colonel T. R. Stanley of the Eighteenth Ohio, the bridge to be placed in position under direction of Captain P. V. Fox, First Michigan Engineers. The troops under Hazen were to take the gorge and hills to the left, and Turchin was to extend from the gorge down the river. Turchin in command of the remainder of the troops marched across Moccasin Point to the ferry, where they were to cross in the same boats, supporting the troops already landed, when the position was to be strongly fortified and held by them until the arrival of Hooker.

At midnight the troops who were to take part in the ex-

pedition were marched to the river and placed in the boats
manned by crews with oars, and on two flat boats. The force
that marched under Turchin moved out under cover of dense
woods over the point to the ferry, where they remained in
readiness to cover the landing of the troops coming down
the river. The artillery accompanied this part of the command and remained under cover.

At 3 o'clock A.M. of the 27th, the boats moved out into the
stream under cover of a slight fog. On arriving at a point
some two miles below the town, these troops reached the
rebel picket line posted on the left bank of the river. The
boats passed on unobserved by keeping close to the right
hand shore until just at the landing, when the troops in the
first boat were greeted with a volley from the rebel pickets,
a station being at this landing. In perfect order, as previously planned, the troops hastily disembarked, moved forward, occupying the crest of the hill immediately in front
and commenced the work of intrenching. Before this was
completed the enemy, heavily reinforced, just beyond this
crest, moved forward to drive Hazen back. Here a stubborn
little fight was had, the rebels making a gallant charge with
partial success on the right of Hazen, when they were met
with the remainder of the brigade under Colonel Langdon,
who charged at once on their lines and after a short engagement drove them from the hill into the valley beyond.
Turchin's brigade having crossed the river was placed in
position on Hazen's right, when the enemy moved from the
front up the valley. The rebel force here was a thousand
infantry, three pieces of artillery, and a squadron of cavalry.

As soon as the last of the troops were over, work on the
bridge was commenced and finished at a little after four
o'clock in the afternoon. For an hour or so in the morning
the work progressed under an artillery fire from the rebel

batteries on Lookout Mountain. Our losses were six killed, twenty-three wounded, and nine missing. The rebels lost six men captured and six of their dead were buried by our men. Our forces captured twenty beeves, six pontoons and some two thousand bushels of corn. The bridge was completed and the position held until the 28th, when Hooker's command arrived. No attempt was made by Bragg to dislodge this force or to destroy the bridge. Hooker moved on the road by the base of Raccoon Mountain into Lookout Valley, driving the rebel pickets before him, and occupied the roads to Kelley's and Brown's Ferries through the valley. Later in the afternoon of the 28th, as Hooker's troops pushed down the valley, Howard's corps in the advance was met with a sharp volley of musketry from a wooded ridge near the Wills Valley Railroad. Two brigades of Howard's command were deployed, and advancing, drove the rebels from their cover with the loss of a few of our men. As the enemy retreated they burned the railroad bridge over Lookout Creek. Hooker then went into camp with Howard's corps at six o'clock in the afternoon about a mile up the valley from Brown's Ferry. Here he learned of the movement to this place and of the building of the bridge.

With the object of holding the road to Kelley's Ferry, Geary's division was ordered to encamp near Wauhatchie, some three miles up the valley from Howard's position. This created two camps—the latter holding the Brown Ferry road—each camp separate and picketed by its own command, as the numbers of the troops would not admit of communication being kept up between them or of their forming one line.

About midnight a regiment that had been ordered by Howard to hold the Chattanooga road across Lookout Creek, had a slight skirmish with the advance of the enemy. This was a portion of Longstreet's corps getting into position for a night attack on the two encampments. Dividing his command into two detachments, Longstreet, about an hour later, with his strong one on his left, assaulted Geary's camp with a fierce attack, driving in his pickets and then charging on the main command. Geary immediately formed his men in line, and for three hours with heavy fighting maintained his position; although enveloped on three sides by the enemy, repelling every attack, and finally charged on the rebels and drove·them from beyond his front. The enemy here attacked in greatly superior numbers, and were only defeated by the skill and coolness·of Geary, aided by the bravery of his troops. As the sound of the heavy fire which the enemy opened on Geary rolled down the valley, Hooker ordered Howard to double-quick his nearest division, Schurz's, to Geary's assistance. The division was started at once, but before it had proceeded far it encountered the other detachment of Longstreet's command, which opened on our troops with a volley of musketry. Hooker now determined that he had two fights on his hands. At once detaching Tyndale's brigade, Howard charged the rebel lines on the hill to the left with it, pushing on the other brigade to Geary. By this time Steinwehr's division of Howard's corps had arrived on the ground, and it was then discovered that the rebels were trying to surround Howard's camp and that they occupied a hill to the rear of Tyndale's brigade. Hooker ordered Colonel Orland Smith with his brigade to charge this hill, which he did up the steep side, almost inaccessible by daylight, reached the rebel intrenchments under a heavy fire and drove the troops with the bayonet, after a severe engagement, in rout from the hill and capturing a number of prisoners. Here General Green and Colonel Underwood were severely wounded. Tyndale also pressing forward occupied the rebel line in his front and drove their forces beyond his lines. The attack on Howard was intended to hold that command from reinforcing Geary until he was routed, and then in turn Howard was to be driven from the field.

During the engagement the enemy opened with artillery fire in the valley, aided by that from the batteries on Lookout Mountain, sending the shells crashing among our troops. Their forces in the valley were repulsed in every charge and our troops occupied the field at all points. Our losses in the attack were 76 killed, 339 wounded, and 22 missing, making a total of 437. The rebel loss is unknown. Geary buried 153 of the enemy on his front alone. One hundred prisoners were captured, with a large number of small arms. Thomas congratulated Hooker's troops for the gallant repulse given to their old enemy, Longstreet, and adds : " The bayonet charge of Howard's troops, made up the side of a steep and difficult hill over two hundred feet high, completely routing the enemy from his barricades on its top, and the repulse by Geary of greatly superior numbers who attempted to surprise him, will rank among the most distinguished feats of arms of this war." Reinforcements were sent Hooker by Thomas from Chattanooga of two brigades under Whittaker and John G. Mitchell, but the fighting was over before they reached the valley.

Work was now pushed rapidly forward on the road from Brown's to Kelley s Ferry, and this being successfully accomplished by the 1st of November, the forces of Nature were overcome and the siege of Chattanooga was at an end as to them. It now remained to raise it on the front, driving Bragg from his strongholds, Lookout Mountain, Chattanooga Valley, and Missionary Ridge.

CHAPTER XIV

CHATTANOOGA, LOOKOUT MOUNTAIN, AND MISSIONARY RIDGE BATTLES.

THESE three detached actions, fought by different portions of our troops, were parts of a series of operations for securing our front and driving the enemy from his position, and are known properly as the Battle of Chattanooga. Grant, late in October, ordered Sherman with the Fifteenth Army Corps to press forward to the Tennessee River, cross at Bridgeport and push rapidly on to Chattanooga. Early in November, learning that Bragg had weakened his forces on our front by sending Longstreet's command into East Tennessee to attack Burnside, Grant was very desirous of making an attack at once on the rebel forces on Lookout and Missionary Ridge, but examining the strong position occupied by Bragg at these points and the length of his lines, Grant became convinced that to successfully operate against the enemy it was necessary to wait until Sherman with his command came up. While this force moved eastward, Grant was maturing his plans for the engagement. He directed Sherman to report in person, which he did on the 15th, and on consultation with him and Thomas the general plan of battle was submitted to them. The main attack was to be made on the 21st, at daylight, by Sherman's troops, on the north end of Missionary Ridge. To accomplish this his command was to be reinforced with one division of the Army of the Cumberland

under Jeff C. Davis. Sherman's troops—four divisions—
were to move from Brown's Ferry through the woods to the
north of the town up to the Tennessee River, opposite the
mouth of Chickamauga Creek, where they were to cross on a
pontoon bridge to be swung there under the supervision of
W. F. Smith, and the crossing of the troops to be protected
by batteries under Brannan, Thomas's Chief of Artillery.
After crossing the river, Sherman was to move rapidly forward, carrying the heights on the north end of Missionary
Ridge as far as the tunnel, if possible, before the enemy
could concentrate on his front, Thomas was to concentrate
all his troops in Chattanooga Valley on his left flank, leaving only the necessary force to defend the fortifications on
his right and centre and to hold a movable column of one
division to move wherever needed. This division was to
make a show of threatening Bragg's forces up the valley.
Thomas was then to effect a junction with Sherman, co-operate with him, advancing his left and moving forward as
nearly simultaneously as possible, and support him. Hooker
on the right in Lookout Valley, was to hold that position
with Geary's division and two brigades under Cruft from the
Fourth Army Corps, ordered to report to him. Howard, on
Friday, the 20th, was ordered with his corps to take position
on the north side of the Tennessee, opposite Chattanooga,
near the pontoon bridge, and hold himself in readiness to
move to Thomas's front or to co-operate with Sherman as
needed. Colonel Eli Long with his brigade of cavalry was
directed to report by noon on Saturday, the 21st, at Chattanooga, to cover Sherman's left flank, and if not further required by Sherman he was then to cross the Chickamauga,
make a raid on the enemy's line of communication in the
rear, doing as much damage as he could.

Sherman made his movement with his troops from Bridge-

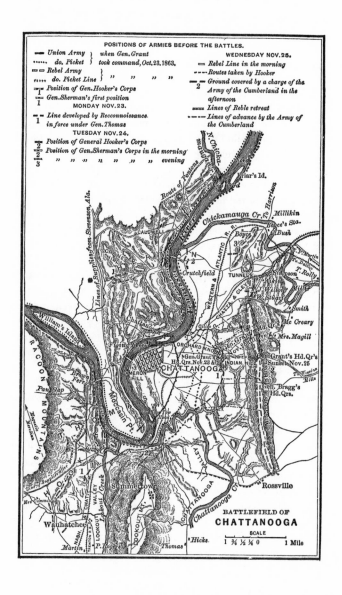

POSITIONS OF ARMIES BEFORE THE BATTLES.

—— Union Army ⎫ when Gen.Grant
•••••• do. Picket ⎬ took command, Oct.23,1863,
◻◻ Rebel Army ⎭
ʃʃʃʃ do. Picket Line ⎰ " " " "

Position of Gen.Hooker's Corps

Gen.Sherman's first position

MONDAY NOV.23.

Line developed by Reconnoissance.
in force under Gen. Thomas

TUESDAY NOV. 24.

Position of General Hooker's Corps

Position of Gen. Sherman's Corps in the morning
" " " " " " evening

WEDNESDAY NOV. 25.

◻◻ Rebel Line in the morning

----Routes taken by Hooker

Ground covered by a charge of the
Army of the Cumberland in the
afternoon

Lines of Reble retreat

Lines of advance by the Army of
the Cumberland

BATTLEFIELD OF
CHATTANOOGA

SCALE
1 ¾ ½ ¼ 0   1 Mile

port through Whitesides. Sending his leading division under Ewing up Lookout Valley, to make a feint on the left flank of the rebel army in the direction of Trenton, he crossed his others at Brown's Ferry and marched up the north bank of the river to the mouth of South Chickamauga Creek. Here they kept concealed in the woods from the enemy until they were ready to effect their crossing. Owing to heavy rains and the state of the roads, Sherman was able to have but one division, under John E. Smith, in position by the 21st, and Grant delayed his plans of battle to give him additional time. Sherman on the 21st moved his second division under Morgan L. Smith over the bridge at Brown's Ferry, and on the 23d, after many repairs to the bridge, rendered necessary by the swollen stream and the raft of logs sent down the river by the rebels, Ewing's division also got safely across. Sherman's fourth division under Osterhaus was not able on the 23d to cross, and this division was then ordered, in the event of not being able to cross by eight A.M. the 24th, to report to Hooker on the south bank of the Tennessee. Davis had reported with his division to Sherman, and on the 23d, the boats of the pontoon bridge were used to effect a landing at the mouth of South Chickamauga Creek by Giles A. Smith's brigade, who captured the rebel pickets at this place, landed his entire brigade, and then sent the boats back for additional troops. By daylight of the 24th, Sherman with two divisions of some 8,000 men was intrenched on the east bank of the Tennessee. A pontoon bridge, 1,350 feet long, was then built over this river, and another over Chickamauga Creek under the direction of W. F. Smith.

Thomas, learning that Sherman's movements across Lookout Valley had been discovered by Bragg, on Sunday, the 22d, directed Howard to cross into Chattanooga to give Bragg the idea that these were Sherman's troops coming to reinforce Chattanooga. Howard made the crossing on Sunday and took position in rear of our front line in full view of the enemy. On the 20th, Bragg notified Grant that it would be well for him to withdraw all non-combatants from Chattanooga. This the latter regarded as a cover for Bragg's withdrawal of his own command, which he was confirmed in by deserters and spies reporting a large number of Bragg's troops as marching to the north. These were two divisions of Buckner's corps sent to strengthen Longstreet in East Tennessee; that last sent, however, was recalled. To determine the truth of these reports, early on the morning of the 23d, Grant directed Thomas to develop the enemy's lines, driving in his pickets, and determine if he still held his force on our front. Thomas ordered Granger in command of the Fourth Corps to form with Sheridan's and Wood's divisions—Sheridan on the right, Wood on the left—with his left extended nearly to Citico Creek, and advance directly in front of Fort Wood, and make this movement. Palmer, commanding the Fourteenth Corps with Baird's division refused, was to support Granger's right and was to hold Johnson's division under arms in the intrenchments in readiness to move as occasion might require. The troops were all in position at 2 P.M. They moved out on the plain as if on parade, and in plain sight of Bragg and his army on Lookout and Missionary Ridge, formed their lines as if in review and moved forward to attack the enemy. Rapidly advancing "in the most gallant style" our troops steadily pushed in the rebel line. They first struck the pickets, drove these on the reserve and then sweeping everything before them they hurled the rebels out of their first line of rifle-pits and sent them on the full run in retreat to the rear, except over two hundred of them captured. Here Granger's troops made themselves secure by throwing up temporary breastworks, while he sent a strong picket line to the front to protect his new line. In this charge Granger's line secured "Orchard Knob" which was then occupied by Bridge's battery. Howard's corps was placed in position on the left of the line to Granger's left and also ordered to throw up breastworks.

Sherman after crossing the river on the 23d, about 1 P.M., placed his command in three columns, following in his advance the general direction of Chickamauga Creek, with his left under Morgan L. Smith resting on the creek. His centre was under John E. Smith and his right under Ewing, all under the command of Frank P. Blair, Corps Commander. In support of these, Davis's division also moved to the attack. Grant and Sherman had supposed that Missionary Ridge was one prolonged even range. When Sherman left the river he passed over the foothills and then pressed up what he supposed was the main portion of the ridge. When he reached the top of this, after a lively skirmish with the rebel pickets, he found a deep depression intervening between this hill and the next, which was the one the tunnel ran through, where the rebels were heavily intrenched, and which he had been ordered to take. On the top of this first hill, finding he could not take the hill beyond where the tunnel ran through, he threw up intrenchments and prepared to hold the ground he had thus far gained. Here about 4 P.M. he had a heavy engagement. The enemy's advance with sharp artillery and musketry fire was gallantly met and repulsed. Sherman then made preparations for the night, posting his command to hold all positions. Howard had reported with three regiments to him, as he crossed the bridge which connected him with the main Army of the Cumberland. Howard leaving these troops with Sherman, then returned to his corps. When his command was placed on the front to Granger's left in the afternoon, he connected with Sherman's right. Here Sherman rested all night, and about midnight received orders from Grant to "attack the enemy at dawn of day," "that General Thomas would attack in force early in the day."

While the main attack was progressing under Sherman on the left, Hooker on the right had been pressing the enemy. On the 23d, Osterhaus, finding that he could not cross the Tennessee in time to engage in the movement with Sherman, reported with his division to Hooker, who was then ordered to take these troops, with Geary's division and Whittaker's and Grose's brigades of the First Division of the Fourth Corps under Cruft, and make a strong demonstration on the northern slope of Lookout Mountain, drawing Bragg's attention to this point and away from Sherman while crossing the river and getting into position. Thomas instructed Hooker if he found he was able to carry the enemy's position here, to do so.

At 4 A.M. of the 24th, Hooker reported his troops in readiness to begin the movement. As he advanced he found Lookout Creek so swollen with recent rains that he could not cross without building a temporary bridge at the main road. He then sent Geary with two divisions and Whittaker's brigade of Cruft's command up the creek to effect a crossing at Wauhatchie. Geary was then to sweep down the right bank, driving the rebels before him. The enemy, watching the construction of the bridge under Hooker, failed to observe the movement of the troops under Geary, by reason of a heavy mist which overhung the mountain, until he was on their flank and threatening their rear. The enemy's force here and on the top of the mountain was under Stevenson, with a command of six brigades posted mainly on the Northern slope midway between the Palisades and

the Tennessee River, on a belt of cultivated land. A con
tinuous line of earthworks had been constructed, with re-
doubts, redans, and pits, lower down the slope, with refer-
erence to an assault from the direction of the river. On
each flank were rifle-pits, epaulements for batteries, walls of
stone and abatis, as against attack from either Chattanooga
or Lookout Valley. In these valleys were still more extensive earthworks.

As Geary moved down on the right bank of the creek, he
soon encountered the enemy's pickets. These gave the
alarm at once, when their troops formed in the breastworks
and rifle-pits. All these positions were soon covered by
artillery planted by Hooker's orders. He then sent Wood's
brigade of Osterhaus's division about eight hundred yards
up the creek to build another bridge, and directed Cruft to
leave a small command at the first bridge, to attract the attention of the enemy, and ordered the rest of Grose's brigade
to cross with Wood's. This bridge was completed at 11
o'clock, when the troops under Wood and Grose crossed, and
joined Geary on the right bank, who had driven the enemy
up to this point. Under cover of the heavy artillery fire,
the entire line advanced, pressing the enemy steadily back.
At noon Geary's advance drove the rebels around the peak
of the mountain. Here Geary was ordered to halt and reform his command, but having the rebels on the run he pressed
forward and drove them in a fleeing, panic-stricken crowd.
Cobham's and Freeland's brigades on the high ground on the
right, near the Palisades, pressed on, rolling their line up on
the flank, closely supported by Whittaker's and Creighton's
brigades. The enemy had been reinforced, but he was not
able to resist the sweep of Hooker's troops as they rounded
the crest of the mountain at Craven's house, where the
enemy made his last stand, and from here, with his line all
    11*

broken and in rout, he was driven over the rocks and precipices into Chattanooga Valley. At this time the mist that had been hanging round the mountain all the day settled still lower down. It was now about 2 o'clock, and Hooker in the mist, unable to see beyond his immediate front, placed his troops in position, threw up temporary breastworks, with his line on the east side of the mountain, the right resting at the Palisades and the left near the mouth of Chattanooga Creek. He then reported to Thomas, who ordered Carlin with his brigade to report to him, when he was placed on the extreme right, relieving Geary's troops. During the night the rebels opened a heavy fire on our right as if intending to break our lines. This was handsomely repulsed, Carlin's brigade taking an active part. Early in the morning, before daylight, several parties were sent up the mountain, in anticipation of the retreat of the enemy during the night, to scale the heights. One from the Eighth Kentucky was the first that reached the summit, and here at sunrise the stars and stripes were unfurled at the extreme point amid the cheers of the entire army. During the night Stevenson abandoned the top of the mountain, while the Summertown road remained open, leaving his camp and garrison equipage. This gave to our army full possession and control of the river and railroad up to Chattanooga.

The mist still clung to the mountain in heavy folds early on the 25th, when Hooker was ordered to press forward on the road to Rossville, carry the pass, and operate on Bragg's left and rear. Advancing down into the valley, he found the rebel pickets still holding the right bank of Chattanooga Creek. Arriving at the creek at about ten o'clock he found the bridges on the Rossville road destroyed. Here Hooker was delayed for some three hours, when Osterhaus in the advance crossed the infantry on the stringers and

pressed forward, driving the enemy's pickets over to Rossville. Hooker found the rebels at this place loading up
their stores. Leaving a force on their front, he sent
Wood's brigade to take the ridge on the right, and William-
son's on the left. After a severe skirmish the enemy hastily
retreated, abandoning large quantities of stores, wagons,
and ambulances. The gap now being under our control,
Hooker ordered the advance of our entire line, Osterhaus
with his division on the east of the ridge, Cruft on the
ridge, and Geary in the valley west of the ridge. This line
advancing soon encountered the rebels under Stewart, occupying the line of breastworks thrown up by our troops
after Chickamauga. Cruft's charged on them, drove them in
all directions out of these works in full retreat. Part of
them ran into Osterhaus's men and were captured. Others
were captured by Geary in the valley. The mass of them
fell back to their second line, from which they were like-
wise speedily driven, when the fight became a running one,
continuing until sunset. Part of the enemy in their endeavors to escape ran into Johnson's division of the Fourteenth Corps, thrown forward to join the pursuit, and were
captured. Hooker's command then went into camp.

Early on the morning of the 25th Sherman made his disposition for his main attack. Holding his centre with
three brigades, he was then to move along the east and
west base of Missionary Ridge with his right and left
flanks. Corse advancing from the right centre moved forward, supported by Lightburn on the left and Morgan L.
Smith on his right, and occupied a crest in the woods about
eighty yards from the intrenched line of the enemy. From
this point Corse assaulted the main rebel line, and for over
an hour maintained a heavy contest, driving the enemy,
and at times being driven back, but still holding his crest as

first secured. Here Corse, Loomis, and Morgan L. Smith fought the rebels under Hardee with Cleburne's, Gist's, Cheatham's, and Stevenson's divisions in a stubborn struggle all day up to three o'clock, holding their own, but making little headway. About two o'clock John E. Smith's two brigades, while moving to the support of Ewing, were driven in some disorder by a charge of the enemy, heavily massed. They were quickly reformed and, aided by Corse's troops taking the rebels in the flank with a hot musketry fire, the enemy was soon driven back into his line of works.

Here Sherman was fighting the heavy column of the enemy on our left, and the main part of the battle had been his share. Grant was waiting for Hooker to reach the rebel left at Rossville, in the hope that this would afford some relief to the stubborn fighting Sherman had encountered. Finding that Hooker had been delayed by the destruction of the bridge longer than was anticipated, and that the diversion was not to come from that quarter, Grant ordered Thomas to move out the four divisions constituting the centre—Baird on the left, then Wood with Sheridan on his right, and Johnson on the extreme right of the line—with a double line of skirmishers to the front, supported by the entire force, press forward to carry the first line of rifle-pits and there halt and await orders, the movement to commence at three o'clock, at a signal of six guns fired in rapid succession from Orchard Knob.

There was some little delay attending the preliminaries of the movement, and it was not until after half past three that the commands having moved out and taken the alignment were in position for the advance, when the guns sounded one, two, three, four, five, six. With this the troops, impatient all the day with being kept in the breastworks while Sherman's men were hard at work, eagerly

pressed onward, divisions, brigades, and regiments striving
each with the other for the advance. With the first movement Bragg at once hurried reinforcements from his right
and left to strengthen his troops in his works to resist the
advance on his centre. Here his line was under the command of Breckinridge, who had his own division under
Lewis, Stewart's division, and part of those of Buckner and
Hindman under Patton Anderson. The enemy had originally four lines of breastworks. The first one on our front
was captured by Thomas on the 23d, when Orchard Knob
was taken. This left three lines of rifle-pits remaining.
The second one was about half a mile to the rear of the
first, near the foot of the ridge. From here to the top was
a steep ascent of some five hundred yards, covered with
large rocks and fallen timber. About half way up the ridge
a small line of works had been thrown up. On the crest of
the hill Bragg's men had constructed their heaviest breastworks, protected on our front by some fifty pieces of artillery in position. As our troops advanced, each command
cheering and answering back the cheer of the others, the
men broke into a double-quick, all striving to be the first to
reach the rifle-pits at the foot of the ridge, held by a strong
line of the enemy's troops. The rebels opened fire with
shot and shell from their batteries, as our troops advanced,
changing it soon to grape and canister, which with the fire
from the infantry made it terrifically hot. Dashing through
this over the open plain, the soldiers of the Army of the Cumberland swept on, driving the enemy's skirmishers, charging
down on the line of works at the foot of the ridge, capturing it at the point of the bayonet, and routing the rebels,
sending them at full speed up the ridge, killing and capturing them in large numbers. These rifle-pits were reached
nearly simultaneously by the several commands, when the

troops, in compliance with their instructions, laid down at the foot of the ridge awaiting further orders. Here they were under a hot, plunging, galling fire from the enemy in their works on the crest of the ridge. Without further waiting, and under no orders from their officers, first one regiment, then another started with its colors up the ascent, until with loud hurrahs the entire line, cheered by their officers, advanced over and around rocks, under and through the fallen timber, charged up the ridge, each determined to reach the summit first. The centre part of Sheridan's division reached the top first, as they were the nearest to the crest, and crossed it to the right of Bragg's headquarters. The rest of the line was soon up, and almost simultaneously the ridge was carried in six places. Here the enemy making a fight for a short time was routed from the last of his lines, and his centre, panic-stricken, broke in full retreat. Regiments were captured almost entire, battery after battery along the ridge was taken. In some cases the rebels were bayonetted at their guns, and the cannon that but a moment before was firing on our troops, were by them captured, turned, and used against the rebels as they were driven in masses to the rear. The charge occupied about one hour from the time of the firing of the guns on Orchard Knob until the troops occupied the rebel lines on the ridge. Sheridan's division reached the ridge a few minutes too late to capture Bragg, Breckinridge, and a number of the rebel generals, who left Bragg's headquarters on the charge of our men up the ridge.

Sheridan advanced with his division, skirmishing with the enemy's rear-guard, but driving them steadily for about a mile on the Chickamauga station road. Here this road runs over a high ridge on which the enemy had posted eight pieces of artillery supported by a strong force to cover their retreat. At this point Sheridan, with Harker's and Wagner's brigades, had an engagement with these troops, but after a movement flanking the rebel's right and left, they hurriedly retreated, leaving two pieces of artillery and a large number of wagons. After this ridge was captured, Sheridan's troops went into bivouac. During the night the full moon flooded the surrounding country with its bright light. At midnight, on Granger's suggestion, Sheridan in the advance was again ordered with his division to press the enemy. He at once advanced his command to Chickamauga Creek, capturing a large number of prisoners and quantities of material and stores.

Wood, on reaching the top of the ridge, with Baird on his left, met with heavy opposition. The enemy was supported by a division from Hardee on the right, advancing just as Baird was getting into position. Here these two divisions were engaged in a sharp contest until after dark. Turchin, with his brigade, which was the left wing of Baird, had taken possession of a small work constructed by the enemy on the ridge when he was attacked by the rebels in a most furious charge, but gallantly repulsed them, when they drew off in the direction of Tunnel Hill. Missionary Ridge was now entirely within our control, with the exception of the point, where Sherman's advance had been so stoutly resisted. During the night, Bragg drew off Hardee's troops from the front of Sherman, where the latter at once placed his command in position for the pursuit the next day.

During the night of the 25th, Thomas was directed to send Granger with his corps, and additional troops to make his command up to 20,000, to march to Burnside's relief at Knoxville, and the other portion of Thomas's command with Sherman's troops to pursue the enemy on the 26th. The latter, on the morning of that day advanced by the road through Chickamauga Station, while Thomas ordered the command under Hooker and Palmer to push on by way of the Greysville and Ringgold road. At the former place the rearguard of the rebels was surprised after night, and three cannon and a large number of prisoners captured. On the next day another piece of artillery was captured at Greysville, and later in the day Hooker's advance again struck the enemy, strongly posted in a pass in Taylor's Ridge. Here, after a heavy fight of over an hour, they were driven from the pass with considerable loss on both sides. The pursuit was discontinued on the 28th. Hooker remained for a few days at Ringgold, while Palmer returned to his camp at Chattanooga.

Sherman's troops, with Davis's division in the advance, pressed through Chickamauga Station, and at about dark struck the rear of the enemy's column, and had a sharp fight. After leaving Greysville, Sherman turned his command to the left, to strike the railroad between Dalton and Cleveland. Howard was sent to destroy this road, which he did in a most thorough manner. On the following day the Fifteenth Corps destroyed the Atlanta Railroad from below Greysville back to the State line. On the 28th, Sherman was ordered to make a reconnoissance to the Hiawassee with his own corps, together with Davis's and Howard's troops of Thomas's command. On reaching Charleston, Sherman received orders to take command of Granger's column, moving to Burnside's relief, and to press forward with all the troops under him in all haste to Knoxville, eighty-four miles distant. Advancing rapidly with his command, Sherman reached Knoxville on the 6th. Longstreet, however, retreated on the 4th of December to Virginia. Leaving Granger's corps to aid in the pursuit of Longstreet, Sherman by easy marches returned to Chattanooga on the 16th of the month, where he ordered Howard and Davis to report with their commands, while he marched west with his own corps to Northern Alabama and placed them in winter quarters.

Sherman with his two days' fighting reports the losses of his command, including Howard's command, but not that of Davis, whose loss he says was small, at 295 killed, 1,402 wounded, and 292 missing—making a total of 1,989. This, however, includes the losses in his first division—Oster-haus's, which fought under Hooker on the right—of 87 killed, 344 wounded, and 66 missing, making 497 to be deducted, which leaves Sherman's loss proper, 208 killed, 1,058 wounded, and 226 missing—a total of 1,492. Thomas's loss in the part taken by his troops, also including How-ard's command and not including Davis's division, was 529 killed, 2,281 wounded, and 141 missing—an aggregate of 3,951. The large bulk of the losses under Thomas were in Sheridan's and Wood's divisions. That of the former was 135 killed, 1,151 wounded, missing, none—aggregate 1,256 ; that of the latter, 150 killed, 851 wounded, missing, none—aggregate 1,001. These two divisions in their one hour's work storming Missionary Ridge met with a loss of 2,287 men, showing hot work. There was captured by the army of the Cumberland 40 pieces of artillery, 58 artillery car-riages and caissons, 6,175 stand of small arms, principally English Enfield, and 5,471 prisoners.

During the winter there were nothing but minor move-ments of the troops. The railroads up to Chattanooga were repaired, and the first "cracker train" that entered the place was greated with many hearty cheers by our troops in the town, as the shrill scream of its whistle woke the echoes among the surrounding mountains, so long silent to this music. The roads into and through East Tennessee were repaired to Knoxville and beyond.

In the early spring the organization of the Army of the Cumberland was changed by Granger being relieved of the command of the Fourth Corps, when Howard was assigned to that command. Palmer was retained in command of the Fourteenth Corps, and the Eleventh and Twelfth Corps were consolidated into the Twentieth Corps, with Hooker in command. The cavalry was organized in four divisions, under the command of W. L. Elliott. The army in the field consisted of 60,773 effective men.

General Thomas ordered the Fourth Corps to Cleveland. The Fourteenth Corps in front of Chattanooga was well thrown forward toward the enemy's front at Dalton, preparatory to the spring campaign to Atlanta, under General Sherman. The Twentieth Corps was stationed in Lookout Valley.

In the general engagement Grant's plan of battle had been for Sherman with five divisions to make the main attack, sweep everything before him down the ridge, and when he had the rebels in full retreat, the Army of the Cumberland was then to aid in the pursuit, after patiently waiting until the fighting was over. Hooker, under Grant's original plan, was to simply hold Lookout Valley secure, and when the enemy was driven by Sherman, he too was to join in the pursuit. All the fighting of the battle was to be done by Sherman and all the glory thereof was to be his. In Sherman's memoirs we are favored with Grant's views of the Army of the Cumberland when Sherman first reported in person to Grant at Chattanooga, to learn of his plan and the part he, Sherman, was to take. Sherman says that Grant told him "that the men of Thomas's army had been so demoralized by the battle of Chickamauga that he feared they could not be got out of their trenches to assume the offensive," and that "the Army of the Cumberland had so long

been in the trenches that he wanted my troops to hurry up
to take the offensive *first*, after which he had no doubt the
Cumberland Army would fight well." So, under Grant's
plan, the Army of the Cumberland was to stand by and be
taught a grand object lesson how to fight, as given by Sherman. During the course of the engagement the plan was
modified twice. Under the original plan, Sherman was to
make a demonstration up Lookout Valley, in the expectation
that Bragg would strengthen his left at the expense of his
right, thereby making Sherman's part of the plan so much
the lighter as the line on his battle front was weakened.
To carry this out Hugh Ewing's division was sent to Trenton,
but this accomplished nothing. Grant fearing that Bragg's
right might be too strong for Sherman to give his lesson to
the Army of the Cumberland properly, finding Osterhaus's
division cut off from Sherman, ordered it to report to
Hooker, who was directed to take it and Geary's division
with Cruft's division of the Fourth Corps and make a demonstration on the rebel left at Lookout Mountain, to attract the attention of Bragg while Sherman was getting into
position to take "the end of Missionary Ridge as far as the
tunnel." Hooker, on the day previous, learning that Howard's corps was going into Chattanooga, and probably into
the fight, asked to be allowed his right to be with his troops
under fire. Under his original order he was simply to hold
Lookout Valley, which he did not relish if part of his command should engage the enemy. When his orders came to
"make a demonstration" he determined he would take
Lookout Mountain and drive Bragg's left out of his works.
With less than ten thousand troops, over two-thirds of whom
were the Army of the Cumberland, Hooker fought his "Battle above the Clouds," that will last in history forever, and
grow in fancy and song as the years roll on. Hooker took

Lookout Mountain and drove the rebel left to Rossville, over five miles, before Sherman reached the tunnel. He made Sherman's task none the easier, however, because Bragg then threw the two divisions Hooker had whipped upon Sherman's front.

Then, when Sherman had been fighting for nearly two days, and had failed to make the headway Grant's plan contemplated, the plan underwent another modification. On the 25th, Grant ordered Thomas to move out his troops from the centre, to make another " demonstration " in Sherman's behalf, so he could take the tunnel in accordance with the original plan. Thomas was ordered to take the first line of rifle-pits and hold his command there, while Bragg was expected to draw off part of his troops from Sherman's front and strengthen his line in front of the "demonstration." Thomas's orders to his corps and division generals were given in accordance with Grant's instructions, and as the orders reached the brigade and regimental commanders, as far as the officers were concerned the movement was only to be a " demonstration." When the troops reached the rebel line, captured it, and then found themselves under the heavy fire from the enemy's lines on the heights above, without orders, and even against orders, the soldiers of the Army of the Cumberland, who were " so demoralized that they would not fight," pressed up the face of the ridge under the deadly musketry fire that greeted them, with cannon in front, to the right and the left raking with converging fire, and won for General Grant the battle of Missionary Ridge, driving Bragg away from Sherman's front and thus enabling him to take the tunnel as ordered. Whenever the victory of Missionary Ridge shall be narrated on history's page, this gallant charge of the brave men of Wood's and Sheridan's divisions, with those of Baird and Johnson on their left and right, will always be the prominent feature of the engagement as told in the coming years, and will be the last to lose its glory and renown.

No wonder that General Grant failed to appreciate this movement at the time, not understanding the troops who had it in charge. When he found these commands ascending the ridge to capture it when he ordered a " demonstration " to be made to the foot of the hill and there to wait, he turned sharply to General Thomas and asked, "By whose orders are those troops going up the hill ? " General Thomas, taking in the situation at once, suggested that it was probably by their own. General Grant remarked that " it was all right if it turned out all right," and added, " if not, some one would suffer." But it turned out " all right," and Grant in his official report compliments the troops for " following closely the retreating enemy without further orders." General Thomas, in his official report, after narrating the events of the 23d, 24th, and 25th of November, quietly says: "It will be seen by the above report that the original plan of operations was somewhat modified to meet and take the best advantage of emergencies which necessitated material modifications of that plan. It is believed, however, that the original plan had it been carried out could not possibly have led to more successful results."

APPENDIX A.

ORGANIZATION OF THE FOURTEENTH ARMY CORPS, DEPT. OF THE CUMBERLAND.

MAJOR-GENERAL W. S. ROSECRANS, COMMANDING.

December 20, 1862.

CENTRE.

MAJOR-GENERAL GEO. H. THOMAS.

FIRST DIVISION.

BRIGADIER-GENERAL S. S. FRY.

First Brigade.—Col. M. B. WALKER, 82d Ind., 12th Ky., 17th O., 31st O., 38th O. *Second Brigade.*—Col. J. M. HARLAN, 10th Ind., 74th Ind., 4th Ky., 10th Ky., 14th O. *Third Brigade.*—Brig.-General J. B. STEEDMAN, 87th Ind., 2d Minn., 9th O., 35th O., 18th U. S. *Artillery.*—4th Mich. Battery, 1st O. Battery "C.," 4th U. S. Battery "I."

THIRD DIVISION.

BRIGADIER-GENERAL L. H. ROUSSEAU,

Ninth Brigade.—Col. B. F. SCRIBNER, 38th Ind., 2d O., 33d O., 94th O., 10th Wis. *Seventeenth Brigade.*—Col. J. G. JONES, 42d Ind., 88th Ind., 15th Ky., 3d O., 10th O. *Twenty-Eighth Brigade.*—Col. H. A. HAMBRIGHT, 24th Ill., 79th Penn., 1st Wis., 21st Wis. *Artillery.*—4th Ind. Battery, 5th Ind. Battery, 1st Ky., 1st Mich. Battery "A." *Cavalry.*—2d Ky. (Battalion), 11th Ky. (Detachment), 4th Ind. (Detachment).

EIGHTH DIVISION.

BRIGADIER-GENERAL J. S. NEGLEY.

Seventh Brigade.—Col. JOHN F. MILLER, 37th Ind., 78th Penn., 21st O. 74th O., Independent Battalion, Capt. Casey. *Twenty-Ninth Brigade.*—Col. T. R. STANLEY, 19th Ill., 11th Mich., 18th O., 69th O. *Artillery.*—1st Ky. Battery "B.," 1st O. Battery "G.," 1st O. Battery "M." *Cavalry.*—7th Penn., 1st Tenn.

SEVENTH DIVISION.

BRIGADIER-GENERAL J. M. PALMER.

First Brigade.—Col. G. W. ROBERTS, 22d Ill., 27th Ill., 42d Ill., 51st Ill. *Second Brigade.*—Brig.-General J. D. MORGAN, 10th Ill., 16th Ill., 60th Ill., 10th Mich., 14th Mich. *Artillery.*—1st Ill. Battery "C.," 10th Wis. Battery. *Cavalry.*—7th Ill. Co. "C."

TWELFTH DIVISION.

BRIGADIER-GENERAL E. DUMONT.

Fortieth Brigade. —Col. A. O. MILLER, 98th Ill., 72d Ind., 75th Ind —— *Brigade.*—Col. W. T. WARD, 102d Ill., 105th Ill., 70th Ind., 79th O. *Artillery.*—18th Ind. Battery. *Cavalry.*—4th Ind. (Detachment), 7th Ky., 11th Ky. (Detachment).

RIGHT WING.

MAJOR-GENERAL A. McD. McCOOK.

SECOND DIVISION.

BRIGADIER-GENERAL J. W. SILL.

Fourth Brigade.—Col. BUCKLEY, 6th Ind , 5th Ky., 1st O., 93d O., 16th U. S., 19th U. S. *Fifth Brigade.*—Col. E. N. KIRK, 34th Ill., 79th Ill., 29th Ind., 30th Ind., 77th Penn. *Sixth Brigade.*—Brig.-General WILLICH, 89th Ill., 32d Ind., 39th Ind., 15th O., 49th O. *Artillery.*—1st O. Battery "A.," 1st O. Battery "E.," 5th U. S. Battery "I." *Cavalry.*—2d Ky. (2 Cos).

NINTH DIVISION.

BRIGADIER-GENERAL J. C. DAVIS.

*Thirtieth Brigade.**—59th Ill., 74th Ill., 75th Ill., 22d Ind. *Thirty-First Brigade.**—21st Ill., 38th Ill., 101st O., 15th Wis. *Thirty-Second Brigade.** —25th Ill., 35th Ill., 81st Ind., 8th Kan. *Artillery.*—2d Minn. Battery, 5th Wis. Battery, 8th Wis. Battery.

ELEVENTH DIVISION.

BRIGADIER-GENERAL P. H. SHERIDAN.

Thirty-Fifth Brigade.—Col. F. SCHAEFER, 44th Ill., 73d Ill., 2d Mo., 15th Mo. *Thirty-Sixth Brigade.*—Col. MOORE, 85th Ill., 86th Ill., 125th Ill., 52d O. *Thirty-Seventh Brigade.*—Col. N. GRENSEL, 36th Ill., 88th Ill., 21st Mich., 24th Wis. *Artillery.*—2d Ill. Battery "I.," 1st Mo. Battery "G." *Cavalry.*— 2d Ky. Co. "L."

LEFT WING.

MAJOR-GENERAL T. L. CRITTENDEN.

FOURTH DIVISION.

BRIGADIER-GENERAL W. S. SMITH.

Tenth Brigade.—Col. W. GROSE, 84th Ill., 36th Ind., 23d Ky., 6th O., 24th O. *Nineteenth Brigade.*—Col. W. B. HAZEN, 110th Ill., 9th Ind., 6th Ky., 41st O. *Twenty-Second Brigade.*—Col. ENYART, 31st Ind., 1st Ky., 2d Ky., 20th Ky., 90th O. *Artillery.†*—Capt. STANDART.

---

* Brigade commanders not indicated on return..
† Batteries not indicated on return.

FIFTH DIVISION.

BRIGADIER-GENERAL H. P. VAN CLEVE.

Eleventh Brigade.—Col. SAM'L BEATTY, 79th Ind., 9th Ky., 19th O., 59th O. *Fourteenth Brigade.*—Col. J. P. FYFFE, 44th Ind., 86th Ind., 11th Ky., 13th O. *Twenty-Third Brigade.*—Col. S. MATTHEWS, 35th Ind., 8th Ky., 21st Ky., 51st O., 99th O. *Artillery.**—Capt. G. R. SWALLOW.

SIXTH DIVISION.

BRIGADIER-GENERAL M. S. HASCALL.

Fifteenth Brigade.—Col. G. P. BUELL, 100th Ill., 17th Ind., 58th Ind., 3d Ky., 26th O. *Twentieth Brigade.*—Col. G. C. HARKER, 51st Ind., 73d Ind., 13th Mich., 64th O., 65th O. *Twenty-First Brigade.*—Col. G. D. WAGNER, 15th Ind., 40th Ind., 57th Ind., 97th O. *Artillery.**—Maj. S. RACE.

CAVALRY.

BRIGADIER-GENERAL STANLEY.

FIRST DIVISION.

COLONEL KENNETT.

First Brigade.—Col. E. H. MURRAY, 2d Ind., 1st Ky., 3d Ky., 4th Ky., 4th Mich., 7th Penn. *Second Brigade.*—Col. L. ZAHM, 5th Ky., 1st O., 3d O., 4th O., 1st O. Artillery, Battery "D."

UNATTACHED FORCES.

1st Mich. Engineers, 9th Mich. (Detach.), 3d E. Tenn., 6th E. Tenn., 15th Penn. Cavalry, 4th U. S. Cavalry (Detach.), Signal Corps, Stokes' Ill. Battery.

GARRISONS.

Bowling Green, Ky.—Brig.-Gen. GRANGER, 129th Ill., 26th Ky., 23d Mich., 102d O., 111th O., 4th Ky. Cavalry. *Nashville, Tenn.*—Brig.-Gen. R. B. MITCHELL, 1st Mid. Tenn., 11th Ind. Battery, 12th Ind. Battery, 1st Mich. Artillery, 5th Battery. 3d Ind. Cavalry (1 Co.)

---

* Batteries not indicated on return.

APPENDIX B.

ORGANIZATION OF TROOPS IN THE DEPT. OF THE CUMBERLAND, COMMANDED BY MAJOR GENERAL GEORGE H. THOMAS. CHATTANOOGA, TENN., OCT. 20th, 1863.

FOURTH ARMY CORPS.

MAJ.-GEN'L G. GRANGER.

FIRST DIVISION.

MAJ.-GEN'L J. M. PALMER.

First Brigade—Brig. Gen'l CHAS. CRUFT, 21st Ill., 38th Ill., 29th Ind., 31st Ind., 81st Ind., 1st Ky., 2d Ky., 90th O., 101st O. *Second Brigade.*— Brig. Gen'l W. C. WHITAKER, 96th Ill., 115th Ill., 35th Ind., 84th Ind., 8th Ky., 40th O., 51st O., 99th O. *Third Brigade.*—Col. WM. GROSE, 59th Ill., 75th Ill., 84th Ill., 9th Ind., 30th Ind., 36th Ind., 24th O., 77th Penn. *Artillery.*—5th Ind. Battery, 4th U. S. Art., Co. " H ; " 4th U. S. Art., Co. " M."

SECOND DIVISION.

MAJ.-GEN'L P. H. SHERIDAN.

First Brigade.—Brig.-Gen'l J. B. STEEDMAN, 36th Ill., 44th Ill., 73d Ill., 74th Ill., 88th Ill., 22d Ind., 21st Mich., 2d Mo., 15th Mo., 24th Wis. *Second Brigade.* —Brig.-Gen'l G. D. WAGNER, 100th Ill., 15th Ind., 40th Ind., 57th Ind., 58th Ind., 13th Mich., 26th O., 97th O. *Third Brigade.*—Col. C. G. HARKER, 22d Ill., 27th Ill., 42d Ill., 51st Ill., 79th Ill., 3d Ky., 64th O., 65th O., 125th O. *Artillery.*—1st Ill. Art., Co." M," 10th Ind. Battery, 1st Miss. Art., Co. " G."

THIRD DIVISION.

BRIG.-GEN'L T. J. WOOD.

First Brigade.—Brig.-Gen'l A. WILLICH, 25th Ill., 35th Ill., 89th Ill., 32d Ind., 68th Ind., 8th Kan., 15th O., 49th O., 15th Wis. *Second Brigade.*— Brig.-Gen'l W. B. HAZEN, 6th Ind., 5th Ky., 6th Ky., 23d Ky., 1st O., 6th O., 41st O., 93d O., 124th O. *Third Brigade.*—Brig.-Gen'l S. BEATTY, 44th Ind., 79th Ind., 86th Ind., 9th Ky., 17th Ky., 13th O., 19th O., 59th O. *Artillery.*—Bridge's Battery Ill. Art., 6th O. Battery, 26th Penn. Battery.

ELEVENTH ARMY CORPS.*

MAJ.-GEN'L O. O. HOWARD.

SECOND DIVISION.

BRIG.-GEN'L A. VON STEINWEHR.

First Brigade.—33d N. J., 134th N. Y., 154th N. Y., 27th Penn., 73d Penn. *Second Brigade.*—33d Mass., 136th N. Y., 55th O., 73d O.

---

* Brigade Commanders not given.

266

THIRD DIVISION.

MAJ.-GEN'L C. SCHURZ.

First Brigade.—82d Ill., 45th N. Y., 143d N. Y., 61st O., 82d O. *S cond Brigade.*—58th N. Y., 68th N. Y., 119th N. Y., 141st N. Y., 75th Penn., 26th Wis. *Artillery.*—1st New York Art., Co. " I," 13th New York Battery, Indt. Co. 8th N. Y. Vol. Infty., 1st Ohio Art., Co. " I," 1st Ohio Art., Co. " K," 4th U. S., Co. " G."

TWELFTH ARMY CORPS.*

MAJ.-GEN'L H. W. SLOCUM.

FIRST DIVISION.

BRIG.-GEN'L A. S. WILLIAMS.

First Brigade.—5th Conn., 20th Conn., 3d Md., 123d N. Y., 145th N. Y., 46th Penn. *S cond Brigade.*—27th Ind., 2d Mass., 13th N. J., 107th N. Y., 150th N. Y., 3d Wis.

SECOND DIVISION.

BRIG.-GEN'L JOHN W. GEARY.

First Brigade.—5th O., 7th O., 29th O., 66th O., 28th Penn., 147th Penn. *Second Brigade.*—29th Penn., 109th Penn., 111th Penn. *Third Brigade.*—60th N. Y., 78th N. Y., 102d N. Y., 137th N. Y., 149th N. Y. *Artillery.*—1st Batt'n 10th Maine Vol. Infty., 1st New York Art., Co. " M," Pennsylvania Batt'y, Co. " E," 4th U. S. Art., Co. " F," 5th U. S. Art., Co. " K."

(MAJ.-GEN'L JOSEPH HOOKER, COM'G 11TH AND 12TH ARMY CORPS.)

LIEUT.-COL. HUNTON, UNASSIGNED ARTILLERY.

2d Ky. Batt'y, 1st Mich. E. and M., 20th Ind. Batt'y., 1st Ky. Batt'y., 1st O. Art., Co. " E," 10th Wis. Batt'y.

FOURTEENTH ARMY CORPS.

MAJ.-GEN'L. GEORGE H. THOMAS.

FIRST DIVISION.

BRIG.-GEN'L. W. P. CARLIN.

First Brigade.—Col. O. F. MOORE: 104th Ill., 38th Ind., 42d Ind., 88th Ind., 15th Ky., 2d O., 33d O., 94th O., 10th Wis. *Second Brigade.*—Col. M. F. MOORE: 19th Ill., 11th Mich., 18th O., 69th O., 15th U. S. Infty., 1st and 2d Batt., 16th U. S. Infty., 1st Batt., 18th U. S. Infty., 1st and 2d Batt., 19th U. S. Infty., 1st Batt. *Third Brigade.*—Col. W. SIRWELL: 24th Ill., 37th Ind., 21st O., 74th O., 78th Penn., 79th Penn., 1st Wis., 21st Wis. *Artillery.*—1st Ill. Art., Co. " C," 1st. Mich. Art., Co. " A.," 5th U. S. Art., Co. " H."

SECOND DIVISION.

BRIG.-GEN'L. JEFF. C. DAVIS.

First Brigade.—Brig.-Gen'l. J. D. MORGAN: 10th Ill., 16th Ill., 60th Ill., 10th Mich., 14th Mich. *Second Brigade.* — Brig.-Gen'l J. BEATTY : 3d East Tenn., 5th East Tenn., 6th East Tenn., 78th Ill., 98th O., 113th O., 121st O. *Third Brigade.*—Col. D. MCCOOK: 85th Ill., 86th Ill., 110th Ill., 125th Ill., 52d O., 22d Mich. *Artillery.*—2d Ill. Art., Co. " I," 2d Minn. Batt'y., 5th Wis. Batt'y.

---

* Brigade Commanders not given.

THIRD DIVISION.
Brig.-Gen'l A. BAIRD.

First Brigade.—Brig.-Gen'l J. B. TURCHIN: 82d Ind., 11th O., 17th O., 31st O., 36th O., 89th O., 92d O. *Second Brigade.*—Col. JAS. GEORGE: 75th Ind., 87th Ind., 101st Ind., 2d Minn., 9th O., 35th O., 105th O. *Third Brigade.*—Col. E. H. PHELPS: 10th Ind., 74th Ind., 4th Ky., 10th Ky., 18th Ky., 14th O., 38th O. *Artillery.*—7th Ind. Batt'y., 19th Ind. Batt'y., 4th U. S. Art., Co. "I."

ARTILLERY RESERVE.

Brig.-Gen'l J. M. BRANNON, Chf. of Art.

FIRST DIVISION.
Col. J. BARNETT.

First Brigade.—1st O. Art., Co. "A.," 1st O. Art., Co. "B.," 1st O. Art., Co. "C.," 1st O. Art., Co. "F." *Second Brigade.*—1st O. Art., Co. "G.," 1st O. Art., Co. "M.," 18th O. Batt'y., 20th O. Batt'y.

SECOND DIVISION.

First Brigade.—Capt. SUTERMEISTER: 4th Ind. Batt'y., 8th Ind. Batt'y., 11th Ind. Batt'y., 21st Ind. Batt'y. *Second Brigade.*—Capt. CHURCH: 1st Mich Art., Co. "D.," 1st M. Tenn. Art., Co. "A.," 3d Wis. Batt'y. 8th Wis. Batt'y. *Coburn's Brigade.*—33d Ind., 85th Ind., 19th Mich., 22d Wis., 9th O. Batt'y. *U. S. Forces, GALLATIN, Tenn.*—Brig.-Gen'l. E. A. PAINE: 91st Ind. (1st Batt.), 50th O. (1st Batt.), 71st O., 106th O., 13th Ind. Batt'y.

NASHVILLE, TENN.
Brig.-Gen'l R. S. GRANGER, Comdg. Post.

Ward's Brigade.—Brig.-Gen'l W. T. WARD : 105th Ill., 129th Ill., 70th Ind., 79th O., 1st Mich. Art., Co. "E." *Unassigned.*—18th Mich. Vol. Inft'y., 12th. Ind Batt'y. *Clarksville, Tenn.*—Col. A. A. SMITH, Comdg Post: 83d Ill. (1st Batt.), 2d Ill. Art., Co. "H." *Chattanooga, Tenn.*—10th O. Vol. Inft'y, 1st Batt. O. S. S.

FIRST DIVISION CAVALRY.
Brig.-Gen'l R. B. MITCHELL.

First Brigade.—Col. A. P. CAMPBELL : 1st E. Tenn. Cav., 2d Mich. Cav., 9th Penn. Cav. *Second Brigade.*—Col. E. McCOOK: 2d E. Tenn. Cav., 3d E. Tenn. Cav., 2d Ind. Cav., 4th Ind. Cav., 1st Wis. Cav. *Third Brigade* — Col. L. D. WATKINS : 4th Ky. Cav., 5th Ky. Cav., 6th Ky. Cav., 7th Ky. Cav. —*Artillery.* Sec. 1, O. Art., Co. "D."

SECOND DIVISION CAVALRY.
Brig.-Gen'l GEO. CROOK.

First Brigade.—Col. R. L MINTY : 3d Ind. Cav. (Detachm't), 4th Mich. Cav., 7th Penn. Cav., 4th U. S. Cav. *Second Brigade.*—Col. E. LONG: 2d Ky. Cav., 1st O. Cav., 3d O. Cav., 4th O. Cav. *Third Brigade.*—Col. W. W. LOWE: 5th Ia. Cav., 1st Mid. Tenn. Cav., 10th O. Cav , Capt. Stokes' Ill. Batt'y, 15th Pa. Vol. Cav., Col. W. J. Palmer. *Miller's Brig. Mtd. Infty.* —Col. A. O. MILLER : 92d Ill., 98th Ill., 123d Ill., 17th Ind., 72d Ind., 18th Ind. Batt'y. *U. S. Forces, FT. DONELSON,*—Lt.-Col. E. C. BROTT : 83d Ill. (Detachm't.), 2d Ill. Art., Co. "C."
Unassigned Infantry.—34th Ill., 80th Ill., 102d Ill., 39th Ind., 51st Ind., 73d Ind., 21st Ky., 28th Ky., 3d O., 102d O., 108th O., 10th Tenn., 31st Wis.

APPENDIX C.

ORGANIZATION OF THE CONFEDERATE ARMY AT THE BATTLE OF CHICKAMAUGA, GA.

RIGHT WING.

LIEUT.-GEN'L. LEONIDAS POLK.

CHEATHAM'S DIVISION.

MAJ.-GEN'L B. F. CHEATHAM.

Jackson's Brigade.—Brig.-Gen'l J. K. JACKSON : 1st Confed. Bat., 5th Ga., 2d Ga. Bat., 5th Miss., 8th Miss., Scogin's (Ga.) Batt'y. *Maney's Brigade.*—Brig.-Gen'l GEO. MANEY : 1st Tenn., 27th Tenn., 4th Tenn., 6th Tenn., 9th Tenn., Maney's (Tenn.) Batt., Smith's (Miss.) Batt'y. *Smith's Brigade.*—Brig.-Gen'l PRESTON SMITH, Col. A. J. VAUGHAN : 11th Tenn., 12th Tenn., 47th Tenn., 13th Tenn., 29th Tenn., 154th Tenn., Scott's (Tenn.) Batt'y. *Wright's Brigade.*—Brig.-Gen'l M. J. WRIGHT : 8th Tenn., 16th Tenn., 28th Tenn., 38th Tenn., 51st Tenn., 52d Tenn., Carnes' (Tenn.) Batt'y. *Strahl's Brigade.*—Brig-Gen'l O. F. STRAHL : 4th Tenn., 5th Tenn., 19th Tenn., 24th Tenn., 31st Tenn., 33d Tenn., Stanford's (Miss.) Batt'y.

HILL'S CORPS.

LIEUT.-GEN'L. D. H. HILL.

CLEBURNE'S DIVISION.

MAJ-GEN'L P. R. CLEBURNE.

Polk's Brigade.—Brig-Gen'l L. E. POLK : 1st Ark., 3d Confed., 5th Confed., 2d Tenn., 35th Tenn., 48th Tenn. Calvert's (Tenn.) Batt'y, *Wood's Brigade.*—Brig-Gen'l S. A. M. Wood : 16th Ala., 33d Ala., 45th Ala., 32d Miss., 45th Miss., H nkin's Batt., Semple's (Ala.) Batt'y. *Deshler's Brigade.*—Brig.-Gen'l JAMES DESHLER, Col. R. Q. MILLS : 19th Ark., 24th Ark., 6th Tex. 10th Tex., 15th Tex., 17th Tex., 18th Tex., 24th Tex., 25th Tex., Douglas' (Tex.) Batt'y.

BRECKINRIDGE'S DIVISION.

MAJ.-GEN'L JOHN C. BRECKINRIDGE.

Helm's Brigade.—Brig.-Gen'l B. H. LEWIS, Col. J. H. LEWIS, 41st Ala., 2d Ky., 4th Ky., 6th Ky., 9th Ky., Cobb's (Ky.) Battery. *Adams' Brigade.*—Brig.-Gen'l DAN'L ADAMS, Col. R. L. GIBSON, 32d Ala., 13th La., 20th La., 16th La., 25th La., 19th La., Austin's (La.) Batt., Slocomb's (La.) Battery. *Stovall's Brigade.*—Brig.-Gen'l M. A. STOVALL, 1st Fla., 3d Fla., 4th Fla., 47th Ga., 60th No. Car., Mebane's (Tenn.) Battery.

WALKER'S DIVISION.*

MAJ.-GEN'L W. H. T. WALKER.

BRIG.-GEN'L S. R. GIST.

Gist's Brigade.—Brig.-Gen'l S. R. GIST, Col. P. H. COLQUITT, 46th Ga., 8th Ga. Batt., 16th So. Car., 24th So. Ca., Ferguson's (So. Car.) Battery. *Ector's Brigade.*—Brig.-Gen'l M. D. ECTOR, Ala. Batt. (Stone's).Miss. Batt.(Pound's), 9th Tex., 10th Tex. Cav..† 14th Tex. Cav.,† 32d Tex. Cav.,† Battery.‡ *Wilson's Brigade.*—Col. C. C. WILSON, 25th Ga., 29th Ga., 30th Ga., 1st Ga. Batt., 4th La. Batt., Battery.‡

LIDDELL'S DIVISION.*

BRIG.-GEN'L S. J. R. LIDDELL.

Liddell's Brigade.—Col. D. C. GOVAN, 2d Ark., 15th Ark., 5th Ark., 13th Ark., 6th Ark., 7th Ark., 8th Ark., 1st La., Swett's (Miss.) Batt. *Walthall's Brigade.*—Brig.-Gen'l E. C. WALTHALL, 24th Miss., 27th Miss., 29th Miss., 30th Miss., 34th Miss., Fowler's (Ala.) Battery.

LEFT WING.

LIEUT.-GEN'L JAMES LONGSTREET.

McLAW'S DIVISION.§

MAJ.-GEN'L LAFAYETTE McLAW.

BRIG.-GEN'L J. B. KERSHAW.

Kershaw's Brigade.—Brig.-Gen'l J. B. KERSHAW, 2d So. Car., 3d So. Car., 7th So. Car., 8th So. Car., 15th So. Car., 3d So. Car. Batt. *Wofford's Brigade.* —Brig.-Gen'l W. T. WOFFORD, 16th Ga., 18th Ga., 24th Ga., 3d Ga. Batt., Cobb's (Ga.) Legion, Phillip's (Ga.) Legion. *Humphreys' Brigade.*—Brig.-Gen'l B. G. HUMPHREYS, 13th Miss., 17th Miss., 18th Miss., 21st Miss. *Bryan's Brigade.*‖—Brig.-Gen'l GOODE BRYAN, 10th Ga., 50th Ga., 51st Ga., 53d Ga.

HOOD'S DIVISION.§

MAJ.-GEN'L J. B. HOOD.

BRIG.-GEN'L E. M. LAW.

Law's Brigade.—Brig.-Gen'l E. M. LAW, Col. SHEFFIELD, 4th Ala., 15th Ala., 44th Ala., 47th Ala., 48th Ala. *Robertson's Brigade.*—Brig. Gen'l J. B. ROBERTSON, 3d Ark., 18th Tex., 4th Tex., 5th Tex. *Anderson's Brigade.*— Brig. Gen'l GEO. T. ANDERSON, 7th Ga., 8th Ga., 9th Ga., 11th Ga., 59th Ga. *Benning's Brigade.*—Brig.-Gen'l H. L. BENNING, 2d Ga., 15th Ga., 17th Ga., 20th Ga. *Artillery.*¶—Maj. FRANK HUGER, Fickling's (Va.) Bat., Jordan's (Va.) Bat., Moody's (La.) Bat., Parker's (Va.) Bat., Taylor's (Va.) Bat., Woolfolk's (Va.) Bat.

---

* Walker's and Liddell's divisions constituted a "reserve corps" under Walker's command, Gist commanding Walker's division.

† Dismounted.

‡ Gen'l Walker reports five batteries, but those of Ector's and Wilson's brigades are not named in reports.

§ Longstreet's corps, organization of these divisions, and of the artillery battalion taken from Return of the Army of Northern Virginia, for August 31, 1863; the artillery is not mentioned in the reports.

‖ Longstreet's report indicates that these brigades were not engaged.

¶ Served in Johnson's division.

HINDMAN'S DIVISION.*

Maj.-Gen'l T. C. HINDMAN.

Brig.-Gen'l PATTON ANDERSON.

Anderson's Brigade.—Brig.-Gen'l PATTON ANDERSON, Col. J. H. SHARP, 7th Miss., 9th Miss., 10th Miss., 41st Miss., 44th Miss., 9th Miss. Batt., Garrity's (Ala.) Bat. *Deas' Brigade.*—Brig.-Gen'l Z. C. DEAS, 19th Ala., 22d Ala., 25th Ala., 39th Ala., 50th Ala., 17th Ala. Batt., Dent's (Ala.) Bat. *Manigault's Brigade.*—Brig.-Gen'l A. M. MANIGAULT, 24th Ala., 28th Ala., 34th Ala., 10th So. Car. and 19th So. Car. consol., Water's (Ala.) Bat.

BUCKNER'S CORPS.

Maj-Gen'l S. B. BUCKNER.

STEWART'S DIVISION.

Maj.-Gen'l A. P. STEWART.

Johnson's Brigade.†—Brig.-Gen'l B. R. JOHNSON, Col. J. S. FULTON, 17th Tenn., 23d Tenn., 25th Tenn., 44th Tenn., 9th Ga. Art., Bat. "E." *Brown's Brigade.*—Brig.-Gen'l J. C. BROWN, 18th Tenn., 26th Tenn., 32d Tenn., 45th Tenn., Newman's (Tenn.) Batt., Dawson's (Ga.) Bat. *Bate's Brigade.*—Brig.-Gen'l W. B. BATE, 58th Ala., 37th Ga., 4th Ga. Batt., 15th Tenn., 37th Tenn., 20th Tenn., Oliver's (Ala.) Art. *Clayton's Brigade.*—Brig.-Gen'l H. D. CLAYTON, 18th Ala., 36th Ala., 38th Ala., Humphrey's (Ark.) Bat.

PRESTON'S DIVISION.

Brig.-Gen'l WILLIAM PRESTON.

Gracie's Brigade.—Brig.-Gen'l A. GRACIE, Jr., 43d Ala., 1st Ala. Batt.,‡ 2d Ala. Batt.,‡ 3d Ala. Batt.,‡ 63d Tenn., Battery.‖ *Trigg's Brigade.*—Col. R. C. TRIGG, 1st Fla. Cav.,§ 6th Fla., 7th Fla., 54th Va., Peeple's (Ga.) Bat. *Kelly's Brigade.*—Col. J. H. KELLY, 65th Ga., 5th Ky., 58th No. Car., 63d Va., Battery.‖

JOHNSON'S DIVISION.¶

Brig.-Gen'l B. R. JOHNSON.

Gregg's Brigade.—Brig.-Gen'l JOHN GREGG, Col. C. A. SUGG, 3d Tenn., 10th Tenn., 30th Tenn., 41st Tenn., 50th Tenn., 1st [20th] Tenn. Batt., 7th Texas, Bledsoe's (Mo.) Bat. *McNair's Brigade.*—Brig. Gen'l E. McNAIR, Col. D. COLEMAN, 1st Ark. Rifles, 2d Ark. Rifles, 4th Ark., 25th Ark., 35th Ark., Culpeper's (S. C.) Bat.

CAVALRY.

Maj.-Gen'l JOSEPH WHEELER.**

WHARTON'S DIVISION.

Brig.-Gen'l JOHN A. WHARTON.

First Brigade.—Col. C. C. CREWS, 7th Ala., 2d Ga., 3d Ga., 4th Ga. *Second Brigade.*—Col. T. HARRISON, 3d Confederates, 1st Ky., 4th Tenn., 8th Texas, 11th Texas, White's (Ga.) Battery.

---

* Of Polk's corps. † See Johnson's Division, following.
‡ Hilliard's Legion. § Dismounted.
‖ It appears that Baxter's (Tenn.) and Jeffress' (Va.) Batteries belonged to this division, but their assignment is not clearly indicated.
¶ This was a temporary organization, embracing Benning's, Johnson's, Law's, and Robertson's brigades, as well as Gregg's and McNair's.
** This organization taken from return for August 31st, 1863.

MARTIN'S DIVISION.

Brig.-Gen'l W. T. MARTIN.

First Brigade.—Col. J. T. Morgan, 1st Ala., 3d Ala., 51st Ala., 8th Confederate. *Second Brigade.*—Col. A. A. Russell, 4th Ala.,* 1st Confederate, Wiggins' (Ark.) Battery.

RODDEY'S BRIGADE.

Brig.-Gen'l P. D. RODDEY.

4th Ala.,* 5th Ala., 53d Ala., Forrest's (Tenn.) Regiment, Ferrell's (Ga.) Battery.

FORREST'S CORPS.

Maj.-Gen'l N. B. FORREST.

ARMSTRONG'S DIVISION.†

Brig.-Gen'l F. C. ARMSTRONG.

Armstrong's Brigade.—3d Ark., 1st Tenn., 2d Tenn., McDonald's Battalion. —— *Brigade.*—4th Tenn., 8th Tenn., 9th Tenn., 10th Tenn., 11th Tenn., Freeman's (Tenn.) Battery, Marion's (Tenn.) Battery.

PEGRAM'S DIVISION.‡

Brig.-Gen'l JOHN PEGRAM.

Davidson's Brigade.—Brig.-Gen'l H. B. Davidson, 1st Ga., 6th Ga., 65th North Carolina, Rucker's Legion, Huwald's (Tenn.) Battery. *Scott's Brigade.*—Col. J. L. Scott, 10th Confederate, 1st La., 5th Tenn., 12th Tenn. Battalion, 16th Tenn. Battalion, Louisiana Battery (1 section).

RESERVE ARTILLERY.§

Barret's (Mo.) Battery, Darden's (Miss.) Battery, Havis' (Ala.) Battery, Le Gardewi's (La.) Battery, Lumsden's (Ala.) Battery, Massenburg's (Ga.) Battery.

---

* Two regiments of the same designation. Lt.-Col. Johnson commanded that in Roddey's brigade.

† Taken from return for August 31, 1863, and Forrest's report.

‡ Taken from Pegram's and Scott's reports and assignments; but the composition of this division is uncertain.

§ With exception of Darden's battery taken from return for August 31, 1863; on that return that battery appears as of Johnson's Brigade.

INDEX.

12*